PrincetonReview.com

WHAT TO DO WITH YOUR HISTORY OR POLITICAL SCIENCE DEGREE

By Sarah Dunham and Lisa Vollmer
and The Staff of The Princeton Review

Random House, Inc.
New York

The Princeton Review, Inc.

2315 Broadway

New York, NY 10024

E-mail: bookeditor@review.com

ISBN 978-0-375-76626-8

Publisher: Robert Franek

Editors: Adrinda Kelly, Michael V. Palumbo

Designer and Production Manager: Scott Harris

Production Editor: Christine LaRubio

Printed in the United States of America.

9 8 7 6 5 4 3 2 1

2008 Edition

ABOUT THE AUTHORS

Sarah Dunham is a former career counselor and pre-law advisor at the Career Center, University of California—Berkeley, and maintains a private career counseling practice in Berkeley, California. She writes and presents on a variety of career development issues in higher education and in the field of disability. Sarah was a founding member of the advisory board for the national nonprofit organization Career Opportunities for Students with Disabilities, and is currently on the Idealist on Campus advisory board for Idealist.org.

Lisa Vollmer is a freelance writer and editor, specializing in business, finance, and career-management topics. Drawing on her previous work experience in both investment banking and management consulting, she authored numerous career guides for San Francisco-based publisher WetFeet Press, including *Job Hunting in San Francisco* and *Beat the Street II: an Investment Banking Interview Practice Guide*. More recently, she has worked as a freelance journalist for the Stanford University Graduate School of Business and as a research editor at Sunset magazine in Menlo Park, California. She is a graduate of the University of Virginia.

ACKNOWLEDGMENTS

This book is the result of encouragement I have received from a wide assortment of Dunham and Lerner family members, including my son Yarrow. I am also most grateful to Grandmaster Sam Tam for the Tai Chi practice which sustains me.

I am indebted to Susan Kishi, Sharron O'Connor, and Betty Walker, as well as a great number of other student affairs colleagues who have dedicated their professional lives in service to students.

I would like to express my deep appreciation to the many graduates of history and political science from University of California—Berkeley and beyond who have contributed to this book. It has been my great good fortune to cross paths with each of them for a few moments. The world is in very good hands.

—Sarah Dunham

This book would not have been possible without the contributions of several members of the Book Publishing team here at The Princeton Review. Our wonderful publisher, Robert Franek, lent his support and expertise to the development of this book; our production dynamos, Christine LaRubio and Scott Harris, transformed the raw manuscript into the finished product now in your hands; and finally, Mike Palumbo, my talented co-editor, merits special thanks for the valuable input he provided along the way.

—Adrinda Kelly, Editor

CONTENTS

CHAPTER 1:

What Will You Do with that Liberal Arts Degree in History or Political Science?

INTRODUCTION

"So ... what are you going to do with that degree?" Your response could be the classic one-liner: "I'm going to frame it and put it up on my wall!" Or, if you're a history major: "Make history!"

As you approach graduation there is a good chance someone may ask you that very question. Are you tired of making jokes about your major? Take heart! There are a ton of career opportunities out there for history and political science majors. In fact, all the stories in this book are about people like you who were drawn to the study of history or political science as undergraduates and are now enjoying successful careers.

The great advantage of the history and political science degree—and any liberal arts degree, for that matter—is the broad skill set it creates. As one graduate said: "I learned to read and digest information quickly and how to write coherently and quickly. ... These skills have been useful at every step of my career."

As a history or political science major, you decided to come to college and engage in the intellectual life on campus. Comparing two eras in history or evaluating diverging views of public policy is not stuff for the fainthearted. You have analyzed and synthesized massive bodies of information and developed basic literacy in economics, government, sociology, law, international relations, and public policy. You've developed keen powers of observation and are trained to observe change and identify broad themes and continuities that arise from these changes. No one would ever accuse you of thinking in black and white; you are comfortable with ambiguity and critical uncertainties. You are a curious and continual learner and resourceful when searching for evidence to back up your point of view.

This is the kind of mind that employers can really use. Rarely do jobs require specific knowledge of a field; instead, they require an ability to learn quickly and convey information clearly and consisely. As one recruiter told us: "Successful liberal arts candidates have presented their majors as foundations in critical thinking and intellectual curiosity. If we find the right candidate, we can teach them the job-specific skills they need to be successful. Their proven ability and desire to learn is more important than the subject they studied." One graduate working in finance put it this way: "Believe it or not, businesses want their most valuable employees to be able to think, analyze, and come up with new ideas. These businesses make money because of good thinkers."

Is it hard to imagine that being a "good thinker" with great reading and writing skills is going to get you a job? Even though you might be suffering from nightmarish visions of your computer science friends laughing at you for making such a thoroughly unemployable academic choice while they cash their six-figure IBM paychecks, the truth is that thinking, reading, and writing are marketable skills that seriously contribute to the "bottom line" in business, government, and nonprofit industries.

Do people read stuff on the job? All the time! They call it information management in some circles. According to one Foreign Service officer in the diplomatic corps, more than 60 percent of his working hours are spent handling reports—assembling facts, writing, proofreading, and reading. "Reading is fundamental and if your writing isn't up to snuff, you'll be selected out—fired, that is." Financial analysts have an equally heavy reading load; they have to stay abreast of news stories, market movements, and industry profiles in financial newspapers, magazines, and books. "Frankly," a public policy analyst told us "a lot of policy work requires copious reading. Monitoring newspaper stories and internet information composes a lot of my daily activity."

Stephanie Hedeline, staff assistant to Congresswoman Doris O. Matsui said, "As staff for a member of Congress, I view the history or political science degree as very valuable for my line of work. I must read multiple newspapers each day to keep on top of issues of interest to my boss, and then I must synthesize that information in a way that makes it readable and digestible for her busy life." Stephanie also spends a lot of time writing: "I write letters on a daily basis on behalf of my boss. I write remarks for the congresswoman and act as her representative when she is not in the district. My major in history provided me with solid written and oral communication skills."

A nonprofit program coordinator told us: "My reading and writing skills have definitely helped me in my current job. I read articles in medical journals, glean the important information, and summarize it for publication in a handbook for health care providers. Political science taught me how to gather the important points from dense material and express those thoughts in my own words."

As you can see, the ability to think critically, read, and write coherently is a hot commodity in the world of work. History and political science majors have those skills in spades.

> "In my opinion the most desirable quality for a new hire is the right attitude (after intelligence, good ethics, and an appealing or interesting personality, of course). The right attitude is equal parts enthusiasm, adaptability to changing circumstance, drive and ambition, maturity, and professional behavior (including decent manners), and, finally, creative abstract thinking."
>
> Ember Martin, Financial Planner

GETTING STARTED

History and political science students are certainly a breed unto themselves. As an intellectually curious history or political science major, you may have been so immersed in studying the critical issues of the past and present that you forgot to attend the job fairs sponsored by your school's career services office. So where does that leave you? Fortunately, your academic efforts have not been in vain, and you can still find a foray into the world of work.

If teaching history or going to law school doesn't do it for you, then now is a good time to really give the question of "What can I do with my major?" the thoughtful investigation and analysis it deserves. History and political science majors are a resourceful bunch and ready to look up and into anything. In your academic life you've been active and willing participants in civil discourse and thoughtfully imagined the variety of perspectives that enter the debate. You can (and should) approach the equally complex variety of careers out there with the same enthusiasm and critical eye.

Let's face it, people may always wonder about your choice of major and its seeming lack of usefulness in the job marketplace, especially when compared to biochemistry or computer science. You may wish you had a convenient answer like "historian" or "politician" to supply to well-meaning family members when they ask you what you are going to do with your degree. While you may not have a packaged response to these inquiries, what you do have is competence in the subject matter. Now all you need to learn is how that competence measures up in the real world.

The challenge for many history and political science students is to translate their major in history or political science from academic language into work-related skills or interests. With the help of this book, you will discover the "market value" of your knowledge and learn how to leverage the analytical tools you've acquired along the way.

> "We've hired history and political science students. Liberal arts students bring a variety of skills and experience that we find useful. Through delving into their area of interest, they demonstrate a high degree of intellectual curiosity, a trait which is crucial in learning the world of finance. Frequently they have a demonstrated ability to tackle an abstract question, take a position, and defend that position with rigorous reasoning and examples. Many liberal arts students have excellent communication and public speaking skills which we find valuable in both internal and client communication."
>
> Jill Hitchcock,
> Recruiter and Group Vice President, Fisher Investments

Reality check: Get out of the classroom and make your mark

You have the flexibility to market your degree and tailor your skill set to a variety of different fields. That being said, you may have to work a little bit harder to show evidence of the practical "real world" skills that you can't learn in a classroom.

Working part-time, taking on leadership positions in a student club, or completing an internship will show that you are a smart history or political science student who recognizes the reality of life outside the classroom. Employers are interested in seeing evidence of students' prior successes, whether that is in their academic, extracurricular, or work life. They don't seem to care what kind of organizations or activities you select; whatever you do, they just want to see you demonstrate leadership and drive, what one recruiter called a "a hunger for responsibility."

Resume entries: Evidence of a hunger for responsibility

Member, University Marching Band
- Organize seasonal activities.
- Lead and teach new members college traditions.
- Teach musicianship and performance professionalism.
- Initiate discourse on marching band policy and propose amendments.
- Perform at two to six venues a week.

Diversity Committee, Residential Life, My University
- Discuss and implement ways to address diverse needs and identities of students within university housing.
- Implemented policies to facilitate comfortable, inclusive living environment for students.

Swim Coach, Community Center, My Home Town
- Trained swimmers (ages 5–18) in sportsmanship, discipline, and ethics along with basic skills and understanding of the sport.
- Planned and executed daily swim programs and weekend invitational swim meets.
- Encouraged and motivated young athletes to identify and pursue goals.
- Communicated with parents and maintained open dialogue.

HISTORY

Profile of a history major: More than memorizing facts about dead people

While history majors come in all shapes and sizes, and have interests and opinions as diverse as the color of the rainbow, there are some commonalities that can be readily identified among history majors. To begin with, history majors love stories. They love telling them, and they love listening to them. "It doesn't matter who it's about or when . . . we're like gossips. We feed off the details and love to speculate," says one history grad currently working in broadcast journalism. History majors have a drive to know things and won't stop until they find the one seemingly obscure fact needed to complete the puzzle or to prove their point. They like to connect the dots. A history major's brain is trained to analyze multiple and differing opinions, and it's entertaining for a history major to work through the conflicting viewpoints and alternative scenarios that present themselves.

History majors take their history very seriously. They can extract high drama from one pivotal occurrence; they understand how a small political deal in history can have the power to alter the course of human events.

Walking by the great cathedrals in Florence, history majors see lessons in physics and their impact on the history of the people there. All evidence of human activity—from buildings and structures to household goods and medical instruments—is up for examination in the eyes of a history major.

History majors are voyeurs. They are the eyes and ears of past lives and events, the flies on the wall, the would-be (and sometimes actual) historians of society's important events. History majors are fantastic researchers. They have a drive to know things. They love libraries! For them, the National Archives are sacred ground. One does not merely glance at original source documents—one uses them to construct visions of a hallowed past.

They prefer nonfiction to fiction and read it for fun. As one history major said "I hate reading bad fiction; at least with nonfiction it's always a good story and you'll learn something important." If they aren't reading historical works then they are secretly penning one. They can be found in every aisle of the bookstore, especially the mystery and biography sections. They like word games and puzzles, read *National Geographic*, and watch shows like *History Detectives* when they aren't listening to NPR.

"The deep background I had from my degree in history accelerated my career as a photographer. I was covering the Balkans when Croatia declared its independence. I had background knowledge about where everyone in the conflict was coming from. Who would have thought that a course in Byzantine Studies would be a turning point of my career, but I understood why the various stakeholders thought the way they did. I'd be let into situations as a photographer when reporters were kept out, but once on the scene I could ask the crucial questions. I'd always get a fuller story because I understood the historical significance of the events unfolding."

Steve Castagneto,

Photojournalist and High School History Teacher

What you learned as a history major and why it matters

> *"Those who cannot remember the past are condemned to repeat it. If anything holds the key to understanding warfare, famine, and social crises, it's the analysis and understanding of history. It's not a recitation of facts. It's the sum total of the human experience—a dramatic, never-ending, entirely uncensored adventure."*
>
> Philosopher George Santayana[1]

The past is very much a part of the present, and no one knows this better than a history major. As congressional staffer (and former history major) Stephanie Hedeline explains, "One class I really liked was on the modern Middle East. At the time, I knew nothing about the region apart from the history of the ancient civilizations. This class really opened my eyes about the effects of colonialism and nationalism on modern Middle Eastern countries. . . . It was because of this class that I knew who Osama Bin Laden and Al Qaeda were before September 11. Without that knowledge, I no doubt would have approached that crisis in an entirely different way. By learning about the history of that area, coupled with involvement from Western cultures, I gained real insight into what was fueling the political crises there."

Some Fun Developments in Twentieth Century History

1906 William Kellogg invents Corn Flakes.

1916 Coca-Cola introduces its curvaceous bottle.

1925 Yale students accidentally invent the Frisbee.

1934 The cheeseburger is unveiled in Louisville, Kentucky.

1942 Tony the Tiger debuts as the Kellogg's Frosted Flakes mascot.

1956 Elvis Presley's "Heartbreak Hotel" hits Number One on Billboard's pop singles chart.

1965 The biggest power failure in history causes a sustained blackout in the eastern United States and Canada. There is a notable surge in national birthrates some nine months later.

1977 *Star Wars* is released.

1982 *Time* magazine names Pac-Man as its "Man of the Year".

---

1 George Santayana. *Life of Reason: Reason in Common Sense.* New York: Scribner's, 1905. 284.

As a history major, you've learned how to separate the relevant from the irrelevant while retaining both. You never know when a useless fact isn't as useless as you thought. Account executives in advertising may secure a new account because of something they recall in their study of history about the culture of the target audience, and can pitch the account with that kind of background information in mind. This is just one example of how the knowledge you gained as a history major might come in handy in the work world.

KNOWLEDGE

There were few multiple-choice exams in your college-level history courses. Instead, you were asked to discuss the silk trade from Beijing to Baghdad, analyze the Civil Rights movement and the New Left in the 1960s, examine the writings of American conservatives from the Founders to the New Right, or delve into the changing roles of class and gender in nineteenth-century France. In addition to becoming good readers, writers, and communicators, you've become experts at distinguishing patterns in large amounts of information.

What you really study is change: why change occurs at particular times in particular places, why other things stay the same, and how individuals and groups deal with change. The question always at the forefront of your studies is: What is brought from the past into the present and what does that mean for future success?

When it comes to your career, Why does any of this matter? History deals with actual people and factual events. There is a need to piece together chronologies out there in the "real world." It's called litigation support in the field of law—from genealogical research for a contested will to gathering evidence for a major civil rights case. Legislators need to determine the original intent of a law or regulation under examination. One historical consulting firm works with legal clients on World War II–era claims arising from looted art, forced labor practices in Germany, and Holocaust assets. A growing number of personal history consulting firms are springing up to document individual and family life stories, as Baby Boomers begin to think about preserving their parents' and their own life histories to pass along to the next generation.

Every field has a history, and every organization within it recognizes the need to cultivate an institutional memory. The past can be a powerful tool for establishing current goals and reaching future objectives. History majors are poised to ask the kind of critical questions which can fuel investigation and documentation. Imagine a strategic planning session at any business in any industry. The questions they ask themselves are historical when you think about it: How was the organization structured in order to develop policies or products? How have successful products changed over time, and what decision-making processes were used to make those changes? What was the economic or political climate which enabled those changes to succeed or caused them to fail?

The analysis of past performance is what one graduate working with an investment research and proxy advisory firm does every day. "We analyze past public companies filings on issues of financial disclosure, corporate governance, and shareholder safeguards, summarize their proposals, and offer voting recommendations to our clients who are some of the largest institutional investors in the world."

"History majors learn to think critically. There is a huge amount of reading required, and you have to distill vast volumes of materials to see the larger themes. I've been hiring interns here at ABC News since 2001, and I appreciate the curiosity of the liberal arts students, their interest and awareness of what is going on. History majors in particular know how to look to find relevant documents. They are not only interested in the world around them but when there is a current event, they know there is also a long history related to the event, a clear recognition that it wasn't just this week's news that caused something to happen. Added to that understanding, they have great reading and writing skills."

Charles Herman,

History major and Producer, ABC News

Learning methods: Identifying and evaluating sources of information

Was a particular event or issue from the past part of a chain of events specific to the time or place? As a history major you can readily search out the information needed to address this kind of question—from volumes of text, to lectures by your faculty, to discussions in small research-oriented seminars. The ability to identify sources that can help you find answers to the tough questions is the mark of a history major.

History majors are expected to know how to find information in a variety of ways. Often history majors turn to secondary sources, which might include faculty and/or the vast literature produced by academic journals and electronic databases. History majors have also been trained to find and use primary sources, which can mean sifting through an undifferentiated mass of material with differing (and often contradictory) points of view. Students of history cannot rely on urban legend. Rather, they have to use complex tools to locate specific archives or manuscript collections in search of evidence to support their assertions.

The ability to identify and evaluate sources of information comes in handy in the "real world"—for example, within the mayor's office in local government where there are various stakeholders with differing perspectives and priorities. To negotiate between neighborhood coalitions lobbying against expansion, while at the same time providing new businesses with incentives to stay in town, requires the ability to see the broader perspective while acknowledging the legitimacy of each group's position. See job profiles in Chapter 3 for other examples of jobs in which the ability to identify and evaluate sources of information is useful.

Although this may be somewhat obvious, the undergraduate study of history makes graduate school a bit less daunting. One history graduate now working on his master's degree in public policy says, "The history degree really helped out with research skills. I could fly through a library catalog or LexisNexis by the time I was done with undergrad, so it made researching papers in grad school a snap. I also developed habits of documenting sources that were helpful. I also learned how to be an excellent 'skimmer' of books and articles with my history degree, and saved time later on reading journal articles."

Contributions to the field

History majors looks for a historical problem worth addressing, delve through many different sources of information, and put all this information together in support of a conclusion. They have to work their way through the argument, match evidence to argument, and anticipate challenges to their assertions. All this investigation of and sifting through sources can lead to some pretty exciting observations. In school, history majors are expected to develop insights from all this investigation and then organize and communicate those insights to others in a convincing way. One history graduate now in law school says, "I have no urge to simplify things. As a history major I was continually searching to find all possible contributions and connections to a given social event or problem. I became comfortable with a diversity of opinions."

The world of work operates in a similar way. There is constant change within the marketplace, the political climate, and human social interaction. There is a need in every employment sector to entertain alternative scenarios and develop contingency plans. As a history major, this is something you excel at.

POLITICAL SCIENCE

Political science majors: Compelling commentators. Natural networkers.

Political science majors put the "social" in social science. They are ambitious and outgoing. They like to both build consensus and engage in spirited debates. They are problem-solvers. They have a way with words and are well-versed in the art of persuasion. Political science majors are compelled to offer opinions on all matters—from the current political climate to which is the best Thai restaurant in San Francisco.

Their fingers are on the pulse of contemporary culture and campus life and they participate in both wholeheartedly. Political science majors are charming and charismatic. You can find them campaigning for student government and often maneuvering the campus bureaucracy to start up a new student club. They easily turn their research paper into an article for the student-run journal, and can't help but stop to read the petition in front of the grocery store or chat up the university clerical workers out on strike. They enjoy controversy and intrigue, and read the op-ed pieces in the *New York Times*. They're crowd pleasers and public speakers.

What You Learned as a Political Science Major and Why It Matters

KNOWLEDGE

In a nutshell, political science is the academic study of politics and government. In one sense, it is an ancient discipline: It remains central to any classical study of the liberal arts, firmly grounded as it is in the work of Plato and Aristotle. In another sense, because it often deals with current events and sophisticated statistical analysis, political science is a cutting-edge area of study. Whether you are analyzing voting patterns in a presidential campaign, the Israeli parliament, or the pros and cons of different systems of government, political science is timely, fascinating, and perpetually changing.

As a political science major, you have studied everything from revolutions to political parties to voting behavior to public policy. You most likely have explored the political issues inherent to different regions of the world, like the Middle East, East Asia, Latin America, and Eastern Europe.

Political science tackles those Big, Serious, Heavy, and Eternal Questions. According to social studies teacher Sean Delgado, "I actually learned that political science has very little to do with the civics that you learn inside your high school government class, but has more to do with the study of power, structures of power, and access to power. I've been teaching high school social science for several years now. Having just completed graduate school at UCLA's Principal Leadership Institute, I have come to discover that a political science degree is extremely beneficial. It gives me a lens to look at power at a public school. Who has access to power at schools? Who is being denied power and a voice? And what can I, as an educational leader, do to allow more people to have access to power over the educational system?"

Why are these questions important? And how does knowing that the government has its hand in everything make a political science major more marketable in the workforce? One political science grad and nonprofit administrator weighs in: "The nonprofits I work for benefit from my knowledge and understanding of the political process, how bills get passed, how funding gets distributed, etc. I have a certain comfort level with how decision-makers and legislators are motivated at the local, state, and federal levels, how bureaucrats operate, and how to get their attention when trying to get funding. Also, when I wrote grants, I understood how to use statistics derived from governmental data to make the case for more funding—and I learned how to collect data from our programs to sustain the funding."

---

2 Plato. "Quotations by Plato." www-groups.dcs.st-and.ac.uk/~history/Quotations/Plato.html.

Learning methods

As a student of political science you have had to develop the ability to consider a variety of perspectives simultaneously: objective, analytical, comparative, and historical. You know how to use various public records—interviews, newspaper clippings, periodicals, case law, historical papers, polls, and statistics—to test theories and develop new ones. You have been trained to analyze, compare, and trace problems back to their sources. You have the ability to look at constructions of power holistically, and are able to break them down into relationships, structures, and networks.

One political science graduate working in the business sector says the degree has served him particularly well: "Political science does not give any person a complete background in business, but it does give a unique perspective to the business world. The political science degree gave me the critical thinking power to set my own rules and create a different way of doing things within my business environments." Another political science graduate, Adam Harris, now a venture capitalist and current MBA student, told us: "Any job that requires research and analysis and written communication—virtually any job in M&A, strategy consulting, or marketing—is right up a political science major's alley. The degree prepares a person to do competitive intelligence or write a business plan as well as any [other] degree. It teaches a person how to conduct research, analyze the processes and meanings of a third party's actions and rhetoric, and then create an argument as to how to campaign with or against this third party. These skills are as applicable for business as they are for politics or law. They are skills for a management-minded person and they are skills for life in general. These skills allowed me to begin my career in research and analysis for an IT strategy firm, then switch into venture capital, which really is just about making an argument as to where to place bets based on a research-based understanding of a particular business."

Contributions

As a political science major, you have learned to ask incisive questions whenever you come across analytical problems. You have learned to write about complex policy issues in a clear and concise manner—most likely with a strong element of empirical analysis. You confidently employ a tight, argumentative style of writing to support your position, building each point and leading to a logical conclusion. This kind of writing is invaluable to busy professionals, whether in a grant proposal, a business plan, or merely in the daily e-mails which require continual sorting through.

COMMON GROUND

History and political science majors are social scientists. What does that mean exactly? You definitely weren't in the bio lab looking at molecules. To begin with, biology is a physical science, and like all physical sciences it deals with the objective aspects of nature and employs an empirical "what you see is what you get" analysis of data.

Investigating the past or present behavior of individuals and groups requires particular methods of observation and reflection that are missing in the physical sciences. While history and political science students do use the scientific method of inquiry and rely on empirical standards of evidence, they've also had to hold both objective and subjective stances and suspend judgment long enough to effectively observe and reach informed conclusions on a complex, ever-changing social system, historical event, or political movement.

History and political science students have brains that are hardwired for analysis. So how does that translate into the analytical skills employers look for in a successful employee? Problem-solving skills—the ability to bring all relevant information to bear on concrete problems —are highly valued by employers. Employers are looking for people who can identify the source of a problem and the key issues surrounding it, weigh reasonable alternatives, and present viable solutions. In some business environments it's the "who, when, what, and key results" process of investigation. In other industries it's called the "where are we going, what we need, what are the barriers, and how do we get through them" approach. However it's described, history and political science majors are quite familiar with the process of problem-solving and should recognize this as a key element of their job marketability.

Research

Both history and political science students have read volume after volume of very dense, interesting stuff—from the history of early Chinese empires to the politics of European integration—but it doesn't stop there. Your professors expected you to examine and be curious about what you read. You were required to develop your own research interests and argue for their applicability to the discipline. Academic research is all about the content of the research, and a good research paper takes the researcher out of the equation. But you need to shift your thinking about research as you begin a job search. While a successful research paper relies on the effective presentation of evidence, a successful resume relies on the effective presentation of you, the researcher. Sometimes the reader of your resume really doesn't care about the topic of your research at all, which can be disheartening after all the time you spent immersing yourself in your research project.

Take heart. While they may not care about the nuances of your topics of interest, employers are looking to find enthusiastic new professionals in their field who have experience collecting and interpreting data. Did you conduct surveys or interviews during the course of your research? Did you review and summarize literature? Think for a moment about what you actually did to bring your research paper to fruition. Chances are, these are the same skills employers are looking for.

Representing your course work and thesis on your resume:

Resume Before

Smart College Guy Job Applicant

Education: BA Political Science

Resume After

Smart College Guy Job Applicant

Education: BA Political Science

Emphasis: International Affairs

Related Course Work: Statistical Research in Political Science, Seminar on Research Methodology, Comparative Government, Human Rights and International Relations, Comparative Immigration Policies.

Senior Thesis: Analyzed the establishment of the 1998 Rome Statute on the International Criminal Court. Research methods included library and internet literature review as well as in-person and telephone interviews with academic experts.

Resume entries: Evidence of analytical skills outside the classroom

Outreach Intern, Scholarships for Inner City Kids Fund

- Analyzed over 100 scholarship applications weekly and determined eligibility.
- Worked with lawyers, social workers and school principals on application process.
- Developed and implemented procedure for reviewing applications.

SKILLS INVENTORY

Skills: The language of job descriptions, resumes, and interviews

All that talk about critical reading and writing earlier in the chapter wasn't just to make you to feel better about your major. Those are skills of interest to employers and we hope that you got the message. We just looked at the skills inherent in the research work you did as a history or political science major. There are other skills of value that you've developed as a college student both inside and outside of the classroom, and there are aspects of your personality that add up to your being an interesting and competitive candidate in the eyes of a prospective employer.

The key is to develop a fluency in the language of skills so you can cultivate a clear sense of what you bring to the table and articulate this to an employer in a succinct and engaging way. Think for a moment about skills you've developed just by being a student: You have the ability to communicate clearly and listen well; you can multitask, manage time, and establish priorities to meet deadlines; you interpret complex material and analyze and evaluate information; you can work in groups; you've learned how to be persistent and motivate yourself.

> **"It'll cost you an arm and a leg."**
>
> In George Washington's days, there were no cameras. One's image was either sculpted or painted. Some paintings of George Washington showed him standing behind a desk with one arm behind his back while others showed both legs and both arms. Prices charged by painters were not based on how many people were to be painted, but by how many limbs were to be painted. Hence the expression, "Okay, but it'll cost you an arm and a leg."

Once you've identified your skills, it then becomes necessary to provide evidence. Somehow just saying "I am a very organized" doesn't make the interviewer a believer. Fortunately, providing evidence is what history and political science majors do best.

Accomplishment Stories: Giving employers evidence

Think of an experience that you feel proud of. It can be anything—it doesn't need to be related to jobs or careers. Scan your experience as a volunteer, a friend, a member of a team. Sometimes the best accomplishment stories start out as your worst nightmares. (Like that time the student club treasurer quit right before the big fundraiser dinner and you were left holding the bag in the middle of midterms.) Jot down some thoughts in response to these questions. You'll be well on your way to crafting your own accomplishment stories.

1. Describe the experience.
2. What led up to it?
3. What did you do?
4. Why did you undertake this experience?
5. Why did you select it as one of your accomplishments?
6. Why did it give you satisfaction?

Writing skills

As a history or political science major, you may be thinking, "Doesn't everyone write well?" Absolutely not. A survey of executives from 120 major American corporations (across a range of sectors that employ nearly 8 million people) cited writing as one of the most neglected skills in the business world, yet one of the most important to productivity.[3] Effective writing skills can be the ticket to success and advancement in the workplace; in a labor force full of mediocre writers, someone who writes well is bound to stand out and succeed. As one CEO we spoke to explained, "My view is that good writing is a sign of good thinking. Writing that is persuasive, logical, and orderly is impressive. Writing that's not careful can be a signal of unclear thinking." According to *Writing: A Ticket to Work . . . Or a Ticket Out: A Survey of Business*, more than half of all responding companies take writing skills into account when making promotion decisions for salaried employees.[4]

It's not just the business world that's in need of good writers. A recruiter from a large nonprofit organization told us, "I hire students from the social sciences because they have learned how to organize the theories and large volumes of reading materials they encounter into coherent thoughts they can express in their own words. This ability to absorb, recall, analyze, and discuss complicated information is a welcome skill that can be applied in many different jobs. I typically ask for a writing sample from the job applicant before accepting the person for an interview. Being able to write clearly is one of the essential skills I would look for in a student who majored in the social sciences."

Look at it this way: All jobs most likely involve some element of verbal *tête à tête*. You are going to be communicating with people (i.e. your boss, coworkers, clients, and the public). You might need to convince, manage, or advocate for them. "Everything you do in public policy requires you to be a strong writer. Creating persuasive and clear letters, analyses and public policies requires the ability to critically read through a lot of source material and sensitivity to different types of writing," says Ellen Dektar, project coordinator for Local Investment in Childcare in Alameda County, California.

Communication skills

Writing counts as communication skills, and good writers ask themselves "To what purpose is the writing, and what was my intention as the writer?" Did you propose something? Address a need? Influence or convince the reader? Did you design a flyer to promote or publicize something for your student organization? Being able to write for a target audience and to a particular purpose are two of the cornerstones of effective communication.

---

3 The National Commission on Writing for America's Families. "Writing: A Ticket to Work...Or a Ticket Out: A Survey of Business Leaders." The College Board: September, 2004. www.writingcommission.org/prod_downloads/writingcom/writing-ticket-to-work.pdf.

4 Ibid.

Communication also involves oral presentations, both formal and informal. Think about the last time you had to make a presentation in class. Classroom presentations are fundamentally no different than those you'll have to make in front of your boss, colleagues, or clients. How about study groups—did you moderate or mediate those meetings in any way? Have you visited your professor during office hours to discuss the class, or negotiate your thesis topic or a new deadline? One recruiter had this piece of advice when it comes to honing presentation skills: "Try to work on collaborative projects, maybe with people you don't know or don't get along with. It will help prepare you for work. Take as many opportunities as you can to give presentations."

Resume Entries: Evidence of communication skills

Telemarketer, Alumni Relations, My University

- Contacted former alumni to reestablish their connection to the university.
- Raised funds by convincing alumni of the importance of their continued support.

Member, Social Committee, My Fraternity

- Planned and implemented social events for a group of 150 students.
- Publicized and promoted events.
- Raised funds for events and operating expenses.
- Invited alumni to be guest speakers at networking event.
- Engaged in various service functions such as working with the homeless and the elderly.

Cashier and Server, Upscale Restaurant, My Town

- Maintained good customer service at busy register.
- Completed extensive training in menu items in order to better serve clientele.
- Trained new employees and managed shifts.
- Designed signs about special offers for consumers' convenience.

Volunteer, Habitat for Humanity

- Volunteered at work site working with contractors and fellow students to design and construct a home for two underprivileged families.

Interpersonal and teamwork skills

These are the "team player" skills and they measure how well you work with others. Have you just been sitting up in the ivory tower for all four years of college? We doubt it. Who have you interacted with? How do you get along in a group? Were you part of a student organization? Were you part of group projects within your course work?

Employers are not interested in hiring a "brain in a jar." They want a smart applicant, yes, but they ultimately need someone who is going to get along with coworkers, has the flexibility to change roles as work priorities shift, and truly understands the meaning of collaboration and cooperation. If you've excelled academically, that's great, but you need to show the employer that you understand of how things get done outside of academia. Examples of working on a team or in a group help get this across.

As groups you've belonged to come to mind, remember that not everyone is the team leader. What roles did you play on the team? Are you the one that came up with the creative ideas? Did you keep everyone on task during meeting times with good facilitation skills? Did you bring the realities of goals and objectives to the project?

Be prepared in an interview to also give examples of teams you've been on that didn't function so well. Teamwork can be difficult, but if you walked away from a bad experience with some understanding of group dynamics and with clear insights into how you handle yourself when things aren't going well, that's great information for the prospective employer to have.

Resume Entries: Evidence of your ability to get along with people

Residence Advisor, My Residence Hall

- Responsible for advising approximately 75 students.
- Coordinated hall activities with team of five other advisors.
- Provided academic and emotional support for students, and helped resolve conflicts.
- Reinvigorated participation in the hall association. Attendance at meetings increased five-fold.
- Represented member concerns to administration.

Officer of Delegate Preparation, Model United Nations

- Promoted member recruitment.
- Instructed members on conference rules and procedures.
- Facilitated and moderated club debates in practice sessions.
- Evaluated delegates based on performance in committee sessions.

Project management skills

As a history or political science major, you have not only had to come up with great ideas in your academic work, but you've had to execute them, through research, analysis, and effective presentation methods—that takes project management skills. Both private and nonprofit organizations are continually engaging in activities to create new and improved products and services. The term "engaging in activities" is key here. Once an idea has been accepted, a whole new set of skills is required to take that idea from concept to implementation, including the ability to observe and evaluate progress, meet benchmark goals, and communicate objectives to other team members. A successful project manager will know how to organize and coordinate the various details of a project in order to achieve a specific outcome.

Top 10 Characteristics Employers Seek in Job Candidates

1. Communication Skills
2. Honesty/Integrity
3. Interpersonal Skills
4. Strong Work Ethic
5. Teamwork Skills
6. Analytical Skills
7. Motivation/Initiative
8. Flexibility/Adaptability
9. Computer Skills
10. Organizational Skills

Source: *Job Outlook, 2005.* National Association of Colleges and Employers. www.naceweb.org/press/display.asp?year=&prid=207#figure1.

Taking an idea from conception to execution also involves expecting the unexpected. History and political science majors understand change and know how to develop and explore contingencies en route to specific aims; they've also witnessed this process in action through their study of social movements. While you may be comfortable taking detours, it's also important to show a prospective employer that you are "results-oriented." This means paying attention to the details that can accelerate or derail your progress toward a specific goal. This is where your organization skills will come in handy.

Resume Entries: Evidence of project management and organizational skills

Teen Tour Coordinator, Outdoor Adventure Organization

- Facilitated entire daily trip itinerary, including accommodations and administrative duties.
- Supervised the overall well-being of 40 teenagers traveling across the United States.
- Planned, purchased, and organized meals for 50 people.

Personal Assistant, Law Professor

- Maintained legal correspondence files.
- Managed article database and updated legal reference books.
- Overhauled extensive filing system, sorting congressional records and securing copyright permissions for over 50 sources for course reader.

Drive, initiative, and a strong work ethic

You don't have to look far for evidence of your drive and initiative. Your experience as a student reflects your work ethic. If you have demonstrated the ability to manage a full course load plus a part-time work schedule and/or involvement in extracurricular activities, that is pretty good evidence of your strong work ethic. It's related to the "hunger for responsibility" that we mentioned earlier in the chapter that employers can't seem to get enough of.

Resume Entries: Evidence of drive and initiative

Secretary, Battle of the Bands, My Student Club

- Scheduled and organized meeting agendas.
- Lobbied student government for money to sponsor first-ever Battle of the Bands.
- Selected final 12 contestants to compete in the show and located official judges. Advertised the event by designing flyers and posting them around campus.

Student Coordinator, Public Service Corps, My University

- Began as a volunteer in an academic support program for elementary school children.
- Assumed additional responsibilities and become program coordinator.
- Trained new volunteers on tutoring.
- Recruited and coordinated volunteers for tutoring, field trips, and other activities.
- Promoted program with university administration to expand support.
- Wrote, compiled, and edited a 20-page manual for training volunteers.
- Expanded program to five additional elementary schools.

Knowledge seekers: Lifelong learners

In order to display this skill, all you need to do as a history or political science major is be yourself! Even as an entry-level professional, you are a representative of the company to clients and the public, and employers need to be able to trust that you will safeguard the company's image. The intellectual curiosity and cultural breadth you have developed as a history or political science student means that you can carry on an intelligent conversation with clients, colleagues, and competitors.

An old adage believed to be authored by a consultant recruiter goes like this: "We are looking for the kind of candidate who I won't mind being stuck in an airport with during a snowstorm." That's the "good thinker" person we described earlier in the chapter. You history and political science students will never run out of interesting things to say during that snowstorm.

CHAPTER 2

Building on What You Know: Advanced Degrees and Fellowships

PURSUING AN ADVANCED DEGREE

Back-to-school special

When you tell people you're about to graduate (or have recently graduated) with a liberal arts degree, many of them will probably ask if you plan to go back to school. For some of you, the answer to that question is a resounding "yes." According to a recent study by the Council of Graduate Schools, more than 1.5 million people enrolled in its member institutions in the fall of 2005. Education and business enrolled the largest numbers of students—about 20 percent of the grad-school population pursued advanced degrees in education and approximately 14 percent studied business. Humanities disciplines (including English, history, and others) accounted for about 7 percent of graduate students, and social sciences (a category that includes both sociology and psychology) accounted for slightly more than 7 percent of the total.[1]

If you've enjoyed yourself as an undergraduate student, the notion of returning to the safe cocoon of campus life might seem appealing. We should point out, however, that even if you pursue an advanced degree in the same subject in which you majored in college (and many people study something different), graduate school will hardly seem like a continuation of your undergraduate education—the purposes of the two degrees are very, very different. Even though you specialized in college to some degree simply by declaring a major, the real purpose of your liberal arts studies was to obtain a body of knowledge in a wide range of fields. The purpose of graduate school, on the other hand, is to explore the body of knowledge in a particular field.[2] The two most common types of advanced-degree programs—master's programs and doctoral programs—are explained below.

The Master's program

As a master's candidate, you'll spend about two years at graduate school. The purpose of this program is to give you a solid education in a specialized field of scholarship. At many universities, you may be able to study part-time while working to support yourself. You'll receive less financial help than declared doctoral candidates do (in fact, it's possible you won't receive any financial assistance at all). In a typical two-year master's program, your academic experience will look something like this:

- **Your First Year:** You'll take courses much as you did in college, fulfilling the course work requirements of your degree. The workload is heavier, the course topics are more specific, and much more is expected than was in college. You'll either be assigned or choose an advisor at the beginning of your program. With your advisor's help, you'll begin to develop an academic focus. A number of professors will supervise the work you do.

1 Council of Graduate Schools. *Graduate Enrollment and Degrees Report: 1986 to 2005.* September 13, 2006. 3–5. www.cgsnet.org.

2 John A. Goldsmith, John Komlos, and Penny Schine Gold. *The Chicago Guide to Your Academic Career.* Chicago: University of Chicago Press, 2001. 20.

- **Your Second Year:** You may take further courses to complete your degree requirements. Deciding on your research focus, you'll direct more and more energy toward your concentration. Taking one semester or an entire year, depending on the program, you complete your master's thesis. The purpose of this thesis is to demonstrate mastery in your field. If you show promise, you may be encouraged to continue toward the doctorate.

The Doctoral program

The doctoral candidate spends five or six years at graduate school. From the university's perspective, the purpose of the program is threefold: to give the candidate extensive knowledge of the field; to train him or her to do original and meaningful research; and to prepare him or her to function as a member of a teaching faculty.

In a typical six-year doctoral program, your academic experience will look something like this:

- **Your First Three Years:** You'll take courses to satisfy your degree requirements and gain a broad knowledge of the field. If you're fortunate, you'll gain valuable experience by snagging a research or teaching assistantship. (Most appointments are filled with fourth- to sixth-year grad students.) You'll gradually focus your research interests, working with an advisor who is usually appointed at the beginning of the program, and you'll develop your working relationships with professors prominent in your areas of interest. At the end of your second or third year, you'll complete a thesis or take comprehensive exams, or both. The thesis or exams will help demonstrate your qualification to continue with doctoral work.

- **The Last Three Years:** Course work becomes a much smaller part of your academic work, and may end altogether as you work at conceptualizing your doctoral dissertation. Your dissertation must constitute a new and meaningful contribution to knowledge in your field. You'll teach more and more classes, and may even teach a course of your own design. You'll collaborate increasingly with faculty members, who may rely on you for research and who will inform you of their own work. You will probably become closely associated with a single professor who will become your dissertation director. You'll devote more and more energy to your own research. Your program culminates in the completion of your dissertation, which may include an oral defense of your work before a faculty committee.

Why me? Reasons to go

The decision to attend graduate school isn't one that should be made lightly. "Over the years, I've come to realize that many, if not most [graduate students] seriously underestimate the enormous investment of time and money that graduate school will require," says Tom Thuerer, Dean of Students in the Humanities at the University of Chicago.[3] If you decide to go to graduate school, you don't want to fall into this camp. As with any investment, you'll want to consider your goals and objectives well in advance to ensure you get the best possible return.

We'll discuss the financial realities of attending graduate school later in this chapter, but it can be an expensive proposition. Pursuing an advanced degree also requires significant personal and professional sacrifice—at least in the short term. And while you may have been encouraged to explore several different academic paths as an undergraduate—trying on various majors to see if they fit with your skills and interests—graduate school doesn't offer the same level of flexibility. In graduate school, the stakes are higher—and the cost of changing your mind is much, much higher. True, just because you've started working toward your degree doesn't mean you're obligated to finish it, but investing the time and money in a program and not having a degree to show for it is a scenario you'd like to avoid.

To ensure you get as much as possible out of the investment—and the experience itself—be sure to give serious thought to whether grad school is the right choice for you. Pursuing an advanced degree can influence your personal and professional life in a big way; therefore, your decision to attend should involve some honest self-assessment and good, old-fashioned soul searching. Grad school isn't the right choice for everyone. Sure, you could probably get through it (you wouldn't be offered admission if you couldn't do the work), but do you really want to white-knuckle your way through a program that's not only expensive and time-consuming, but one that's supposed to be intellectually stimulating and enriching? There are numerous reasons people go to grad school; if you're like most people, these are the ones most likely to apply to you:

Because you have to go

In many fields, graduate-level studies are part of the drill if you want to obtain the licenses and certifications necessary to work in your chosen profession. Medicine and law are two obvious examples—if you want to be a doctor, there's no way around medical school (which is a good thing for everyone), and if you want to be a lawyer, law school is in your future for sure. Teaching often requires a graduate degree, too; though the educational requirements will vary depending on the subject and grade level you hope to teach, you'll probably need to complete some level of postgraduate work, whether it's a required teacher-training program, or (if it's a tenure-track college professor career you're thinking of) a master's degree or PhD.

3 John A. Goldsmith, John Komlos, and Penny Schine Gold. *The Chicago Guide to Your Academic Career.* Chicago: University of Chicago Press, 2001. 30.

Career advancement

In some industries and organizations, graduate studies are required—either officially or unofficially—for upper-level or management positions. Even if it's possible to get in the door of an organization without an advanced degree, you many find that you can only move so far up without one. In some cases, an advanced degree is actually a prerequisite for a step-up in seniority; in others, it's more of an unwritten rule. Either way, think of an advanced degree as a type of currency—depending on where you work (or where you'd like to work), you might just have more purchasing power when it comes to getting promoted. And it's not necessarily because the skills or knowledge you picked up in grad school are directly applicable to the everyday responsibilities of your job. "I enjoyed my master's program immensely," says Mary, a 28-year-old analyst with the U.S. government who obtained her master's degree in public policy. "But I wouldn't necessarily say I'm using what I learned in my job every day. Even so, I probably wouldn't have this position if I hadn't gone to grad school. The department that I work for is pretty stringent about its master's degree requirement." The good news is that if you're considering grad school as a possible way to move up within your current organization, there's a good chance your employer will foot at least part of the bill. Many companies offer generous tuition reimbursement programs.

Because you're switching careers

You probably already know that people switch jobs more frequently today than they ever have before—and not just across organizations or functions, either. In fact, not only are job changes becoming more frequent, but they're becoming more dramatic, too. It's not uncommon to see dancers and artists become journalists or doctors, bankers become small-business owners, teachers become therapists, or investment analysts become CIA operatives. As we've said before, careers don't always evolve in a linear fashion. Sometimes, the position that we once considered our "dream job" becomes less satisfying over time. Other times, our personal priorities or circumstances change, making the career path we're currently on seem less appealing. And for some folks, taking a class, attending a lecture, or getting a part-time job transforms a one-time hobby or interest into the focus of their professional aspirations. The reasons behind people's career changes are as varied as the occupations in which they move in and out. In many cases, pursuing an advanced degree provides a bridge between two disparate careers. Graduate school provides much more than just expertise when it comes to establishing your credibility with future employers; the very fact that you took the time to pursue an advanced degree proves you're committed to building a career in the field.

For the love of money

When it comes to graduate school, there's no money-back guarantee. In fact, the only thing that earning an advanced degree guarantees is a few extra letters at the end of your name. And while U.S. Census Bureau data supports the notion that earnings increase with higher educational levels, there's no question that some letters are worth more than others—at least when it comes to salaries. According to Census Bureau research, people with professional degrees (MD, JD, DDS, and DVM) earn higher salaries on average than any other segment of the U.S. workforce. For the rest of the working world, progressively higher education levels correspond to higher earnings, all other things being equal. These salary trends make sense; like any other market, the labor market is driven by supply and demand. Higher demand for your skills—and/or a scarcity of supply when it comes to your particular skill set—will drive up the "price" that employers will pay for your efforts (in other words, your salary). In general, the higher your level of educational attainment, the higher your level of specialization—and the more scarce your skills, knowledge, and experience generally becomes.

However, depending on the specific graduate degree you're pursuing, the dollar increase in your new salary might not be enough to offset the cost of obtaining the degree in the first place. With the cost of higher education increasing each year, students are carrying more debt upon completion of their undergraduate degrees than they ever have before. Tack on the cost of funding a graduate degree, and you'll quickly find that all of this learning comes at a steep price. If your interest in graduate school springs primarily from the promise of a fatter paycheck, proceed with caution: You'll need to conduct a pretty thorough cost-benefit analysis to figure out whether the enhanced earning potential justifies the substantial costs. The Bureau of Labor Statistics' website, BLS.gov, includes hiring projections in addition to salary ranges for various occupations; by reviewing resources such as this one, you'll learn what factors influence the job market in your field—and what the landscape might look like by the time you graduate.

Network connections

As we'll discuss in detail in Chapter 5, networking is an important part of your job search whether you have an advanced degree or not. The connections forged in grad school, however, could potentially give you a leg up when it comes to learning about job opportunities in your field. Even if they can't hook you up with a full-time job, grad-school classmates will often be able to provide you with professional advice that's just as valuable. "Not only did the 23 other people in my MFA program become some of my closest friends, but they've become a powerful network of professional contacts that I continually rely on," says Lisa, currently a senior travel writer with a consumer lifestyle magazine. Lisa, who earned her MFA in fiction writing, recently co-edited a collection of anthologies and is currently working on a book scheduled for publication in the spring of 2007. "The people who were in my writing program were able to put me in touch with agents and publishers who would be able to help me put a book deal together," she says. "I don't know if I would have been able to get that done without them."

Connections like these will pay off whether you're intending to stay in academia or not; as always with job-hunting, it pays to know people and to have them know you, too.

You just can't get enough . . .

. . . of school, that is. Many people pursue graduate studies purely because they're absolutely fascinated by their chosen field of study, and they want to develop a highly specialized area of expertise. Whether you eventually want to teach at the college level or you just want to eat, sleep, and breathe your academic passion for a while, graduate school will enable you to fan your intellectual flames. Those who go all the way with their studies and earn their PhD are a unique breed—a species of intellectual omnivores that enjoys learning for its own sake. Such individuals are visibly charged by scholarly debate and discussion and have the patience and single-minded focus to endure half-a-dozen years or more in an academic environment.

Because it's the path of least resistance

Just because there are many perfectly legitimate reasons to go to grad school doesn't mean there aren't a few bad ones, too. Pursuing an advanced degree as a default option (i.e., you still haven't decided what you want to do and are hoping to postpone the inevitable transition into the real world) isn't a great idea. And if you're simply frustrated with the way your job search is going or hoping to use graduate school to wait out a downturn in the economy, think again. Graduate-school is hardly a quick fix for a broken job search, and the economy may very well pick up long before you've even made a dent in your student loans.

So how can you tell if you're using grad school as a stall tactic? Well, only you know for sure, but if you find yourself contemplating graduate school but haven't really narrowed in on a field of study, that's definitely a warning sign. It's possible that the relative security of being a student—and not necessarily a commitment to a particular field—has captured your interest. That doesn't mean that you shouldn't explore grad school as an option, but you should consider your other alternatives, too, to be sure that fear isn't the only factor motivating your decision. Trust us, there are other ways to bide your time—and most of them require far less time, energy, and money than graduate school. For the grad-school experience to be worthwhile for you, it should make sense as part of some larger plan for your career.

Do you have what it takes?

When deciding whether grad school is something you'd like to do, it helps to consider the skills and attributes successful grad students consistently demonstrate—not just the attributes that make them capable of doing the work grad school requires, but the personal qualities that make them gush with enthusiasm when they describe the experience ten years down the road. Across disciplines and institutions, graduate students who both succeed in their programs and seem to genuinely enjoy them typically have these four things in common:

Compound interest

Far and away, experts say a genuine passion for the subject matter is the single most important factor determining which grad students thrive and which become frustrated and disappointed with their decision. A genuine passion is very different from a peripheral interest—in other words, pursuing a masters' degree in linguistics because you took a single English Literature class probably doesn't represent the most well-informed choice. In order to make the most out of your graduate-school experience, you need to have a deep, enduring interest in the subject, the profession, and its literature. When you apply to programs, admissions staff will examine your transcript and resume not just for evidence of academic achievement (though the importance of solid grades and test scores can't be overstated), but for classes and extracurricular activities that demonstrate an interest in—and a commitment to—the field.

Not-so-idle curiosity

In addition to an inveterate desire to study the field you've chosen, it helps if you're an intellectually curious person in general. In other words, do you enjoy exploring concepts and ideas, whether or not they specifically relate to your chosen field of specialization? Do you enjoy the process of pulling things apart—literally or metaphorically—to understand how they work? Are you intrigued by the challenge of understanding—and expressing—two or more seemingly contradictory perspectives on the same issue? Is your pursuit of knowledge driven largely by your interest in the question more than the practical application of its answer? Whether you're pursuing a two-year master's program, a six-year PhD program, or a full-fledged career in higher education, you'll enjoy your time in academia a lot more if you're excited by the process of learning—not just the degree you'll have in hand when you graduate.

Perfect timing

Well-honed time management skills are another prerequisite for graduate-school success. If you're attending school full-time, you'll probably be balancing competing academic priorities within the classroom walls and possibly the demands of extracurricular involvements, a part-time job (whether it's related to funding your studies or not), a family, and some semblance of a social life. Samantha, who completed a master's degree in English, juggled a couple of different jobs in order to finance her graduate education. As part of the fellowship she was awarded during her first year, she participated in a program known as "Artists in the Schools," where she taught writing to elementary, middle, and high school students throughout the state. "I also worked as a reporter for the university press office," she says. "And I did freelance work for the daily paper, doing book reviews. And I also worked part-time at a café serving lattes. Thinking about it now, it's no wonder I didn't produce as much writing as I would've liked." If you're pursuing your degree on a part-time basis, the demands of a full-time job are most likely in the mix. Either way, you're likely to have a lot on your plate, so understanding how to prioritize is key if you want to finish your program with your sanity intact.

Eyes on the prize

Somewhat paradoxically, the ability to work on a single task for an extended period of time—whether it's a dissertation, thesis, or any long-term research project—is just as important as the ability to juggle multiple tasks at once. The research and writing required in graduate school is highly focused—much more so than in undergraduate studies—so grad students devote a seemingly inordinate amount of time exploring a highly specialized area of interest within their field of study. By its very nature, work like this requires a great deal of autonomy—not to mention a better-than-average attention span. Successful degree candidates are therefore highly motivated, unusually self-disciplined, and comfortable working independently. A good dose of patience doesn't hurt, either—even the most exciting and ground-breaking research projects usually involve some fairly monotonous tasks. In general, the road to completing an advanced degree and seeing it pay off is long and arduous. If instant gratification is important to you when it comes to your academic pursuits, a professional degree might be a more suitable choice than an advanced degree in the liberal arts.

Ask and it shall be answered

We know what you're probably thinking: "Of course I have all of those skills and attributes! I am literally bursting with excitement about my field of study, I can handle multiple competing priorities, I love monotony, and I have the self-discipline and patience of a saint!" If you have a killer transcript, and a resume full of related extracurricular activities and work experience to boot, then it's time to sign you up. All you need to know is where to send the check, right?

Not so fast. We said that considering graduate school required a great deal of introspection and honest self-assessment, but we didn't say that was all that was required before you jumped on board. In Chapter 5, we'll stress the importance of networking and conducting informational interviews to make informed decisions about your career—just because you're thinking of applying your talents to academia for a while doesn't mean you're off the hook where this type of legwork is concerned. You need to ask questions before you decide to apply to school—not only will this type of research make your applications more compelling, but, more importantly, you're far more likely to choose the right program—and the right field of study, for that matter—if you've taken the time to look before you leap. In the *Chicago Guide to Your Academic Career*, the book's three authors (all distinguished professors and scholars themselves) emphasize the importance of seeking advice from as many informed perspectives as possible before you apply. Here are some specific questions they suggest you ask as you begin to gather information:

- To professors (past or current) who know your work well: Do you think graduate school, in this particular field, would be a good choice, given my level and kinds of talents? Do you think I would have a contribution to make?

- To professors in your field who have completed graduate school within the last five years or so: What are the current issues in the field? Where do you see the field going? What is graduate school like these days?

- To graduates of your own college or university who are now in graduate school in a field close to yours or who have recently obtained jobs (your undergraduate teachers, the Career/Placement Center, and/or the alumni office should be able to provide you with names and contact information): How have you found the graduate school experience? Were you well prepared for the program you entered? Is there any advice you wish you'd received before entering graduate school?[4]

4 John A. Goldsmith, John Komlos, and Penny Schine Gold. *The Chicago Guide to Your Academic Career.* Chicago: University of Chicago Press, 2001. 22.

Two words: Manage expectations

Even if you've determined that you'd probably succeed in graduate school—meaning you'd not only do well academically, but you'd probably really enjoy it—you may not be entirely convinced you should go. If you're trying to decide whether the investment would be a worthwhile for you, you're not alone. Formulating realistic expectations—in terms of the graduate-school experience itself and its expected payoff in the long run—is one of the best ways to assess whether attaining an advanced degree is the best possible next step. If you take the time to speak with current grad students, recent alumni, professors, and other prospective grad students (like yourself), you'll probably find that people's objections to graduate school fall into two categories: the practical and the personal.

Practical Concerns

The practical reasons all relate to two things: the cost of school and the likelihood of getting a job afterward. Together, these two factors will determine whether graduate school makes sound practical sense for you. It's possible to land a job easily after earning an advanced degree and still struggle to pay back your loans. It's also possible to complete a graduate program with no debt and still have trouble finding work. Many people would find each of these scenarios unacceptable. To avoid any nasty surprises, spend some time researching the probable cost of your graduate program and study the state of the job market in your field. The most important aspects of the job market are the availability of positions and the salary range. Together, these pieces of information give you some idea of what your professional future (and loan-paying power) might look like. The more information you dig up, the better you'll be able to appraise the practical obstacles to graduate education.

Personal Concerns

The personal pitfalls of graduate school are a little more complicated. They depend on your likes and dislikes, and your powers of endurance. Many people begin graduate programs and never complete them. This is especially true for those pursuing doctorates: Some of these people quit for financial reasons, but many leave because they find that the life they're living is unacceptable. Beginning a graduate program you never finish is the worst-case scenario. Investigating graduate programs should involve not only research into the broad academic outlines, but also research into what your daily life as a graduate student will be like. In an informal survey of hundreds of graduate students, these are the top five lifestyle complaints students made.

- It's hard to make ends meet financially.
- There is little or no free time.
- There is not enough socializing in the department/school.
- There is nothing to do in the university community or surrounding area.
- Fellow graduate students are neurotically competitive.

When making your decision, be sure to consider these aspects of graduate life as well as anything else that could have a substantial effect on your quality of life. Once you can clearly articulate why you want to go to graduate school, you'll be able to make an informed decision as to whether the advantages of an advanced degree outweigh the sacrifices you'll need to make in order to get one.

Timing is everything: When to go

When you started thinking about college, you probably knew when you were going to be attending—about three months after you graduated from high school, most likely. With graduate school, there's a little more variation in this regard. Some unusually focused college grads pursue their advanced degree immediately after obtaining their bachelor's degree (which means, of course, they're going through the application process while they're still in school). Most graduate students, however, have taken at least one year off between their undergraduate and graduate programs— usually to work, sometimes to travel or volunteer, occasionally just to take a break. In fact, more often than not, practical experience—particularly as it relates to the advanced degree you're hoping to pursue—makes you a more desirable applicant than one who has little to no work experience to speak of.

So when should you go to grad school? Well, the short answer is: it depends. On one hand, many people find the years between college and graduate school to be an extremely valuable time for exploring professional options—and for doing some important self-exploration, too. Because you've had a few years in the workplace, you'll probably bring a more informed perspective to bear on your academic pursuits. You might also have saved a little bit of money during your working years—or at least been able to pay down some of your undergraduate debt, if you had any. But more important than any nest egg is the greater sense of clarity and purpose you'll have since you've had some time to consider what you really want to do—and what's especially important to you in your career. No matter how much you enjoyed college or how much you excelled there, perhaps there wasn't ever really a question you would go. When you enroll in graduate school—particularly after you've taken a few years off to work—you're usually there because you want to be there. And if the pure love of learning isn't enough, the fact that you've taken out loans or depleted all of your savings to finance your higher education will probably motivate you to squeeze every last drop of value out of the experience.

On the other hand, taking time to work in between your degrees means you'll have to adjust to life as a student again, which can be difficult for some folks who have been out of an academic routine for several years. And if you've been earning a regular paycheck, you might find it difficult to give up that income and learn to live more modestly as a graduate student. The longer you wait, the more likely it is that personal commitments—a spouse, a significant other's job, children, or mortgage—may complicate your decision of what program to attend (or whether to go at all).

There's no magic formula when it comes to deciding whether to take time off between your undergraduate and graduate studies, or (if you decide to work for a few years) how many years you should work (or travel, or do whatever it is that you're doing between degrees) before you go back. The only absolute guideline is that you go to graduate school when you're absolutely certain it's what you want or need to do. As we've belabored in the preceding pages, pursuing an advanced degree isn't something you should take lightly, so you shouldn't apply until you're sure it's right for you. The option to go to grad school will always be there, and spending time in the "real world" can actually make you more interesting to graduate schools once you decide what you want to do and are ready to apply. The richness of your life experiences will cause the most difficult part of the application—the personal statement—to write itself. You will have cultivated a sincere interest in a particular degree that you need in order to advance your career or gain more influence in a particular field. Your enthusiasm and ability to convey how the degree fits into your long-term goals will leave Admissions Committees inspired and ready to offer you a spot in their next class.

That said, finding out what's typical for other students in the programs you're considering doesn't hurt. Most of the time, graduate programs will post statistical information about their current students on their websites: Oftentimes, the average age of entering students is listed. Again, you shouldn't feel discouraged to apply if you're a few years off the mark (these numbers are averages, after all), but they can help to shape your expectations of what your experience will be different. Kurt, who recently began a MFA program in writing after working as a teacher for nine years, was surprised how old he felt on the first day of school. "Not only have I been working for a while, but I've been married for three years, and my wife and I are expecting our first baby. A lot of my classmates are 23 or 24. I feel so old!" Conversely, if you're attending grad school right after college, you may find that you're the only 22-year old single person in your class. Again, the extent to which you do or don't fit into the prevailing demographics is only one data point, but it's one that will definitely shape your experience in and out of the classroom.

A law school insider's observation: Waiting might have been a better option

"Plenty of law school students have gone directly from college into their legal education. Many do just fine, and have no regrets. Others wistfully wish that they had taken some time off to travel the world, serve the community, campaign for candidates, or read for pleasure. For the train really picks up speed as it pulls away from the law school. Commencement stage—first stop is preparation for the bar exam, and then many years of long hours in the office before there is time and opportunity to pursue other interests. Still others may find themselves unhappy in law school or in law practice and wish that they had taken some time to explore other possible paths before taking the jump into law school. Finally, taking some time off before heading to law school may make one a stronger candidate by virtue of the experience gathered and maturity gained."

Bill Hoye, Associate Dean of Admissions with Duke University School of Law

What to consider when deciding where to apply—and where to go

Like deciding whether or not to go to graduate school, selecting target schools is more complex than it first seems. Filling out applications is a huge demand on your time and energy, and whether you're taking undergraduate exams or holding down a job, you probably can't afford to spend weeks dealing with a large pile of applications.

Applications are a financial drain as well: Grad-school application fees range from $20 to $90 and average about $50. These high fees are no accident. Many universities, with Admissions Committees swamped by record numbers of applications, have raised their fees in order to prevent less-motivated applicants from applying and reduce the number of incoming applications. Given today's fees, you can expect ten applications to cost you about $500—and that's before you figure in postage, transcript handling fees, photocopying, and so on. It can really add up.

Economically speaking, you can see the saturation-bombing technique that a lot of people use to apply to college isn't very practical for grad school. It pays—in time and money—to narrow your field down to four or five good target schools. To figure out which institutions make the cut, you'll probably want to consider the following six factors:

Academic fit

In selecting schools, the most important aspect of any school is its academic fit—that is, how well-suited the school is to the research you want to do. If you're a prospective grad student in, say, philosophy, then it's certainly a good idea to find out where the leading philosophy departments are; but to have a really good graduate school experience, you need more than just a respected department. You need individuals on the faculty who share your research interests, and who will become involved in your work and involve you in their own.

The importance of finding professors to work with varies according to your degree ambitions. If you're looking for a master's degree to round out your education or give you that professional edge, then the overall quality of the faculty may be more important to you than finding the ideal mentor. Because your grad-school experience will probably involve more course work than research, you'll want to make sure the classes offered are relevant to your interests and will give you some background for your research. If you are decided on doctoral work and an academic career, however, the specific research interests of professors become much more important. If you already have an area of academic specialization in mind, you need to find out whether that subspecialty is well represented in the departments you're considering. In any case, graduate work will always be more profitable and enjoyable if there are professors in your program who will take a personal interest in what you're doing.

As you gather information about your prospective professors, remember that the most brilliant scholars in the world are not always the best teachers. No matter how celebrated the scholars are that you'll work with, it won't really matter if teaching isn't their scene—or if they're rarely accessible to students. Make no mistake about it: The quality of teaching can make or break your experience. "I was surprised by the lack of professionalism exhibited by some of my well-paid teachers," laments one recent master's grad. "Overall, I'd give the experience a '6' out of '10'. I wish I had gotten an MBA." To avoid any nasty surprises, talk to other students to gauge their level of satisfaction with the teaching. Also, try to schedule interviews with the faculty members you are most interested in working with.

Reputation

To a greater extent than our undergraduate education, graduate schools represent an affiliation with a specific department, just as much (if not more than) an affiliation with a specific university. Keep this in mind as you consider which programs you'll apply to. When it comes to reputation, the excellence of a particular program doesn't always correspond to the institution's overall reputation—or the strength of its undergraduate programs. Harvard, Princeton, and M.I.T. might vie for the tops spots of the various undergraduate rankings each year, but when it comes to department-specific rankings there's a lot more variety.

Most of the people we spoke to relied—at least to some extent—on department rankings, which are published annually for graduate programs in much the same way they are for undergraduate institutions. (Keep in mind, though, that rankings aren't available for every advanced-degree program you might consider). And while rankings can provide some useful information as you make your choice, remember that they represent just one data point. Be sure to read the fine print about research methodology as you interpret ranking information. Consider the following excerpt from the 2007 edition of *U.S. News & World Report's America's Best Graduate Schools*: "Rankings of doctoral programs in the social sciences are based solely on the results of peer assessment surveys sent to academics in each discipline."[5] There's nothing inherently wrong with this approach, but you should be aware that that these particular rankings do not incorporate the quality of teaching (mentioned above) or the availability of job-placement resources (mentioned below). If that information is relevant to you, you'll need to obtain it through additional research.

5 "Social Sciences & Humanities: PhD Programs Ranked Best by Department Chairs and Senior Faculty." *U.S. News & World Report: America's Best Graduate Schools* . 2006. 65.

Irene, who completed a one-year master's program in journalism, considered the overall reputation of the school to be more important than the reputation of the program. "I wasn't sure I was necessarily going to stay in journalism forever," she explains, "so I wanted to go to a school where the overall reputation of the university would mean something to employers outside of journalism. There were probably better journalism programs out there, but, when deciding where to go, I placed a lot of importance on the overall quality of the school—not the quality of the program alone."

Job Placement

When you're considering which programs to apply to—and, eventually, when you're deciding which school to attend—be sure to visit the Career Center and ask what resources are available to graduate students. While some universities have excellent, program-specific, career-planning resources devoted to their graduate students exclusively, others do not. Talk to students currently enrolled in the programs you're considering and ask if they've found the resources available to them to be satisfactory. Many students enroll in programs assuming that job placement—or at least career counseling—is part of the deal, and they're unpleasantly surprised to find out how few resources actually exist. Regardless of whether you're hoping to snag a position in private industry or make a career in academia, ask questions. Find out whether employers visit the campus to recruit graduate students in your program. If you're going the academic route, ask whether recent grads have gotten academic positions, how long their searches took, and where they're working. In the end, you may not lean on the resources your program provides—in fact, you may not use them all. As we've said before, though, it's important to develop realistic expectations before you sign up.

Students

To really figure out whether a particular program might be a good fit, you need to talk to the students currently enrolled in it. As you make your final decision among programs, you'll ideally visit each campus and talk to current graduate students. Ask them about the faculty's level of commitment to the graduate program, whether they enjoy working with their professors, and whether they feel they've been given enough guidance and opportunity to develop their own research. Ask them to describe the good points and the bad points of the department and the school. If you can, schedule time to speak with a graduate advisor; ask how well the program is organized and what the ratio of graduating students to entering students is. If you take the time to gather qualitative and quantitative information like this, you'll make a much more informed decision than you would if you relied on rankings alone.

While you're on campus, be sure to ask students about their quality of life too. Your lifestyle will not necessarily resemble the one you enjoyed as an undergraduate student. ("Grad school is mostly devoid of the cultural and social atmosphere that is so intoxicating about undergrad life," says Scott, who recently completed a two-year master's program in urban planning. "And the football was worse in grad school, too.") Still, you want to enjoy your experience as much as possible, and that means taking the time to consider what your life will be like outside of the classroom as well as in it. Ask whether there are opportunities to socialize and whether there's a strong sense of community among graduate students. As you talk to people who are attending the programs you're considering, give some thought to whether you can see yourself fitting in at each place. Not only are you going to grad school to advance your formal education, but you're going to be building a network of friends and supporters, too—your fellow students should ideally be people you like and respect. The impressions you get as you visit different campuses are a valuable part of this decision-making process.

Years of Work Experience Prior to Elliott School

Years	# of Grads	percent of Responses
None	71	30 percent
1 to 3 Years	119	49 percent
4 to 6 Years	35	14 percent
7 to 10 Years	11	5 percent
11 to 15 Years	3	1 percent
More than 16 years	3	1 percent

Source: "2004–2005 Employment Survey Summary." The Elliot School of International Affairs, The George Washington University 2004–2005 Employment Survey Summary. www.gwu.edu/~elliott/careerdevelop ment/employmentresults/resultssummary0405.htm.

Geography

This one's pretty straightforward: The geographic location of the university should influence your decision to attend. If you have a particular aversion to rain, then you might prefer not to spend the next few years of your life in Seattle; if you're especially claustrophobic, New York City might not be the place for you. But the question of geography isn't just about personal preferences: there are practical implications, too. For example, depending on your field of study, it might be considerably easier to secure part-time jobs (or jobs between academic years) in some parts of

the country than in others. And if you have your heart set on settling down in a particular region, then you'd probably be best
served attending graduate school there (or somewhere close by).
And if you have a spouse or significant other who's going to
accompany you, your partner's career prospects in each of the
locales you're considering will also influence your decision.

Advice for making the most of your experience

In 2001, about 32,000 graduate students participated in a survey conducted
by the National Association of Graduate-Professional Students (NAGPS).
When asked what specific advice they would provide to entering students,
getting a head start on career planning was the suggestion that survey
respondents offered most frequently. Building a network of personal and professional contacts—by attending professional conferences, joining student
organizations, and actively seeking the support of professors and advisors—
was another popular recommendation.

Source: Adam Fagen and Kimberly Sudekamp Wells. "A Little Advice from
32,000 Graduate Students," *The Chronicle of Higher Education*. January 14,
2002. http://chronicle.com/jobs/2002/01/2002011401c.htm.

"Rapunzel, Rapunzel": Getting into the ivory tower

While you might think the graduate school application process begins when you
start trawling around various schools' websites and committing program rankings to
memory, it really begins months earlier—albeit only informally. The process starts
when you begin to consciously seek out and nurture relationships with your undergraduate professors and advisors as well as professors or researchers at your target
graduate institutions. It continues when you prepare for and then take the GRE, a
topic discussed in more detail below (while not a required application element for
every program, the GRE is compulsory for admission to most programs). Whether you
start thinking about your applications six months or six years before they're due, one
thing is certain: With all the pieces that go into a graduate-school application, it's definitely not something you can whip up over a weekend or two.

Many universities have a single application form for all their graduate programs
and a set of basic application requirements to which individual departments may add.
At some schools, individual departments have their own applications. At these
schools, you will have to request an application from an individual department rather
than a central office.

Once you've accessed and reviewed the admissions materials, it's time to complete the applications to your target schools. Before you dig in, take some time to consider all the application pieces (we discuss these below) and set a schedule with self-imposed deadlines that are possible to meet. The applications themselves typically require a general information form, GRE scores, transcripts, recommendations, and a personal statement. Some programs may have additional requirements, such as an interview or portfolio.

Due to differences in departmental requirements, it is difficult to make generalizations about applications. Still, application processes across institutions and programs usually involve the following:

- **Deadlines.** First things first: Meeting your schools' deadlines is one of the most important details of the application process. You don't want to be rejected from a school for which you might otherwise have qualified simply because you were late in filing your application. Check with each individual department to which you are applying to find out their specific deadlines. Also be aware that there may be separate (usually earlier) deadlines for those students seeking financial aid. Get your applications in as early as possible.

- **Test Scores.** Almost all graduate schools ask applicants for applicable standardized test scores, such as the GRE General Test, a GRE Subject Test, or the Test of English as a Foreign Language (TOEFL). Here again, you must check with individual departments to ensure you meet their specific requirements. Although there are a few programs that don't require the GRE General Test, most do. Only a few programs require a GRE Subject Test. All foreign students from countries where English is not the native language are required to take the TOEFL.

  Preparing for the GRE may require the single biggest investment of time when it comes to applying for graduate school, so get started early. Ryan, who recently completed a two-year master's program, says he prepared for the GRE by completing a single section of a practice test "maybe every other day at work. My boss was very encouraging." (If you are currently working full-time, we should point out that few managers are likely to be as supportive of practicing for the GRE while you're on the clock).

  No matter when and where you prepare for the test, however, make sure you've budgeted enough time for it. The weight placed on your GRE score in relation to the other factors Admissions Committees consider (e.g., undergraduate GPA, letters of recommendation, relevant experience in your chosen field, etc.) will vary from school to school and from program to program, but it's never insignificant. The scores from these tests (like SAT scores when you were applying to undergraduate schools) are one of the few objective metrics that help Admissions

Committees evaluate candidates with very different academic and professional backgrounds. In addition to influencing admissions decisions, GRE scores are an important factor in the awarding of teaching and research assistantships and merit-based financial aid.

- **Transcripts.** A transcript is a certified, official copy of a student's permanent academic record. All graduate schools require official transcripts of your grades from any colleges you attended. Most schools ask that transcripts be sent directly to them, but some ask that you collect the information and send in a complete application package. Contact the registrar's office (at every undergraduate institution you have attended) to request that your transcript be sent either to you or directly to the school to which you are applying. If your school used an unusual grading scale, you will often need to translate your transcript into the requested format.

- **Application Fee.** Application processing fees range from moderate (around $30–$45) to expensive (over $75). As mentioned earlier, these high fees are no accident—they are designed to discourage less-serious applicants from bombarding busy Admissions Committees. Fee waivers are occasionally offered by a school for applicants who can prove financial need. A good rule of thumb: If you failed to qualify for a fee waiver for the GRE, you are unlikely to qualify for a fee waiver from an institution. Check with the graduate admissions office of the schools to which you are applying to find out if you qualify for a fee waiver.

- **Letters of Recommendation.** These letters are one of the most influential aspects of your application to a graduate program. Committee members use them to get a more personal perspective on an applicant. Keep this in mind when choosing your recommenders. Their words will (hopefully) be what set you apart from the other applicants. A borderline student is often pushed into the acceptance pile because of excellent recommendations.

    Some application packets include recommendation forms that ask a recommender to rate your abilities in various categories; such applications generally also provide blank spaces for open-ended comments on an applicant's personality and potential. Other applications simply ask recommenders to write their own letters. Most schools require two or three letters. Try to get three, or even more, in case one is lost or submitted late. Some programs require more recommendations for PhD applicants than they do for Master's degree applicants. Others require additional recommendations for students applying for funding. Be sure you know the specific procedure for the department to which you are applying. If there's any doubt in your mind, call the dean's office or the admissions contact for that department.

If you've been out of school for a few years, you might find it difficult to approach professors from your alma mater and ask them for recommendations, and understandably so: Their recollections of your academic performance aren't exactly fresh. Jessica, who applied to master's programs three years after she completed her bachelor's in sociology, asked for a few recommendation letters before she completed her undergraduate course work— even though she wasn't sure exactly which degree programs she'd eventually apply to. If you're still in school, you might consider this approach: This way, even if the specific applications require that your recommenders fill out additional forms, your professors will have some record of all the nice things they said about you when your academic prowess was still fresh in their minds. If it's too late for that, consider drafting a sample letter— or even an outline—that can serve as a map for the person writing your recommendation. In it, you'll want to include the points you'd most like your recommender to cover, including any specific academic achievements—in his class or otherwise—and the topics of any research projects you undertook during the class. Also provide your recommender with a copy of your transcript.

And no matter what your circumstances—and no matter whom you approach—give your recommenders plenty of warning when you ask them for letters! If you ask the week before the letter is due, chances are your professor (or manager or coworker) won't be able to devote enough time to crafting a compelling recommendation.

- **Personal Statement.** While applicants to medical, law, and business school are often asked to submit fairly lengthy essays about their motivations, goals, greatest achievements, character flaws, and/or solutions to hypothetical problems, applicants to other graduate programs are usually asked to submit a personal statement only. The personal statement may be called anything from the Autobiographical Statement to the Letter of Intent. Whatever its name, if you are required to write one, do it well. No matter what type of graduate program you are applying to, Admissions Committee members will evaluate the following: how clearly you think, how well you have conceptualized your plans for graduate school, and how well your interests and strengths mesh with their programs.

- **Interview.** Of major importance for admission to some graduate programs, interviews are not required for entrance to others. However, many schools encourage you to visit the campus and set up appointments to speak with admissions officers and individual faculty. It's a good idea for you to check out the places at which you're thinking about spending the next several years. You'll get insight into the school and the programs that you just can't get on paper. And if an interview is optional, take advantage of the opportunity to make a personal impression.

Tips from a faculty member for getting letters of recommendation

- Get to know the professor early on. Get to know the professor early on. Get to know the professor early on.
- Thoughts on how to hold a conversation with your professor in office hours:
  - ○ Tell me that you like the class.
  - ○ Tell me a thought you had about the lecture.
  - ○ Recommend a book I might like.
  - ○ Just show up so I can get an idea of who you are. I need to speak to your personality a bit—are you energetic? Do you talk in class?

GRE at a Glance

WHY TAKE IT?	Most graduate schools require it
HOW LONG IS IT?	2.5 hours
WHEN IS IT OFFERED?	Most weekdays and weekends, year-round
HOW TO REGISTER?	www.GRE.org
HOW IS IT SCORED?	Scoring is based on your:

- Verbal Score (200 to 800 points)
- Math Score (200 to 800 points)
- Analytical Writing Assessment (0 to 6 points)

GRE: Section by Section

ANALYTICAL WRITING	• 2 essays
	• 30 minutes for one essay and 45 minutes for the other
QUANTITATIVE	• 28 multiple-choice questions
	• 45 minute section
VERBAL	• 30 multiple-choice questions
	• 30 minute section

Source: PrincetonReview.com

Your unwritten application

As we've said several times now, the application process begins long before you start filling out all of those forms (and paying all of those fees). A large part of your application is never put down on paper. It consists of the contacts you've made with faculty at the programs to which you're applying, your conversations with them, and the impressions you've made. Put this "unwritten application" on your checklist right beside "Bother Professor So-and-So for a Recommendation" and "Study for the GRE." It's that important.

With all the piles of paper involved in applying to graduate schools, it's easy to conclude that paperwork is what it's all about. You spend weeks poring through faculty listings, course offerings, and graduate bulletins to choose your schools, and then you start filling out application forms, requesting transcripts, and writing essays. Of course, all of these documents are important, but in the graduate admissions game, you have a big advantage if you talk to people.

Unlike undergraduate schools, a typical graduate program receives only hundreds—not tens of thousands—of applications each year. From this applicant pool, a program might extend offers of admission to a few dozen, expecting some of those admitted to choose other schools. It's a group of applicants small enough that the Admissions Committee can reasonably expect to meet—or at least talk to—a fair number of them. Some graduate programs receive fewer than 100 applications annually, making an individual applicant's chance of making personal contact better still. At the same time, some popular graduate programs do receive several thousand applications each year, and the Admissions Committees in charge of these programs won't necessarily have time to chat. In general, however, there's a lot of room in the graduate admissions process to talk with professors and other members of the department.

To put together the strongest possible application, you've got to be a go-getter—or at least pretend you're one. This means talking to professors in a way that makes your research interests and career intentions clear to them. If you've done some thinking about what you want from a graduate program, professors will sense your clarity and direction and get a better feel for you as a prospective student.

There are two steps to developing personal contacts within a department: First, know what program you hope to enter and what field you want to work in, as well as what you want to learn from your conversations with faculty; and second, pick up the phone and make some calls—even if it makes you nervous.

Footing the bill

Okay, now it's time for a pop quiz to see if you've been paying attention: do you remember what the average starting salary was for a recent graduate with a degree in the liberal arts? In case you don't remember, it's approximately $31,000 per year. According to *U.S. News & World Report,* $31,000 also represents the average cost of attending graduate school for one year.[6] While that figure includes tuition and living expenses, it doesn't include the cost of being out of the workforce if you're attending graduate school full-time (and according to the Council of Graduate Schools, more than half of graduate students—around 55 percent—attend full-time).[7]

When considering the cost of graduate school, you can't ignore the implicit costs as well as the explicit ones: you're not just foregoing a real income, but you're also delaying possible career advancement opportunities. Even if your graduate program is related to the job you left behind—or the job you aspire to get—you're out of the workforce to one degree or another while you're in school. And, depending on your degree program, you may not be getting any on-the-job training that's directly applicable to what you'll be doing once you finish.

6 Kristin Davis. "The Hunt for Money." *U.S. News & World Report: America's Best Graduate Schools*. 2006. 13.

7 Council of Graduate Schools, *Graduate Enrollment and Degrees Report: 1986 to 2005*. September 13, 2006. 3. www.cgsnet.org.

The simple truth is this: Whether you're hoping to attend grad school before the ink has dried on your undergrad diploma, or whether you've been out of school for several years and would like to return to school as a way to improve your earning potential or even change careers entirely, grad school is an expensive proposition.

That said, the cost of attending graduate school alone shouldn't deter you from pursuing a graduate degree. The fact is, you have many options for financing your education, and, if an advanced-degree program is where your professional and personal stars align, then the investment will eventually pay off. However, it's important to understand how the investment will influence other decisions in your life: It's not uncommon for graduate students to postpone major milestones—like purchasing a house or starting a family—in order to fulfill their educational aspirations (and the ensuing financial obligations). While only you can decide whether choices like these are worth it—or whether they're even necessary, you need to research the implications of attending school so that you're not unpleasantly surprised once you've got your hard-earned degree in hand. To help alleviate some of the financial pressure of graduate school, the primary ways of financing a higher education (other than calling a wealthy relative, of course) are listed below.

- **Earn it.**

  For many graduate students—especially doctoral candidates—fellowships and assistantships go a long way toward paying the graduate-school tab. At the graduate level, grants like these are usually awarded based on merit. The most generous award packages not only cover tuition and fees, but also pay a stipend and provide health-insurance coverage. Not all awards represent a totally free ride; while fellowships usually have no work requirement, graduate assistants typically work up to 15 hours a week teaching, grading papers, leading discussion groups, supervising lab courses, or assisting faculty with research. If your financial aid package involves an assistantship, teaching responsibilities will place significant demands on your time. Completing your academic work will already take a major amount of time and energy, so consider whether the academic intensity of the program you choose—not to mention your time-management capabilities—will enable you to get everything done.

  The amount of fellowship and assistantship aid available to you depends on the field of study you're pursuing. In the humanities, for example, only about half of full-time PhD students and 40 percent of full-time master's degree students have assistantships, and the stipends awarded are usually lower than they are in other disciplines, such as engineering, math, and computer science. To make the financial picture even more sobering, keep in mind that high-paying internships between academic years—par for the course in professional degree programs—aren't as commonplace in liberal arts fields.

The first step toward getting a fellowship or assistantship is to indicate on your admissions application that you want to be considered for all forms of financial aid. The choicest awards are often made by departmental committees on the basis of application materials and sometimes supplemental recommendations. To find other awards or assistantships, check with your school's financial aid office, graduate school office, and fellowship coordinator (if there is one), or seek out faculty members in your department who are directing research funded by outside grants. Several government agencies and private organizations also sponsor outside fellowships that students can apply for on their own.

As part of the process of researching individual schools and programs, ask what percentage of students in the program are funded through fellowships, grants, and assistantships, and ask whether that changes after the first year. Some programs fund only a small percentage of students during the first year and provide funding in subsequent years based on academic performance (it's definitely worthwhile to ask whether the programs you're considering employ this approach, since it inevitably creates competition among students).

- **Borrow it.**

Most graduate students will borrow money to pay some or all of their graduate school costs. According to the National Center for Education Statistics, 69 percent of full-time master's degree students borrow to cover their expenses; on average, they carry a total of $32,500 of debt (including remaining undergraduate debt) once they finish their master's program. Some degree candidates have no choice but to finance their degrees with savings or loans; for those who earn their degrees part-time while continuing to work full-time, assistantships are impractical, and their income typically disqualifies them from subsidized student loans.

Of the borrowing options available, subsidized Stafford loans represent the cheapest type of student debt available. Interest rates are currently 5.3 percent, and you can borrow up to $8,500 per year ($65,500 in total). The federal government pays the interest on your loan while you're in school and for six months after you graduate or drop below half-time status. Even if interest rates rise significantly by the time you need to repay, they can't exceed 8.25 percent.

Students qualify based on financial need, so it's necessary to file the Free Application for Federal Student Aid (FAFSA) to get subsidized loans. If your need is high, you may also be offered a subsidized Perkins loan, with an interest rate of 5 percent. You can borrow an additional $10,000 a year in unsubsidized Stafford loans (and up to $138,500 in Stafford loans overall). Rates are the same as for the subsidized Stafford, and you can defer making payments, but interest begins accruing right away.

If your school participates in the Federal Direct Student Loan program, you'll borrow directly from the federal government. Otherwise, you can choose your own lender. Rates are usually the same no matter where you go, but some lenders waive up-front fees or offer attractive repayment incentives that make loans even cheaper.

For students who own a home, a home-equity loan or line of credit is another choice. Many banks were recently offering lines of credit at 6 percent or less, and the interest you pay is generally tax deductible. (So is up to $2,500 a year in student loan interest if you earn less than $50,000 as a single taxpayer and $105,000 if you file a joint return. A lesser amount of interest is deductible if you earn up to $65,000 or $135,000, respectively.)

If loans like these don't entirely meet your needs, keep in mind that many commercial lenders typically offer private education-related loans at rates only slightly higher than those for federal loans. Not only are the rates competitive, but you can typically borrow substantially more money with private lenders than you can with government lenders, whose maximum loan amounts may not provide you with the funding you need to cover all your expenses. For information on connecting with private lenders (and for general advice on financing your graduate education), check out the Scholarships & Aid section of the Princeton Review's website—PrincetonReview.com/grad/finance.

However much you borrow, make sure you know exactly how much it will eat into your monthly expenses once you graduate. Several websites—including FinAid.org—provide online calculators that will let you know how much debt you can afford to take on in order to fund your master's or doctoral program.

- **Ask your employer for it.**
  If you're currently working and can make a compelling case that your advanced degree is job-related, it's possible that your employer may be able to foot at least part of the bill. According to *U.S. News & World Report*, approximately 49 percent of private firms offer tuition-reimbursement programs for job-related educational expenses as an employee benefit. About 14 percent will help employees pay for courses that aren't job related. The percentages are significantly higher for professional and technical employees and for employees of large and medium-sized firms. While employer-sponsored funding is more common among business-school students financing their MBA, it's often a compelling option for employees of colleges and universities,

too. Educational institutions often offer significant tuition breaks for employees—so if you're currently working at a college or university (as a research assistant or an administrator, for example), remember that your employer might help fund your advanced degree. Even if you're not pursuing an advanced degree, many schools allow their employees to take a certain number of credit hours—or continuing education classes—for free, which is something to keep in mind. No matter who your employer is, however, be sure to read the fine print before you tap into this kind of funding, because you typically can't just take the money and run—there are usually restrictions on how long you must stay with the company once you've obtained your degree.

- **Tell Uncle Sam about it.**
  Students paying out of pocket for tuition and fees can take advantage of the federal Lifetime Learning tax credit, worth up to $2,000. The credit equals 20 percent of the first $10,000 you spend in tuition and fees each year. If you file a single return, you're eligible for the full tax credit if your income is $45,000 or less and for a partial credit with income up to $55,000. For married couples filing jointly, the tax credit is fully available with income up to $90,000 and partially available with income up to $110,000. You can use the credit even if you don't itemize deductions, and it reduces your tax bill dollar for dollar.[8]

ADVANCED DEGREE PROGRAMS FOR HISTORY AND POLITICAL SCIENCE MAJORS

Master's and PhD program opportunities are numerous and diverse; housed in a variety of home institutions, these programs reflect the full continuum of theory to practical application, and blend scholarship with social science research methods. Of course having lots of options may not make your situation any easier. That's where we come in. This section will identify some of your advanced study options and help you start thinking about the path that might be a good fit for you.

Academic vs. professional degrees

A traditional "academic" graduate school program focuses on work that will generate original research in a particular discipline. You may believe that a PhD is a "stronger" degree than a master's, but it really depends on your individual career objectives. A master's curriculum focuses on applied topics, while the theoretical and technical topics at the heart of a doctoral education train scholars for careers in academia and in high-level positions within research institutions. Some master's degrees

8 Kristin Davis. "The Hunt for Money." *U.S. News & World Report: America's Best Graduate Schools* . 2006. 13–15.

are designed to lead to a doctorate degree while others are the "terminal" degree for a profession (e.g., Master of Library Science; Master of Business Administration). For full-time students, completing a master's degree usually takes two years. As a part of a master's degree, you may be required to write a master's thesis or complete a project in the field and in some cases there is an additional certification or licensing requirement after graduation.

A "professional" degree program, on the other hand, is designed to provide relevant skills and knowledge to future professionals in a particular field. Professional schools provide a quick foundation of academic course work relevant to the field coupled with a specialization. The curriculum includes academic course work, exposure to advanced analytical tools, and fieldwork.

Many academic and professional advanced-degree programs adopt an interdisciplinary approach to focus on a particular problem or interest area. By digging a little deeper into what's out there, history and political science students have found some interesting programs. You can combine disciplines within one degree program—for example, a master's in law and diplomacy or a master's in history and museum studies. Even if you are committed to one degree—let's say law school—you are often able to take graduate courses in other departments on campus—for example, environmental science or public health—to enhance your legal education training. And of course there are the official joint-degree programs—the graduate level version of a double major—where you can leave a university with two degrees under your belt.

Maybe you have identified the advanced degree you'd like to pursue but are not sure where to apply. A good place to start is by talking with the faculty on your own campus and at other institutions who teach in the field you plan to pursue. Read professional and academic journals related to your area of interest—the authors of those articles are most likely faculty members in graduate programs which may interest you. Talk with current graduate students, alumni, and professionals to gain insider information about your programs of interest.

It really does pay to shop around because there are interesting intersections of study and research across disciplines. It's a good thing that you are great researchers, because most likely there is a program which will really capture your imagination. It just takes a little digging.

Academic programs: PhD history or PhD political science

In order to complete a doctorate degree, you will need to be able to conduct independent research resulting in the creation of new knowledge. Including the time it takes to write and defend a dissertation, this degree can take anywhere from five to seven years to complete. Progress towards the degree can be slow, and a few major hurdles need to be overcome early—qualifying exams, course work in the first couple years, and the defense of a dissertation idea before a self-selected panel of professors.

If you want to tackle the hard problems in society and have activist instincts, you may want to go elsewhere (like Capitol Hill). Academia may not be the agent for social change it used to be, but you can expect to make a very positive difference on a small segment of the academic community and your students. As one graduate student told us, "I would encourage anybody who is thinking about going to graduate school with the intention of pursuing an academic career to try something else for a while and see if your passion for the subject leads you back to it. If it does, then you are in the right place."

You may have gotten to know the graduate teaching assistants in your history or political science classes. But life as a graduate student involves quite a bit more than teaching undergraduates. Once you enter a PhD program you are not a "student" in the same way you were as an undergraduate. You are part of the academe, and you are treated by professors as a colleague. There is no pressure for grades, and you probably won't take tests, but the workload is very demanding. The general absence of hard and fast constraints means that self-discipline is essential for finishing the degree. However, you are still a "student" in some ways, and as such, you'll enjoy all the rich opportunities for culture and fun that are part of campus life. Most graduate students we talked to agreed that, despite the many challenges, the path is vastly rewarding.

Interview: Ryan Enos, PhD Candidate, UCLA Department of Political Science

Had you always known you were bound for graduate study in the field or did you decide to pursue an advanced degree later on?

I did consider it as an undergraduate and did research on the idea during my senior year. I actually think that it is a difficult decision to make as an undergraduate because the application process takes so long that you have to have essentially made that decision by the beginning of your senior year, and there is actually a lot of changing of priorities that can happen in that year alone. After I started working, I always assumed I would go back to graduate school, but it was actually a very difficult decision to make. I was fortunate enough to have a lot of options available outside of academia and I considered those too.

After graduating, I joined Teach for America and worked for an organization called Teach First that is based out of London and has a similar mission as Teach for America. During my second year of Teach for America, I applied for graduate school, was accepted, and considered going, but I decided to put it off for one year to teach another year. I am very glad that I made that decision. When I finally did go to graduate school, I was sure that I wanted to go, even though I missed teaching.

What are the rewards and challenges of being a graduate student in political science?

The first obvious challenge of being a graduate student is that you don't make a lot of money. It is okay because your graduate student friends don't either and you can adjust your lifestyle. But be warned, if you have friends who are not in graduate school, like I do, it can be annoying always being the poor person when you are out together.

The other challenge, and this one is not so obvious, is that you will have to get used to the fact that you do something that people don't really understand and that can be frustrating, especially if you study something like political science because people think they understand and they usually don't. You will have to deal with the frustration of people thinking that you are a "teacher" and not understanding that your primary occupation is research. You will also be doing something that is highly specialized and cannot easily be explained so it is hard to have those small-talk conversations with people in the seat next to you on that flight across the country. And finally—and this can be really frustrating—people think you are doing graduate school because you basically don't want to work hard or don't know what you want to do in life; it is really difficult to convince people that you probably work much longer hours than they do.

Other challenges worth noting (and anybody going into graduate school should definitely ask if they want this type of lifestyle) are that it can be very solitary. It can also be a very slow process—there is practically no immediate gratification. And it is generally a very competitive type of work environment. There is always pressure to publish and be at the top of the game. This is not true of all disciplines and schools, but if you enter a highly regarded program with the intention of earning your PhD, then be prepared for it.

The rewards are that, hopefully, you are able to be immersed in something you find fascinating. You are surrounded by brilliant people. You get to be your own boss. And you are working towards a prestigious career choice.

How does life change along the way towards the PhD?

I am beginning my third year of graduate school, and my life has changed in many ways. I don't make much money so I have definitely had to change my spending habits. My bookshelf is a lot more crowded. I no longer take classes, so my time, other than teaching, is very unstructured. I have also acquired skills that I never would have imagined having when I first started graduate school.

Any advice for undergraduate political science students in terms of advanced study in the field, or advice in general about career decision-making?

You should only do it if you are really passionate about it, not just because it seems like fun. You are devoting your life to the study of this subject, which is often very narrow, and you better really think it is important. Secondly— and this is important to me but not to everybody equally—is study something that matters to the world. Choose a subject that has an impact on our lives and how we understand ourselves. If you are doing that, I think you will be able to go to work everyday with the feeling that you are accomplishing something valuable, and there is no reason that an intelligent, talented person should not have that feeling.

Remember that you are really young. I have been out of Cal for five years now and I have had so many experiences since then that I am almost a completely different person than I was when I graduated. I am looking forward to seeing who I am in another five years. So, if advanced study is where you want to be, then just know that there is no need to rush into it, or any other career for that matter. Be smart, make good decisions, but let your experiences build and guide you along your career path.

Going all the way: An academic career

The traditional employment objective of PhDs is a tenure-track faculty position. While these positions aren't impossible to obtain, landing one is far from a sure thing—and the path toward getting one is arduous. A master's degree may be sufficient to qualify to teach in a two-year college, but a doctoral degree is required to teach in four-year colleges and universities. While the PhDs dissertation is the most important element of her search for a first job as a professor, postdoctoral experience—teaching or research done by PhDs after they've earned their doctorates but before they've landed tenure-track teaching positions—is also crucial. For the coveted tenure-track positions, virtually every successful job candidate now boasts at least one and usually two "postdoc" years, and these are necessary to remain competitive, which means gathering a sufficient backlog of publications and writings in progress. Personal relationships with faculty are also critical in this hunt for a first job, as teaching positions in many areas (particularly the humanities) can be scarce. While approximately 80 percent of college jobs are in four-year institutions, about a third of all college faculty are employed part-time or in non-tenure track positions, and this percentage has risen in recent years as colleges attempt to control costs.

It's worth noting that landing your first job after you've completed your PhD is far from the end of the road. You'll spend at least five or six years as an assistant professor. In your seventh year, you'll be evaluated for a tenure position on the basis of teaching and research (which almost always means published work). Institutions vary in the relative importance they place on these criteria, but it's always some combination of the two. Those who earn tenure are—for the most part—virtually guaranteed job security until they retire. Tenure also effectively separates junior faculty from senior faculty at most institutions. Senior, tenured faculty members have far more discretion when it comes to deciding what to teach as well as when (or whether) to conduct research than do junior faculty.

Folks who are jazzed enough about their studies to go this route aren't necessarily motivated by money or the certainty of getting a job—and that's a good thing. Not only do most doctoral candidates live pretty frugally while they're working toward their degree, but, unlike advanced degrees in business or medicine, there's no guarantee of recouping the financial investment. According to a recent article in *U.S. News & World Report*, roughly 30 percent of PhDs who earned their degrees in 2004 were still seeking employment or planning further studies in 2006, thanks in large part to a perennially tight job market for tenured professors. According to the same article, PhDs in the humanities and liberal arts face a particularly formidable challenge when it comes to landing a job. In 2001, for example, there were more than twice as many newly minted PhDs as there were available tenure-track teaching positions. Of course, non-academic jobs are an option, too; in fact, approximately 4 out of 10 PhDs go the private-sector route. Still, the relative scarcity of available jobs—especially when compared to the investment of time and money that a PhD requires—leads to a fairly high attrition rate among doctoral candidates. Roughly 40 to 50 percent of matriculating students never earn their PhD.[9] And some master's degree candidates who toy with the idea of pushing forward for a PhD decide against it when they take a hard look at the job prospects. Lisa, who we mentioned earlier, enjoyed her MFA in fiction writing so much that she briefly considered pursuing a PhD in literature. She eventually decided against it. Looking back, she's glad she did. "I'm pretty sure I

9 Silla Brush. "Beyond the Ivory Tower." *U.S. News & World Report: America's Best Graduate School.* 2006. 54–55.

would have been miserable," she says. "And I would have just finished a few years ago with a mountain of debt and limited and depressing job prospects—with guaranteed low salaries at all of them."

The good news, however, is that the job outlook for future professors is considerably brighter than it was even a few years ago. According to the Bureau of Labor Statistics, employment of postsecondary (i.e., college and university) teachers is expected to grow much faster than the average for all occupations through 2014. And that's good news if you're in for the long haul: The BLS predicts that "PhD recipients seeking jobs as postsecondary teachers will experience favorable job prospects over the next decade."[10]

Though job prospects will vary significantly depending on the field you're in, there are a few demographic trends working in your favor if you want to be a professor. First of all, significant numbers of current professors (many of whom were hired in the late 1960s and the 1970s) are expected to retire over the next few years. And not only is the supply of professors expected to shrink, but demand for professors is expected to increase. The BLS predicts higher enrollment numbers at colleges and universities, which stems mainly from the expected increase in the population of 18- to 24-year-olds (who make up the majority of the college-student population).[11]

Even with the decreasing supply and increasing demand for college-level professors, however, it's important to remember that a significant proportion of the resulting job opportunities will be part-time positions. The BLS predicts that while competition will remain tight for tenure-track positions at four-year colleges and universities, there will be a considerable number of part-time or renewable, term appointments at these institutions and positions at community colleges available to them.[12]

10 Bureau of Labor Statistics, U.S. Department of Labor. *Occupational Outlook Handbook,* 2006–2007 Edition. Teachers—Postsecondary. www.bls.gov/oco/ocos066.htm.

11 Ibid.

12 Ibid.

Interview: Amy Speckart, American Studies Program, The College of William & Mary

Did you always know you wanted to go on for the PhD in history?

I did not feel ready to apply in my fourth year, so I compromised with my parents—who were pressing me to apply to graduate school—by doing half of a fifth year, thereby delaying graduate school applications by a year. In retrospect, I may still not have been ready emotionally, but I did not see that then.

What have been the rewards and challenges of life as a graduate student?

How has my life changed from my first year in grad school? Whew, do you want real answers? First of all, Cal prepared me well in my knowledge and in the "hard knocks" of attending any school. Connections made with my professors in college have served me well in life after college. The rewards of grad school have been: meeting very interesting, bright people; challenging myself; being able to travel as a student. The challenges have been: the "lower caste" status of not having a PhD while operating in academia, summoning the commitment and dedication necessary to stay in school.

Any advice for the history or political science student?

Be aware of the gains and risks of going into graduate school. For my career interests, I had to get a PhD (museums, public history, now editing of historical documents for publication). You have to be dedicated, and in some respects, time out of school can help. On the other hand, for fast-trackers, it is good to have it behind you. I think advanced study in any field is a terrific opportunity in the U.S., where those opportunities exist for most anyone. I did a summer internship before my last year in college that helped me see the need for graduate school.

And now the good news . . .

While a career in academia isn't the right choice for everyone, it can prove to be an immensely satisfying, rewarding profession for many people. (If there weren't an awful lot to recommend it, why would so many people be clamoring for it?) If you love reading, observing, and figuring things out, then there are few careers that offer greater opportunities for indulging your unique intellectual interests. And as a professor, you're not just developing an area of expertise, a significant portion of your time and energy will usually be devoted to knowledge creation. The profession is therefore best suited for motivated self-starters, and its highest rewards are given to those who can identify and explore original problems in their fields.

In academia, you're also paid to teach that material to people who are interested in learning it—and for many professors (including—hopefully—the ones you'll be working with) the opportunity to contribute to other people's learning and growth provides the greatest source of professional fulfillment.

There's also a lot of variety in an academic career: Many full-time faculty engage in outside professional activities. Economists consult with governments and corporations; engineers and academic labs develop products for private industry; humanities professors write articles which appear in newspapers and magazines. Many find this ability to work professionally on terms they define, while remaining in their institutions, to be among the most satisfying aspects of the profession. In addition, the significant administrative positions in colleges and universities are usually filled by former and current professors, and it is not uncommon for careers in university administration to develop from teaching careers.

Apart from the career satisfaction many professors enjoy, there are other, more practical, perks that come with the job. In addition to the time spent teaching in the classroom (which amounts to as few as three hours a week in graduate schools, up to 12 to 16 hours a week in undergraduate schools), professors spend time meeting with students during designated office hours, sitting on committees, and completing any number of administrative duties associated with teaching a class or running a department. But they can allocate the rest of their time as they see fit. Professors get summers off too—or they at least get a three-month break from their teaching and administrative responsibilities. In actuality, few professors spend three months on the beach every year; many devote the majority of that time to conducting their own research, catching up on journal reading, and planning the courses that they'll be teaching the following semester. Still, they can complete that work whenever—and wherever—they choose. It's worth pointing out, however, that this degree of flexibility can be a double-edged sword. "Academic work is both flexible and all-consuming," says Penny Gold, a history professor at Knox College in Illinois. "One can read a book or journal article anywhere, and so it's a challenge to keep work from creeping into every available space. Sometimes I think wistfully of a nine-to-five job, where I would come home at the end of the day and be done with it."[13] But despite those occupational hazards, most consider this flexibility—certainly greater than what most non-academic jobs allow—to be one of the real benefits of an academic career.

Job security is another big draw. A tenured-professor gig isn't the guaranteed job for life it once was (post-tenure review is now required at most universities, and those who fall behind on teaching and independent scholarship may not be as secure as they would have been 10 or 20 years ago). Still, once professors earn tenure they have considerably more job security than their counterparts in the private sector. Of course, they typically don't earn the same fat paychecks, either. In 2004–2005, salaries for full-time faculty averaged $68,505. Specifically, the average salary was $91,548 for professors, $65,113 for associate professors, $54,571 for assistant professors, $39,899 for instructors, and $45,647 for lecturers. Educators in four-year institutions earned higher salaries, on average, than did those in two-year schools. In fields with high-paying non-academic alternatives—e.g., medicine, law, engineering, business—

13 John A. Goldsmith, John Komlos, and Penny Schine Gold. *The Chicago Guide to Your Academic Career*. Chicago: University of Chicago Press, 2001. 9.

professors tended to earn higher-than-average salaries, while professors in others fields—e.g., the humanities, education—typically recorded salaries on the lower end of the range.[14]

Interview: Neil Ruiz, PhD Candidate in Political Science, MIT

Had you always known you were bound for the PhD in the field or did it come to you later on?

When I was a child, I always wanted to do a PhD since I thought that it might lead to a political appointment (like a Secretary of Labor) in the future. I will be the first PhD in my family so I do not come from a family of academics (which is the usual story I noticed among my colleagues). I did consider doing a professional degree, such as a MPP and/or a law degree. But I realized that my interests in continuing school were more theoretical and empirical, rather than practical. But I did acquire practical skills by starting up several organizations (we do have a lot of time on our hands and a lot of autonomy as PhD students). I feel like my training is a good balance of research skills, [knowledge of a] breadth of academic literature, and also some practical understanding of policy.

Did you go straight through from your BA?

I was admitted directly as an undergraduate student, but MIT allowed me to defer my admission for two years to go to Oxford after winning a scholarship from the English-Speaking Union called the Winston Churchill Scholarship. It was an opportunity I couldn't refuse since it came with two years of funding. The MS was a great experience since it helped me define my research interests.

Any advice for your fellow political science undergrads in terms of advanced study in the field or related fields?

I would advise students to ask if they enjoy discovering new ideas. You must be passionate about research and theory in order to do a PhD. You also have to be self-disciplined/self-motivated since academicians and PhD students have a lot of autonomy. If you like to be your own boss from the very beginning, doing a PhD is great! You will learn a lot about yourself—how to motivate yourself, how to manage your time on your own since many of your deadlines are loose, and how to translate your theoretical research interests into practice.

---

14 Bureau of Labor Statistics, U.S. Department of Labor. *Occupational Outlook Handbook*, 2006–2007 Edition, Teachers—Postsecondary. www.bls.gov/oco/ocos066.htm.

Professional degree options

It may be hard for you to wrap your brain around this concept, especially when waiting one to two years to go to grad school may seem like an eternity, but the option for an advanced degree does not have an expiration date. There are amazing opportunities for professionals who have been in their field for a while to go to graduate school and get their jobs back after their degree program is over. After teaching for a while, one history graduate decided that he preferred the administrative side of education. He enrolled in UCLA's Principal Leadership Institute, an intense 15-month program for teachers which resulted in a Master's in Education with a Preliminary Administrative Service Credential. Another graduate with a career path in business continues to work at his financial services firm while attending an Executive MBA program. After 19 months he'll have the MBA along with even greater opportunity for advancement at his current job.

The professional degree programs described below are at the master's level, and most take about two years to complete (law school is three years). Some history and political science students may find themselves interested in going on for a doctoral degree in policy, public administration, law, urban planning, or other professional arenas. These students should expect to complete many of the same requirements of academic doctoral degree programs, including the completion of a dissertation and comprehensive oral or written examinations in their area of focus.

Law (JD)

The Juris Doctor, or JD, is the most common degree conferred by law school and usually requires three years of full-time study. Some law schools also offer part-time programs that generally take four to five years to complete. In addition, many schools offer joint degrees, such as a JD/MBA or JD/MA that may take four to five years to complete, but generally take less time to complete than would enrolling in the two degrees separately.

Law school is not merely an extension of an undergraduate degree in political science. At law school, you will learn how to "think like a lawyer," and your studies will be more focused than they were as an undergraduate. Attending law school is an enormous personal and financial commitment and one that should not be entered into without adequate self-assessment. Observing how lawyers operate in the professional setting will provide valuable insight for you as you make your decision. No matter what anyone says about the JD being a "versatile degree" that will allow you to advance in many careers, most doors to alternative careers do not open until you have at least some amount of experience and training as a lawyer.

As a first-year law student at virtually every law school throughout the United States, you don't get to choose your classes. Instead, you'll be assigned to something called a section, which is a good-sized group of students who have all the same classes with all the same professors at all the same times. Those classes will include Torts, Civil Procedure, Contracts, Property, Constitutional Law, and probably Criminal Law. In addition to these course requirements, many law schools require first-year students to participate in a moot-court exercise. As part of this exercise, students—sometimes working in pairs or even small groups—must prepare briefs and oral arguments for a mock trial (usually appellate). This requirement is often tied in with a Methods class, sometimes called Legal Writing or Legal Research and Writing.

LSAT at a Glance

WHY TAKE IT?	Most law schools require it
HOW LONG IS IT?	4 hours
WHEN IS IT OFFERED?	Upcoming dates
HOW TO REGISTER?	LSAC.org
HOW IS IT SCORED?	Scoring Information

LSAT: Section By Section

READING COMPREHENSION	• About 27 multiple-choice questions
	• 35 minute section
LOGICAL REASONING (Arguments)	• Multiple-choice questions
	• 2 sections, about 25 questions each
	• 35 minute sections
ANALYTICAL REASONING (Games)	• About 25 multiple-choice questions
	• 35 minute section
EXPERIMENTAL	• About 25 multiple-choice questions
	• 35 minute section
ESSAY	• 1 essay
	• 35 minute section

Source: PrincetonReview.com

Law school professors want you to be prepared for class and they set up elaborate schemes and scare tactics to ensure that you've done your reading. During the first year and sometimes beyond, you will probably encounter the case method of teaching, also known as the Socratic Method. You will be assigned to read hundreds of pages of judicial opinion and write summaries of them called briefs. Then you may be called upon in class to answer a series of questions about the facts, legal principles, and reasoning used to formulate the opinions. The case method tests your ability to synthesize information and to apply knowledge to new situations. Throughout your law school career, you will face this awkward rite of passage. The classic method—and the clear favorite among especially sardonic, old-school law professors—involves randomly calling on students throughout the semester. New age, touchy-feely professors ask for volunteers or proceed through the seating chart in a democratic and more predictable fashion.

Preparing for a Legal Degree: Core Skills and Values

- Analytic/Problem-Solving Skills
- Critical Reading
- Writing Skills
- Oral Communication/Listening Abilities
- General Research Skills
- Task Organization/Management Skills
- Public Service and Promotion of Justice

Source: "Preparing for Law School." American Bar Association. www.abanet.org/legaled/prelaw/prep.html.

Several law school admissions directors we talked to revealed a few key points that make candidates stand out beyond the numbers (GPA and LSAT scores) as they evaluate the large pile of law school applications on their desks. The consensus is that undergraduates who have dedicated themselves to their undergraduate work and have demonstrated academic excellence as well as passion for something outside of themselves make a great impression. As one put it, "We aren't looking for brains in a jar."

While there isn't one cookie-cutter profile of the successful applicant, evidence of intellectual curiosity is crucial, as is some evidence that students have challenged themselves and succeeded. There are many different ways to demonstrate these qualities. For one applicant, it may be having a truly outstanding academic record. For another, it may be his or her leadership in campus organizations. For still another, it may be a solid academic record while working full-time and raising a child. Internships can help, but only to the extent that they are part of a compelling package.

Put yourselves in their shoes. Their job is to put together a first year class that will bring a variety of life experiences and skills to their law school. They understand that students learn a great deal from each other and therefore want people who have had interesting and unique experiences.

Interview: Armilla T. Staley, JD Candidate, Boalt Hall School of Law

What are the rewards and challenges of being a law student?

The biggest challenge of being a law student is learning how to balance academic and personal responsibilities. The first year of law school is extremely time-consuming, and it is very stressful to think about staying on top of your homework while making time for family, friends, and loved ones. Additionally, you are constantly thinking about job prospects for the upcoming summer and what type of law you want to specialize in. Nothing can really prepare you for the amount of work that you will be doing during the first year of law school, and the heavy amount of reading that a law student has per night is overwhelming to all law students.

There are several rewards of being a law student. The first is learning a different way to think, analyze, and articulate oneself as a lawyer. It is also nice to be a student for an additional three years before having to enter, or re-enter, the real world. The critical and analytical skills that I have acquired during law school are priceless. Also the ability to make better oral presentations and arguments, as well as to write concisely and effectively has been a reward of being a law student.

Did you always know you wanted to go or was law a career path that opened up after you were out in the "real world?"

I pretty much always knew that I wanted to attend law school, but right after college I began to doubt whether it was truly necessary for me to obtain my JD for the career path that I wished to pursue at the time. I was initially very interested in pursuing a career in criminal law and/or law enforcement, such as working for the FBI or the federal government, so I actually applied to graduate schools in Washington, DC to pursue a Master's in Criminal Justice before I decided to apply to law school.

I postponed law school for a year to participate in the Judicial Administration Fellowship Program [see "Fellowships" section at the end of this chapter]. The fellowship was a good way to obtain work experience without completely removing myself from an academic environment. My hope was that the fellowship would help solidify my decision to attend law school. Upon completion of the fellowship, I finally decided that I wanted to attend law school, so I continued to work part-time for the courthouse where I worked as a fellow in order to attend LSAT classes and begin the law school application process.

Master's in Business Administration (MBA)

Graduate business schools teach the applied science of business, combining the latest academic theories with pragmatic concepts, hands-on experience, and real-world solutions. There are many paths that lead to b-school. One MBA student at UPenn's Wharton School of Business was a committed nonprofit professional before applying to business school: "I decided to pursue an MBA because of my interest in the intersections of business and social responsibility. An MBA will provide me with the business knowledge and credibility to complement my experience in the social sector."

The application to b-school is intense. It usually involves a series of 250- to 500-word essays on anything from how you value creativity in your work to an ethical dilemma you have faced. Most MBA applicants have several years of work experience under their belts—four to five years is typical. These real-world experiences will help you better understand the types of cases presented in class. Take the GMAT—but only when you're well-prepared. Great GMAT scores won't necessarily get you into the school of your choice (there are too many other factors), but low scores will almost certainly keep you out. If you are applying without the four to five years of work experience, your GMAT score will be scrutinized closely, as will your GPA, because the Admissions Committee has no work experience to consider that might otherwise help to balance out the other factors.

To equip students with the broad expertise they need to be managers, most business schools start new MBAs off with a set of foundation or "core" courses in what are known as the "functional areas": finance, accounting, management, marketing, operations, and economics. These courses introduce you to the basic vocabulary and concepts of formal business culture. Next, you acquire knowledge of tools such as ratio analysis, valuations, and pro formas. Finally, you experience action-based learning in the form of case studies, role plays, and business simulations.

Business schools employ two basic teaching methods: case study and lecture. Usually, they employ some combination of the two. Case study, the most popular approach, presents students with real or hypothetical business scenarios and asks them to analyze them. Students often find case studies exciting because they can engage in spirited discussions about possible solutions to business problems. Which brings us to another point: In addition to practical knowledge of basic business functions, b-schools teach the analytical skills used to make complicated business decisions. You learn how to define the critical issues, apply analytical techniques, develop the criteria for decisions, and make decisions after evaluating their impact on other variables.

After two years, you're ready to market a box of cereal. Or prepare a valuation of the cereal company's worth. You'll speak the language and know the tools of the trade. Your expertise will extend into many areas and industries. In short, you will have acquired the skills that open doors.

Interview: Adam Harris, Political Science BA, MBA Candidate, Berkeley-Columbia Part-Time Executive Program

Did you always know you wanted to go for an MBA?

I wasn't sure I wanted to pursue an MBA until just within a year of applying. In fact, as an undergraduate, I was not very fond of the idea of being in business at all. It did not seem exciting enough. I did not want to live a cookie-cutter life, and this is what I envisioned a business career to be. This changed as I learned more about business and entrepreneurial life: the ultimate gamble.

What are the rewards and challenges of being an MBA student?

My major challenge in being an MBA student is finding time for both work and school, since I am in the part-time Executive MBA program. The major reward for me is getting to know many other amazing people and in learning business skills that will benefit me in the future. Political science does not give any person a complete background in business, but it does give a unique perspective to the business world for which an MBA program may be looking. My political science degree and my own entrepreneurial spirit took me to a point in my career [at which] I needed to learn the finer points of accounting, finance, etc. that are not common knowledge. I suppose the political science degree helped me along my path by not burdening me with preconceived notions about how to do business or what was possible in a business environment. I learned quickly that the cookie-cutter businessman did not exist, or if he did, most businesses did not want him. The poly sci degree gave me the thinking power to set my own rules and create a different way of doing things within my business environments. The achievements that resulted from this different perspective were invaluable in gaining admission to the Berkeley-Columbia program because they provided me with great stories and insights to benefit the program and my fellow students.

Master's in Public Policy

In a Master's of Public Policy (MPP) degree program students acquire more complex analytical tools in order to evaluate and develop alternative approaches to policy problems or issues. Sometimes, this kind of training and study results in a master's degree in political science. Course work includes core requirements designed to help students develop and refine research methodologies. These include: statistics and quantitative methods and data analysis, public finance, microeconomics and macroeconomics, research design, program evaluation, organization and management concepts and behavior, and ethics.

In addition, students must choose to concentrate or specialize within a particular policy area. Some examples of areas of concentration include: environment, education, health, transportation, economic development, international development, urban affairs, criminal justice, and science and technology policy. Several policy graduates told us that the alumni networks alone were worth the intense work they did in graduate school: "I've run across several alums from my program who hold prominent positions in government and are working in amazing places nationally and internationally."

Others choose the degree program because of its potential to help advance their careers: "I was in Washington, DC working for the Clinton administration for a member of the president's cabinet. I had a ring-side seat to amazing policy and international diplomacy debates and decisions. But I really wanted to take the next step to be the person helping to make those decisions rather than just getting to watch. It seemed that one of the best ways to do that was to go back to school and get a higher degree. The MPP appealed to me because it added a very analytical and statistical approach to dealing with complex problems. It was also about making our government and society work better, not just making money or winning court cases. I liked that broad approach."

Interview: Greg Kato, Graduate Student, MPP program, Goldman School of Public Policy, UC—Berkeley

Had you always known you were bound for the Master's in Public Policy or did you decide to pursue it later on?

I decided on a Masters in Public Policy after working for two years. After my undergraduate degree in history, I had been working as an outreach coordinator for UC—Berkeley, recruiting high schools kids for the campus. That means I ran a summer camp for high school kids, visited high schools to talk about college, and also worked with donors to support the program. After working very closely with students, I decided I wanted to do something more quantitative and on a larger scale, so I went for the MPP. The diversity of my experiences was helpful in my application to the MPP program

What are the rewards and challenges of your work as an MPP student?

The rewards were learning the method of analyzing public problems that the Goldman School teaches. The challenges were working on quantitative skills after not really engaging that part of my brain for a while. Also, graduate school was a very consuming time. As for my fieldwork, my project was with the Oakland Police Department—I worked on a report on overtime. They were way over on overtime and we interviewed a bunch of cops to determine where they could make improvements.

Any advice for your fellow history undergraduates in terms of advanced study in the field?

Working for a few years was great for helping me clarify what I wanted out of my career, and made graduate school more productive than if I had attended graduate school straight after college.

Master's in Public Administration (MPA)

If you are committed to public service but find yourself more interested in management positions than research, you may find the MPA degree of interest. In an MPA program, you are trained to develop skills necessary to promote public policy agendas while taking on the challenges of running an organization, including budgetary and financial concerns, internal information systems, and human resources management. Emphasis is on the operation of public and nonprofit organizations and the development of the decision-making and analytical skills required of management. Students in MPA programs are often involved in significant group project work to gain exposure to a managerial work environment. These programs provide management techniques that include greater analytical and quantitative grounding.

Core courses in the MPA program include: human resources, budgeting and financial processes, information systems, policy and program formulation, implementation and evaluation, decision making and problem solving, organization and management concepts and behavior, and ethics. Specializations within schools of public administration vary widely and could include health care or environmental management, urban affairs, criminal justice, or philanthropic development.

History graduate Mark Lewis got his MPA at Harvard's Kennedy School of Government: "As I studied history as an undergraduate, I began to notice how we have made a lot of mistakes by not examining current policies well. I grew up in Los Angeles and have always been committed to improving things. Through my work after my BA degree, I saw academic PhD graduates come into public administration who really couldn't relate to the issues and see the interconnectedness of the different levels of government and the nonprofit-government relationship. I wanted advanced training in managing the type of complex projects such as the one I am doing now with the city of LA. I got that through the MPA degree at Harvard. It provided me with the administrative tools to understand and work effectively within the public sector."

If you want to be a competitive candidate for a master's degree in public policy or public administration, you'll need a combination of strong academics combined with practical and relevant experience. Because the degrees are not licensing degrees (like an MSW, JD or MD), field experience is incredibly important in this arena. Jobs, internships, and volunteer experience that are related to your area of interest (whether it be economic development, policy analysis, children and youth, housing, the environment, social justice, or any other issue that is your passion) will elevate your candidacy and demonstrate your interest in public service.

Master's in International Affairs (MIA)

International Affairs graduate programs offer a mixture of detailed instruction in theory combined with practical field experience. The core curriculum provides the foundational studies, and may include: theory, policy analysis, courses in oral and written communications, macro and microeconomics, management, and quantitative methods/statistics. Grad students in international relations can choose to focus in a variety of different areas. Some might take a regional interest and concentrate their studies on a particular geographic area (for example, Southeast Asia), while others might take a more functional approach and concentrate on an issue area such as international security, trade, or finance. As in public policy and public administration graduate programs, MIA graduate programs combine project management and research exposure. A political science major really appreciated the balance of academic and practitioner faculty available in his MIA master's program: "You could be having class in the morning with a leading academician in political science and in the afternoon be taught by the former ambassador to Moscow or a CNN anchor."

Master's Degrees in Museum Studies, Public History, and Archival Studies

There is a variety of advanced degree options providing training in the theory and practice of museum work, sometimes terminating with a master's degree and a certification in museum studies. The core curriculum provides the student with knowledge of all of the museum's functions, and is supplemented by elective courses and an internship or master's project focusing on the student's specialized area of museum work. Potential areas of focus include: curation, exhibition design, museum education, museum fundraising, museum management, and registration/collections management.

Public history programs focus on the practice of history outside of university classrooms. Not all history departments offer public history, but the number of programs is growing, and museums are looking to hire graduates of public history or museum studies programs. Some master's programs in historic preservation (which are often housed in public history programs) offer academic training in preservation law and preservation theory and practice. The specific focus of the programs vary widely; some emphasize the role of the historian, some stress the legal and planning elements, and others emphasize museum education and other administrative functions.

For those interested in both history and the library profession, a few graduate schools offer students the opportunity to complete both a master's in history and a master's in library science. Archival education programs have grown in number over the years. Traditionally housed in both history and library science environments, this program provides training in the identification and protection of archival records and in procedures required to make these records accessible to the public. Some programs educate "generalists" with knowledge of all areas of archival administration. Other programs prepare specialists in one or more areas of archival administration including electronic records management, historical manuscripts, and management of institutional archives. Other programs offer a more interdisciplinary approach and include library science and museum-related course work in the curriculum.

Master's of Information Studies, Master's of Library Science (MIS, MLS, MLIS)

University programs in library and information science have been pioneers in the application of digital technology to meet the growing public demand for access to information. Course work may include: classification, cataloging, computer courses, and reference work. Some graduate programs require students to know a foreign language. While popular perception links such training to a career in librarianship, these degree programs offer various approaches to the management of information, whether generated in the past or the present, and in the case of the archivist, particular technical skills needed to preserve historical records.

One library science graduate student decided on the MLIS in part because there were so many career paths open to her with the degree, and so many kinds of organizations she could potentially work for: "The other great thing is that I can work in the field as I go to school. I started working for an agency that sends me out to about five law firms per week. At some firms I am the lowly assistant and I sit and file the updates to the law books (this means replacing the pages where a law or opinion has changed, and it can be pretty tedious). At other firms I am the only library staff they have, so I do everything: check in the mail, maintain the catalog, process new books, reconcile the bills, etc. Although law librarianship is not a career that I intend to pursue, I've learned a lot in the last year doing this."

Master's in Journalism

Journalism school teaches you how to be a reporter in various communications media: radio, television, print, and online. Although some argue that good reporters are born, not made, proponents of journalism school will tell you that one of the most critical lessons you'll learn as a graduate student in journalism is how to be an ethical reporter which, according to the Society of Professional Journalists, is defined as someone who properly represents facts, identifies sources, and supports the open exchange of views. Because faculty in most programs are former or current industry professionals, journalism school students have access to a broad network of field contacts, and are often engaged in fieldwork for the duration of the program.

In order to be a competitive applicant, you must be able to demonstrate superior writing and critical-thinking skills, and be able to impress the Admissions Committee with published clippings or other writing samples. If you haven't already interned at your college newspaper or local radio station, choose academic writing samples that show your ability to form and defend an argument, especially one that revolves around hotly debated issues.

Journalism schools tend to favor applicants who have several years of work experience behind them. Applicants who are able to demonstrate an abiding interest in journalism and communications will have an edge over those who lack any exposure to the field. Prospective students who have years of professional experience in a niche area that they intend to explore as reporters, (a former museum curator or ballerina who intends to become an arts journalist) will also be viewed favorably. It's a good idea to show that you have a well-rounded liberal arts education by taking a broad range of course work, from political science, to psychology, to world history.

"Graduate journalism study isn't for every aspiring journalist. There are many ways to establish a journalism career, and most good degree programs are aimed at exceptionally smart, curious people who have had enough experience in the field both to know this work is what they want and to understand what kinds of skills and practice a graduate program can offer them. We look favorably at most kinds of undergraduate degrees, although journalism and mass communication degrees are not regarded as an advantage; we tend to think those are redundant. Strong writing skills and personal statements and backgrounds that show us a natural journalist in the making, matter more to us than high grade point averages or GRE scores."

Cynthia Gorney,
Associate Dean and Professor from the UC—Berkeley
Graduate School of Journalism

Master's in Education/Teacher Credential Programs:

Want to pass along that love of history or political science to the next generation? Other history and political science grads are out there teaching some version of social studies within K–12 public or private schools. Opportunities to teach history as a separate subject are available at the junior-high and high-school levels.

All 50 states and the District of Columbia require public school teachers to be licensed. The specific requirements vary by state, but include completion of a teacher training program with a prescribed number of subject-specific academic credits, and several hours of supervised student-teaching. A number of states require that teachers obtain a master's degree in education within a specified period after they begin teaching.

Many school systems are implementing performance-based systems for licensure, which usually require a teacher to demonstrate satisfactory teaching performance over an extended period in order to obtain a provisional license, in addition to passing an examination in their subject. Private schools are generally exempt from meeting state licensing standards.

Many states also offer alternative licensure programs for recent college graduates who did not complete education programs. States may issue emergency licenses to individuals who do not meet the requirements for a regular license when schools cannot attract enough licensed teachers to fill positions.

FELLOWSHIPS: KEEPING THE DREAM ALIVE

Fellowships are great opportunities to feed your love of academics while you decide if and when graduate school makes sense. One history graduate puts it this way: "It is perfectly okay to feel like you don't know what you are going to do with your life after you graduate from college. In fact, I saw my fellowship as an opportunity to obtain a good job without long-term commitments."

Fellowships tend to be short-term opportunities lasting anywhere from a few months to several years. Fellowships often provide an important and often missing training function within the nonprofit and government community. These sectors recognize the need for new talent and are making a commitment to provide support for people coming out of college to start their careers. Well-run fellowship programs can provide you with the experience and training you need to be successful over the longer term.

The postbaccalaureate programs discussed below are designed to support a range of activities including: graduate study in a specific field; research to advance work on a particular issue; development of a new community-based organization or initiative; training and reflection to support the fellow's growth; opportunities to further explore a particular field of work; or support for leadership in a particular region or within a particular cultural group.

Fellowships are structured to provide significant work experiences, and fellows are often expected to take on a great deal of responsibility quickly. Generally, fellows are provided with unique experiences that are not typically available to someone starting out in an entry-level position. Below are a few fellowships of possible interest to you as a history or political science major. See Appendix A for more ideas.

What do you do on a fellowship?

The fellowship experience varies from program to program, but many include:

- An apprenticeship with a senior-level nonprofit professional
- A research project designed and implemented by the fellow
- A part-time or full-time internship in an organization chosen by the fellow
- Short-term field placements in various segments of the public affairs arena: nonprofits, labor, the media, the private sector, and government entities
- A team project developed by the group of current fellows
- An independent project proposed by a social entrepreneur and funded by the fellowship program

Interview: Carrie Donavan, Alumni, Congressional Hunger Fellowship

Why did you decide to do a fellowship?

Around the midpoint of my senior year, I began to wonder about jobs and what I would do after graduation. I thought that I wanted to go to graduate school and pursue a PhD, but I had heard from numerous people that it was a good idea to take time off, gain work experience, and explore the real world for a little while. This sounded like wise advice. The only problem was, I was interested in many different things and did not know exactly what I wanted to dedicate my time and energy to. I wasn't sure if I wanted to work locally in an advocacy organization or nationally in a policy organization. I wasn't sure if I wanted to do research, program planning/development, or work directly with people in more of a service delivery role. So, I decided the best thing to do was to find an opportunity that would expose me to diverse experiences. Ideally, I hoped to get a taste for different types of work and to gain exposure to jobs and careers that were out there.

I began researching fellowships and programs, and found the Congressional Hunger Center's national fellows program. The fellowship was a great match for me for three reasons: First, I gained both grassroots and national policy experience and was better able to assess where my own interests lie. Second, I learned a lot about different types of organizations, projects, and the range of first jobs available from the experiences of others in the group. Finally, the fellowship created a natural setting for me to learn networking skills. By learning and talking to one another, our group developed a strong peer network that we still turn to—many years later—for career advice, job references, and moral support.

What did you actually do on your fellowship?

For the grassroots portion of my fellowship, I worked at a food bank in St. Paul, Minnesota. The food bank provided food to many different local organizations who were interested in finding out more about the cultural diversity of the individuals who eventually ate the food. The Twin Cities have among the highest populations of Hmong immigrants and urban Native Americans in the country, in addition to large numbers of immigrants from Latin America and Africa. My job was to research each site, conduct interviews with staff, and organize focus groups with community members to find out whether the food bank was meeting the basic need of supplying culturally appropriate food.

In Washington, DC, I worked at the National Association of Community Action Agencies where I tracked legislation related to poverty issues and helped organize a policy conference and journal. In Washington, all of the Fellows worked Monday through Thursday and would organize professional development seminars with invited speakers and presenters on Fridays, which allowed for even greater exposure to organizations and issues.

Popular Fellowship Programs for History and Political Science Students

- **The Bill Emerson National Hunger Fellowship**
  HungerCenter.org/national/national.htm
  This fellowship is a project of the Congressional Hunger Center and lasts 12 months. Fellows are placed for six months with urban and rural community-based organizations and then move to Washington, DC to complete the year with six months of work at national organizations involved in the anti-hunger and poverty movement, including national advocacy organizations, think tanks, and federal agencies.

- **CareerWays Fellowship, NYU Wagner School of Public Service**
  NYU.edu/wagner/partnership/careerways
  CareerWays is a seven-month development program which brings together up to 40 young people from across the country, who are currently working or plan to work in a public service organization in New York City. Fellows gain experience and exposure to a range of career exploration activities that will help them define their path into public service. These activities include monthly workshops, speakers, guidance from professionals in the field, and participation in events held at NYU Wagner and New York City.

- **Capital Fellows Program, Sacramento State Center for California Studies**
  CSUS.edu/calst/Programs/about_programs.html
  The Capital Fellows Program consists of the Jesse M. Unruh Assembly Fellowship, Executive Fellowship, Judicial Administration Fellowship, and California Senate Fellows programs. Fellows receive an opportunity to engage in public service and prepare for future careers, while actively contributing to the development and implementation of public policy in California. Fellows in each program work for 11 months as full-time members of a legislative, executive, or judicial branch office, and are typically given assignments with a significant amount of responsibility and challenges.

- **Fellows Program in Public Affairs, Coro Center for Civic Leadership**
  CORO.org/programs/programs.html
  The Fellows Program with Coro is a nine-month, full-time, postgraduate experiential leadership training program which includes field assignments, site visits, interviews and special individual and group projects and consultancies. According to one Coro

Fellow now in law school: "The Coro Fellowship was helpful for developing my inquiry skills and helping me learn to work with others in a professional environment. Coro taught me to constantly question my assumptions and to work to develop consensus, while still being able to advocate a particular position. I find these skills were crucial in my day-to-day work in every job I've had since and in law school now."

- **Greenlining Institute—Academy Fellowship Program**
  Greenlining.org/program/academy/alumni/index.php
  The Academy Fellowship Program is an annual leadership training program for multi-ethnic students who have at minimum completed their undergraduate studies and want experience working on low-income and minority economic development.
  Fellows conduct research, write reports and position papers, help organize community events, and interface regularly with multi-ethnic community, corporate, and government leaders. They write articles for various papers, represent the Greenlining Institute on television and radio, and give presentation and testimony at policy hearings.

- **The Herbert Scoville Jr. Peace Fellowship**
  CLW.org/scoville/index.html
  This fellowship provides college graduates with the opportunity to gain a Washington perspective on key issues of peace and security. Supported by a monthly stipend, the Fellows spend six to nine months in Washington serving as full-time junior staff members at the participating organization of their choice. The program also arranges meetings for the Fellows with policy experts.

- **The New York City's Urban Fellows Program**
  NYC.gov/html/dcas/html/employment/urbanfellows.shtml
  The Urban Fellows Fellowship provides opportunities for young professionals to gain meaningful work experience in public policy, urban planning, and government operations as they consider careers in public service. Components of the Urban Fellows Program includes weekly seminars and symposia. Through the weekly seminar series, the Fellows examine critical issues and meet a wide range of commissioners, elected officials, and people at all levels of New York City government who share their insights and experiences. The program also explores the relationship between local, state, and federal government and typically provides Fellows the opportunity to meet with both state and federal officials, affording them a perspective of New York City from the vantage points of both Albany and Washington, DC.

ANOTHER OPTION: YEAR OF SERVICE PROGRAMS

There are other ways to spend some time out in the "real world" before applying to graduate school. Below are a couple examples of "year of service" programs. These are often "in the trenches" jobs that involve teaching or working in the community. These programs are very highly regarded by both employers and graduate schools and can give you serious hands-on experiences with which to shape your graduate school and career objectives. Another great benefit of these programs is that participants may be eligible for federal loan forgiveness and/or loan deferment programs.

- **AmeriCorps**

  AmeriCorps is a network of local, state, and national service programs that connects more than 70,000 Americans each year in intensive service to meet the country's critical needs in education, public safety, health, and the environment. AmeriCorps members serve with more than 2,000 nonprofits, public agencies, and faith-based and community organizations. Since 1994, more than 400,000 men and women have provided needed assistance to millions of Americans across the nation through their AmeriCorps service.

  Full-time members who complete their service earn an education award of $4,725 to pay for college, graduate school, or to pay back qualified student loans. Some AmeriCorps members may also receive a modest living allowance during their term of service.

- **Peace Corps**

  Do you think of the Peace Corps and imagine teaching in a one-room schoolhouse or farming in a remote area of the world? While education and agriculture are still an important part of the Peace Corps' many initiatives, today's volunteers are just as likely to be working on HIV/AIDS awareness, helping to establish computer learning centers, or working on small business development.

  Peace Corps volunteers work in the following areas: education, youth outreach, and community development; health and HIV/AIDS; agriculture and environment; business development; and information technology. Within these areas, the specific duties and responsibilities of each Volunteer can vary widely.

  All Peace Corps volunteers commit to 27 months of training and service overseas. The Peace Corps provides volunteers with a living allowance that enables them to live in a manner similar to the local people in their community. The Peace Corps also provides complete medical and dental care and covers the cost of transportation to and from your country of service. When you return from your 27 months of service, you will receive just over $6,000 toward your transition to life back home.

AmeriCorps members address critical needs in communities throughout America, including:

- Tutoring and mentoring disadvantaged youth
- Fighting illiteracy
- Improving health services
- Building affordable housing
- Teaching computer skills
- Cleaning parks and streams
- Managing or operating after-school programs
- Helping communities respond to disasters
- Building organizational capacity

CHAPTER 3

What's Out There? Popular Jobs for History and Political Science Majors

THE BIG PICTURE

It's a wide open field "out there." The world of work is complex and ripe with possibilities, and history and political science grads are right there in the mix, hard at work in a variety of interesting roles.

Maybe you already know what you want to do and that's great; we hope to provide some good job-search strategies for you in this book. But maybe the big "a-ha!" moment will not arrive by the time you walk across the stage to get your diploma. For some strange reason, graduation dates rarely coincide with a clear understanding of what you want to do for the rest of your life. All is not lost, even if you find yourself watching the soaps as the fall semester begins without you.

The professional world is not made up of 15-week semesters, and entering the job market is not the same as arriving on campus and deciding on a major. The fact is there is a lot "out there," so it might be worth having a bit of a direction when you do finally set sail. Sometimes it begins with a bit of looking around. You might ask yourself, "I want to do what that person does, how did she get there?" or "Can I really keep doing research and pay the rent?" Keep looking around. Just a kernel of an idea will release the initiative to get you off the couch. History and political science students are natural investigators and researching career options from an initial "that sounds interesting" point of view is a good way to get started on a promising career path. And it's a good strategy as well. Think about it: Employers are basically interested in two things, "Why are you here and what are you going to do for me?" If you're drawn to a position because "it sounds interesting" it will become easier to fashion a focused resume and provide evidence of the mysterious "good fit" during an interview. The due diligence that has led you to their door will provide a compelling story.

And there's more good news. The first thing you do after graduation is not what you have to do for the rest of your life. At your first job you will meet many different people, and networking can lead to more interesting opportunities. So don't think that what you decide to do now is necessarily going to be what you'll be doing for the rest of your life. For better or for worse, career paths are easily (and frequently) readjusted.

Quick and dirty self-assessment exercise: The other side of the "what's out there" equation

There are people who have carved out a place for themselves making a living doing exactly what makes them happy. So what really floats your boat? As crazy as that might sound, it's a practical place to begin. Employers can spot an unfocused "I'll do anything" applicant from a mile away, and they usually aren't interested. They want to see that spark in your eye (i.e., motivation) as proof that you won't run screaming from the room right after they've trained you.

Ask yourself the following questions:

- When was the last time you lost all track of time? What were you doing?
- If you won 5 million dollars in the lottery what would you do (after buying stuff and sitting on the beach on a tropical island)?
- If you could switch places for one week with anyone, who would it be?
- If you had six months with no obligations or financial constraints what would you do?

Your answers to these questions may reveal important clues about the things that make your eyes light up.

Talk to 10 people about your answers to these questions and the potential for it turning into a job. After that, the question becomes "How do I get there?"—which any smart history or political science student can figure out!

BREAKING IT DOWN

Work gets done within broad arenas including public (government), private, and nonprofit sectors. Within each sector, there are a myriad of organizations—large and small—with different missions and a variety of functional areas supporting these missions. If you glance behind a desk in any of these places along the continuum, you are bound to find a history or political science graduate working there.

The boundaries are not fixed, and there is a great deal of cross-breeding between sectors, creating interesting work opportunities. Much like the interdisciplinary nature of history or political science, each sector informs and influences the other. No one has to tell you, the history or political science major, how the government influences commercial life and social systems. Both private and nonprofit organizations offer jobs in government relations. In turn, government agencies contract with nonprofit research institutions, mayors hire economic development staff, and nonprofits hire corporate donor relations managers. One graduate now working in education policy research told us that "People are doing a variety of things within education besides teaching because of the changing nature of professional employment. People often move from teaching to policy and back again because they want and expect to be challenged in a way that encourages frequent career moves."

Career paths of history and political science majors reflect these fluid boundaries and many folks go back and forth across sectors during the course of their individual careers. Decisions about which career path to pursue can be approached in different ways. You might look for a job that matches up to a particular interest, such as museums, education, or international affairs. Or there might be a particular skill you want to use or enhance, such as management, writing, or research skills. Taking management as an example, how that skill is deployed will play out differently in different settings. You might oversee membership services for a museum, work as an education administrator, or coordinate a project within an international NGO (nongovernmental organization). Some history and political science grads have interests in broad arenas like communications, which may lead them into careers in journalism, public affairs, or even as a member of the communications staff of an elected official.

Interests (Government + Law) = Legal Assistant, Department of Energy

"The Chicago Office, U.S. Department of Energy, is a Cabinet-level agency with missions spanning science, energy resources, environmental stewardship, and national security.

The incumbent will serve as a Legal Assistant to the Deputy Chief Counsel in the Intellectual Property Law Division, Office of Chief Counsel performing various administrative and technical legal functions."

Source: USAjobs.opm.gov, keyword search "legal assistant"

To add to the mix, within each sector—public, private, and nonprofit—individuals have jobs which require them to communicate across sectors. For example, a nonprofit professional who helps provide grassroots social services may be responsible for managing the government contract or private foundation grant that funds those services. And within a financial services company, someone has to monitor community affairs to shape the public's perception of the way that company does business. You've heard about management and strategic consulting firms whose clients are the *Fortune* 500 companies. Well, nonprofits and politicians hire consultants, too, and there are historical preservation consulting firms hired by city governments. The list goes on and on.

Interests (Political Science + Business) = Regulatory Affairs Director, Department of Government and Legislative Affairs, Biotechnology Company

Job Description
- Ensure that regulatory strategies are defined and efficiently implemented.
- Develop and implement strategies to proactively influence legislation/guidelines with impact on organization.

- Provide regulatory leadership and expertise to licensing colleagues.
- Provide strategy and direction to teams involved in agency activities and/or hearings.
- Ensure that all existing marketed product registrations are maintained in line with business needs.

Interests (History + Government) = Historical Interpretive Coordinator, Old Town, USA

Job Description

- Spearhead interpretive projects, including development of living history program.
- Write interpretive text and design graphics for use in-house, on marketing materials, and on the website.
- Conduct historical research and develop interpretive reference materials.
- Plan, create, and execute thematic programs, demos, and activities.
- Assist Interpretive Manager with staff training and developing training materials.
- Supervise and coach interpreters with program research, development, and organization.
- Conduct evaluations of interpretive programs, events, and activities.

In this chapter we will present some options for you to consider as you begin your search for a rewarding career path. First we'll look at a few jobs in government, politics, and public policy where history and political science grads have found satisfying careers. Then we will move on to the field of law, the nonprofit sector (including museums and libraries), and some career paths within education. We then include several business career options that history and political science grads have found to be a good fit and, finally, on to the broad field of communications—public relations, journalism, publishing.

No attempt has been made to uncover every option. These are just a few examples of where some history and political science majors have found themselves. And as one graduate now working as a financial planner said: "Remember that your first job doesn't have to be your last job. You may have to bounce around a little bit before you find your niche . . . and that's okay."

WORKING FOR THE GOVERNMENT

Government jobs make up a complex network of organizations, departments, bureaus, agencies and commissions on local, state, and federal levels. People in these positions often make lateral transfers to other agencies with similar missions, to other locations (both national and internationally), and may also move from one level of government to another. Half of the nation's 1.8 million federal employees will become eligible to retire in the next five years, and the government has developed a national initiative "Call to Serve" to encourage smart recent grads like you to consider working for the federal government.

Government jobs should not be viewed any differently than the jobs you are considering in the private sector. Keep your options open and focus on determining the individual "personality" of the organization and whether or not it would be a good fit. Do your homework. Go to the agency's website, educate yourself, and contact the local offices to make an appointment to meet with someone to get more information.

Investigating jobs in government can be beneficial even if you are ultimately headed for the private sector. Government jobs offer great exposure to one part of the job market and your experience within a government organization could be of value to a private sector employer.

Uncle Sam pays well with a regular series of raises— often the equivalent of 20 percent every two years.

Most entry-level positions for a bachelor's degree are at the GS 5-7-9 salary level.

Annual Rates by Grade and Step

Grade	Step 1	Step 2	Step 3	Step 4	Step 5	Step 6	Step 7	Step 8	Step 9	Step 10
5	$25,195	$26,035	$26,875	$27,715	$28,555	$29,395	$30,235	$31,075	$31,915	$32,755
6	$28,085	$29,021	$29,957	$30,893	$31,829	$32,765	$33,701	$34,637	$35,573	$36,509
7	$31,209	$32,249	$33,289	$34,329	$35,369	$36,409	$37,449	$38,489	$39,529	$40,569
8	$34,563	$35,715	$36,867	$38,019	$39,171	$40,323	$41,475	$42,627	$43,779	$44,931
9	$38,175	$39,448	$40,721	$41,994	$43,267	$44,540	$45,813	$47,086	$48,359	$49,632

Look at locality differentials as well. For example, the San Francisco Bay Area federal government salary levels are 19 percent above the general pay scales listed above.

Source: USAjobs.opm.gov website maintained by the Office of Personnel Management

Demystifying the federal government job application process

The government application process has never been particularly easy but things are definitely looking up. As Lynn Kim, Office of Human Resources with the U.S. Department of Justice puts it, "The federal government has made great efforts to attract outstanding applicants. The government has become more 'savvy' in how they market to students and the application process is more 'user-friendly' with online applications. In addition, there are new development programs—such as the Federal Career Intern Program—that offer employees an opportunity to gain valuable skills and acquire meaningful work experience. Along with one of the most generous benefits packages and a good work/life balance—the government is one of the best places to work."

Tips for federal resume writing: Forget everything you ever learned about resumes

- The average federal resume is 3–5 pages long.
- Be sure to provide evidence that you meet the minimum qualifications. Include dates, especially when they ask for a certain number of years of experience.
- Course work and volunteer activities count as experience.
- Pay special attention to the "Evaluation Factors" (sometimes called "Selective Factors" or "Qualification Requirements") section of the job listing.
- Submit an attachment addressing every single KSA (knowledge, skills, and abilities) mentioned there.
- Respond thoroughly to this. It's no time to be modest. You will be assigned points for every example that addresses those factors. It's the top three candidates with the most points who get a referral to the hiring manager.

Working in state and local government

Public issues are addressed differently by state and local governments and the nature of the work may be different as a result. According to one graduate, "Local government has the advantage of being very real. You can impact people's lives on a direct and on-going basis. You are very accessible, and your actions are insanely reviewed, which is hard. You can also get things done relatively quickly. Higher levels of government have more resources and, in many cases, more power."

Federal Jobs by College Major

Any of these sound interesting? They are from the "Federal Jobs by College Major" section of USAJobs.gov under "History" and "Political Science":

- Civil Rights Analyst
- Program Analyst
- Administrative Officer
- Management Analyst
- Paralegal Specialist
- General Investigator
- Archivist
- Intelligence Specialist
- Foreign Affairs Specialist
- Public Affairs Specialist
- GAO Evaluator

Pick one and do search of job openings by job title on the USAjobs.opm.gov site. Interesting options guaranteed!

Source: "Employment Information" section of USAJobs.opm.gov

GOVERNMENT JOB PROFILES

Diplomat/Attaché/Foreign Service Officer

Number of people in profession	5,800
Average hours per week	70
Average starting salary	$32,000
Average salary after 5 years	$45,000
Average salary after 10–15 years	$89,000

Life on the job

The Foreign Service represents the United States around the world. Members interact with local governments as emissaries of the United States, staff U.S. embassies and consulates, and provide resources for Americans traveling abroad. Strong communication skills are absolutely essential for anyone thinking about entering the profession. Diplomats are posted to positions abroad for terms of two, three, or four years with nine-month stateside stints every two to four years, but they can be recalled at the discretion of the State Department at any time.

The Foreign Service handles all problems of Americans abroad, including negotiating with local governments for individual United States companies who wish to manufacture, produce, or do business abroad; providing information about the host country; and issuing replacements for lost documentation. Foreign consulates also issue visitation and residency visas to foreigners wishing to enter the United States. These tasks consume a minimum of 30 hours of the work week. Since additional internal duties (including writing reports) and social functions (which are an important part of the job) can take up another 40 hours per week, people who are looking for a sinecure are ill-advised to enter the Foreign Service. Members who are satisfied with their profession enjoy the responsibility, and the ability to look at a host country from the inside, write a considered opinion of the state of that country, and have it seriously regarded by officials making decisions about international relations.

Individuals who pass all the tests are given a ranking and put on a list of eligible candidates for future posting. As positions become available, candidates are offered suitable postings. Note that at most, a few hundred slots open up each year. While many start their tenure with a nine-month stint in Washington, DC to learn the protocols of being a diplomat (termed the "pregnancy period"), others begin in the field and are trained on the fly. Be aware that if you are listed on the sheet of eligibles, and no position opens up within 18 months, you will have to begin the process again. All names are removed from the list after a year and a half of inactivity.

Insider tips

To enter the Foreign Service, you must be an American citizen between the ages of 20 and 54 and have a bachelor's degree. Applicants must pass the competitive Foreign Service exam, offered once a year in most major urban centers and at consulates abroad. Individuals who pass take a secondary exam, which includes a day-long assessment: a physical, a rigorous background exam, and a final review of all the candidates' strengths and weaknesses. Candidates are expected to be familiar with another language, but fluency can be acquired after posting.

FBI Agent

Number of people in profession 17,420

Average hours per week 40

Average starting salary $21,400

Average salary after 5 years $33,200

Average salary after 10–15 years $47,100

Life on the job

Do you see yourself as Clarice Starling tracking Hannibal Lecter in *Silence of the Lambs*? Do you want to fight for truth, justice, and the American way on American soil? FBI agents investigate people suspected of violating federal law, including serial killers, kidnappers, bank robbers, bombers, and perpetrators of mail fraud. Strong deductive reasoning skills, flexibility, and irreproachable moral character are key traits for people who want to succeed in the FBI. The sensitive nature of the work requires a person with sound judgment and discretion. The application process is one of the most rigorous and selective in the nation.

Agents research and gather evidence about suspected criminals. Duties include surveillance, transcription, research, coordination with local authorities, and report-writing. Individuals in the scientific division work in labs and in the field, collecting and analyzing evidence and working with private labs. Many agents in the profession feel that the variety of tasks keeps the job fresh and exciting. By themselves, FBI agents have limited power to arrest and no power to punish people suspected of violating federal law. An FBI agent investigates and reports, and when other government agencies make the arrest, they often invite the FBI agent or agents who were involved with the case as a courtesy. It is common for the agent to move on to another case before any arrests are actually made.

The most difficult part of being an FBI agent is the sense of isolation it can foster. Most agents work by themselves or, if necessary, in pairs. They often travel for long periods of time. The project-based nature of this career may keep it exciting, but the uncertainty of it can lead to frustration. One agent from New York describes his experience, "My wife and I were married on May 25 of last year. I was assigned to a case two days later and couldn't tell her where I was or when I would be back or what was going on. I next saw her July 14." Even with all the pressures the work entails and the lifestyle limitations it demands, only 4 percent of agents leave each year (not including retirees). There must be something great about being an FBI agent—but of course it's a secret.

Insider tips

The FBI is not looking for a particular kind of special agent. They are not just looking for people with military or law enforcement experience, but for history and political science majors as well. Even minimal language ability adds a plus to your application. All applicants must be U.S. citizens, between 23 and 36 years old, with a four-year degree from a college or university. Applicants must also pass a variety of tests, including vision, hearing, and polygraph.

The FBI has five entry programs: law, accounting, science, language, and diversified; and each program has its own specific academic requirements. The application process is renowned for its rigor and thoroughness.

In addition to giving each applicant difficult written tests and interviews, the FBI conducts intensive background checks including criminal record checks; credit checks; interviews with associates, roommates, and landlords; professional references; and academic verifications. Each candidate takes a drug test, physical exam, and, at the discretion of the FBI, a polygraph (lie detector) test.

Interview: Mark Lewis, Acting Field Director Department of Neighborhood Empowerment, City of Los Angeles

How did you end up working for the city of Los Angeles?

I was born and raised in Los Angeles and knew early on I wanted to continue to work and live here. I was deeply involved in community service beginning with youth advocacy, and eventually expanding into quite a range of community activities including youth violence prevention. I realized that to move into positions of greater responsibility it was necessary to have the credentials, so I went to UC—Berkeley and majored in history. I was selected to be a Public Policy and International Affairs Fellow [see Appendix A] which financed my graduate education at Harvard's John F. Kennedy School of Government where I earned my Master's in Public Administration (MPA).

After getting my MPA I returned to Los Angeles and began working with the Los Angeles Police Department. After that I worked for the Carter Center doing research on handgun reform. When the opportunity became available, I moved into the Department of Neighborhood Empowerment for the City and have proceeded through the ranks to become Acting Field Director.

What do you actually do on the job?

The City of Los Angeles has set up a model of grassroots democracy, with neighborhood councils being written into the city charter in 1999. These councils are made up from a diverse group of stakeholders, including everyone from the Disney family to housewives. I work with the mayor and his staff, city council, private businesses, nonprofits—anyone and everyone. We do outreach and education for these groups and provide technical assistance on everything from potholes to airport expansions.

WORKING IN POLITICS

A career path in politics differs from other government career paths. You need to rely on informal networks and personal contacts and pay your dues by volunteering on a political campaign or interning with your local representative. But all the working for free stuff does pay off in the end. As one staffer explains, "The institutional memory in the world of politics is a long one. Once you have proven that you are willing to work in a team and pitch in to get things done, your reputation will open many doors."

To sustain your commitment during the long hours of work (often for no money), it's crucial to have the right motivation. If you end up in elected office, that's great. But starting out, it's important to think about how you would improve the community around you, what issues are important to you, and how you might influence change in that direction.

The long and winding road of a political career

"After college, I worked on political campaigns in California. Then, I went to DC sort of on a whim because I was interested in the work going on there. I did a bunch of odd jobs and ran up a lot of debt while volunteering for the Clinton/Gore reelection campaign. I ended up working for the campaign press secretary and then got shipped off to Pittsburgh to help set up the Clinton/Gore Headquarters there. About two months before the election, I was hired into the Department of Transportation to work for the Secretary of Transportation. When he became Secretary of Energy, he asked me to move over with him and I did. I was there until grad school. During my graduate studies in public policy I worked for the California State Legislative Analysts' Office doing research in education policy. After grad school I surprised myself and everyone else by getting back into politics by joining a political consulting firm and running campaigns as well as doing other PR for companies. Now, I am Chief of Staff to the Mayor of Berkeley, California."

Cisco DeVries

BA Political Science, MPP

Chief of Staff, Mayor Tom Bates, City of Berkeley, CA

Political consultant: The business side of politics

Political consulting is a growing private sector business in which consultants advise and assist political campaigns in everything from research to field strategy. Political consultants can do everything or specialize in one specific service. General services include overall strategic expertise, survey research, TV or radio production or placement, telemarketing, direct mail, fund raising, and media relations. Political consultants may manage campaigns and write and implement strategy, media production and placement, and polling.

The demand for political consultants is growing beyond just individual politicians who need help managing their election campaigns. Corporations, public interest groups, labor, and other entities also hire political consulting firms. What you do as a political consultant can vary depending upon the size of the firm and the clients served. One political consultant interviewed is a sole practitioner hired out to manage school campaigns. As you might imagine, this involves serious grassroots organizing for a very focused local audience. He manages phone banks and works with volunteers when initiatives or candidates are on the ballot. "I really have to pound away on the fund-raising piece."

Campaign consultants may do debate preparation, write speeches, work with the media, and do some hand-holding of candidates, anything to keep all the cogs in the wheel moving. Consultants are increasingly offering assistance with creating and maintaining an organization's or candidate's overall online communications strategy and website management. Websites are an integral part of an organization's communications, fundraising, and outreach strategies, and they often outsource this to political consultants.

Internship: Political Strategy and Communications Firm

Responsibilities

Responsible for scheduling, completing extensive internet research, assisting with and visiting local campaign events, and general administrative duties

Qualifications

- A professional demeanor and style.
- Good communication and interpersonal skills.
- Ability to manage various projects at the same time.
- Motivated self-starter and able to work well without constant supervision.
- Interest in public affairs, current events, and politics is desirable.
- An excellent sense of humor.

Paying your dues: Spending time in Washington, DC

If you want a ton of networking contacts (and experience in an intense social scene in a city swarming with people like yourself) then you should spend some time in DC. You can get some amazing experiences—from an inside look into legislative politics on the Hill to the real-life ramifications of work within a major policy think tank. Going to Washington even just for the summer or for a semester will gain you a ton of business cards and a substantive new entry for your resume. Employers in DC work their interns hard. "As an intern with the Asian Pacific American Institute for Congressional Studies I researched bills, assisted staffers in compiling the Congressman's legislative record, and assisted staff members when they wrote letters and speeches for the Congressman. I was allowed to sit in on meetings, attend committee hearings, and go to evening receptions with the Congressman or staff. Because the office wanted me to experience every facet of life on Capitol Hill, I was treated like the other staff members. I was given a key to the office, I had set hours, I had deadlines for projects, and the Congressman always called on me during staff meetings to ask about the progress of my projects."

Interests (Politics + Communications) = Press Secretary

Job Description

- Manage day-to-day press outreach for busy Capitol Hill office.
- Reach out to press (electronic and print).
- Manage website content and web-based outreach.
- Produce direct mail and e-mail.
- Work with legislative staff to draft press releases and op-ed pieces.
- Must have the ability to manage several media requests simultaneously while pitching original ideas to local and national media.
- Must have significant Hill or political experience, take a creative approach to pitching press ideas, have a team-player attitude, utilize the latest technology, and possess top-notch writing skills.

Online Resource: Capitol Hill Job Guide

Visit the website for the Opportunities in Public Affairs (www.opa.com) to find out about the types of jobs available on Capitol Hill, get formal addresses for the House and Senate, learn where to look for jobs and what you can expect, and connect with other Hill job resources.

POLITICAL JOB PROFILES

Political Campaign Worker

Number of people in profession ....N/A

Average hours per week 50

Average starting salary $5,400

Average salary after 5 years $32,100

Average salary after 10–15 years $64,200

Life on the job

Political campaign workers specialize in the art of winning elections. The profession includes many subspecialties: press and public relations, polling, opposition research, fund-raising, logistical organizing, and a wide range of other responsibilities to deal with the crises of a campaign. In large campaigns, specialists representing all of these specialties work together to develop integrated campaign strategies; in smaller, local elections, one or two professionals will serve as jacks-of-all-trades, putting to use this entire range of skills and developing their expertise. Technical and tactical skills are extremely important in campaign management, but the ultimate emphasis in the profession is on winning. Campaign professionals with a reputation for victory can have lucrative, prominent careers; individuals who participate in too many losing campaigns will have trouble finding work.

This is a career for people who love the thrill of the chase. Many individuals get into the profession by volunteering for a particular candidate they support and falling in love with the excitement of campaigns. In the weeks preceding elections, campaign professionals work full-time, 24 hours a day, seven days a week, as they plan and coordinate down-to-the-wire campaign strategies. Deadline pressure is intense, as Election Day provides a final test of the staff's campaign work. Many people in the profession thrive on the pressure; others burn out and find other work.

Campaign management is also highly public work. Pollsters and researchers may work behind the scenes; but the press and public relations specialists and those who wish to rise to the position of campaign manager must feel comfortable working with the media. At the highest level of political campaigns, statements and actions of senior campaign aides are as important as those of the candidate. Some relish being in the public eye; others are more comfortable working behind the scenes.

Insider tips

The career campaign professional's first exposure to politics is usually as a volunteer for a campaign, perhaps over summer vacation while still a student. Volunteers perform the bulk of the low-level jobs in every campaign, but they are often found in positions of substantial responsibility in smaller, local campaigns. A bright, hardworking volunteer can rise rapidly in a reelection staff, and this is often the best way to acquire the credentials that can lead to a career working on major political campaigns.

In some of the profession's job roles, educational or career background is extremely important. Training in statistics is a prerequisite to polling and voter analysis work; many influential pollsters have doctorates in statistics. Many political workers begin as journalists and then put their knowledge of the media to use as press aides and campaign spokespeople. A degree in political science can be very useful. Some universities offer master's degrees in political management. This can also be an effective route into the profession.

Political Aide (Staffer)

Number of people in profession............1,500,000

Average hours per week 50

Average starting salary..........................$18,000

Average salary after 5 years $30,000

Average salary after 10–15 years $50,000

Life on the job

"Politics is all-in-the-staff work," said one Senate aide. Politicians are the visible faces of political life, the personalities who spark public debate; but the overwhelming bulk of the processes by which political decisions are made are handled by political staffers. Staffers prepare the reports, conduct the research, draft the legislation, and prepare the negotiation briefs that allow political life to happen. The pay is average, and the hours are long, but many staffers report great satisfaction with work that enables them to have a central role in important public decision-making.

Legislative staffers research, analyze, draft, amend, and manage legislation. They also coordinate meetings and consult with lobbyists, government agencies, and community groups to build support for legislation. They may write committee and floor statements and brief elected officials on issues related to legislation. As one legislative staffer explains, "The long hours and sometimes stressful work environment definitely took some getting used to, but the camaraderie and support of my colleagues more than made up for any initial challenges."

Aides must keep abreast of both of the political developments in their field and of the needs of the home district, and they must be aware of likely public reaction to the various positions in a political debate. An effective aide is a valued advisor and resource, and elected officials frequently develop a core senior staffer whom they take with them from office to office throughout their careers. There is a high turnover rate among more junior staffers, however, as they maneuver to work for candidates or officeholders whose careers are on the rise.

Attachment to a particular politician, who often serves as a mentor, is perhaps the most striking aspect of a career as a political aide. The development of long-term commitment and loyalty to a single party or candidate can be extremely rewarding, but an aide's ambitions must be aligned with those of the boss. Moreover, political egos are such that staffers who seek the limelight frequently find themselves seeking alternative employment. In addition, the success of a staffer's career is tied to that of the politician; if the politician changes jobs, so must the staffer, and if the politician loses a reelection bid, the staffers are out of jobs. Despite these uncertainties, however, the life of a political aide can be extremely satisfying, and the dangers of getting turned out of office are offset by the wide range of experiences afforded a political aide.

Insider tips

Competition for entry-level jobs can be intense; aspiring aides who have worked on major campaigns or interned in government offices have a good chance of being hired. Frequently, though not always, legislators hire aides from their home districts or states as a means of maintaining contact between their constituents and Washington or the state capitol.

If you are interested in having a career in politics, you should gain experience through interning or working on political campaigns. Stay on top of what is happening in your local community. Think of how you would improve the community around you, what issues are important to you, and how you might influence change in that direction. Once you identify those issues, locate organizations that are already doing that work, get to know the people involved in that work, and volunteer or work with that organization.

Conduct informational interviews with elected officials whose work you admire and with staff in organizations that are doing work in issue-areas in which you are interested.

Lobbyist

Number of people in profession 106,000

Average hours per week 55

Average starting salary...........................$21,400

Average salary after 5 years $53,500

Average salary after 10–15 years $85,600

Life on the job

Whether lobbyists work for a large organization, a private individual, or the general public, their goals and strategies tend to be similar. First and foremost, lobbyists must be adept at the art of persuasion, which is the mainstay of their job. They must figure out how to sway politicians to vote on legislation in a way that favors the interests they represent. This means tailoring appeals to specific individuals as well as to group voting blocs, such as Southerners or pro-choicers. Lobbyists also occasionally lobby one another. When opposing groups find a common area of interest and can present a united front, they are extremely effective.

Lobbying can be direct or indirect. Direct lobbying means actually meeting with members of Congress and their staffs and providing them with information pertinent to a bill being voted on. The lobbyist imparts his or her information with the help of graphs, charts, polls, and reports that he or she has hunted up or created. Needless to say, this is usually information that the politician may not otherwise have access to and casts the matter in a light favorable to the interest the lobbyist represents. Sometimes, lobbyists will even sit down and help a politician draft legislation that is advantageous for their interest.

Maintaining good relations with politicians who can be relied upon to support the lobbyist's interest is key. While their employers cannot themselves make large campaign donations to politicians, lobbyists can raise money from other sources for reelection campaigns and be affiliated with political action committees. The resulting core of relationships a lobbyist has with the decision-makers of this country is what makes a lobbyist worth hiring. To be successful at all of this, the lobbyist must be well-informed, persuasive, and self-confident.

Indirect lobbying, sometimes referred to as grassroots organizing, is a bit less glamorous. Grassroots lobbyists enlist the help of the community to influence politicians by writing, calling, or demonstrating on an organization's behalf. This means long hours spent on the phone and writing letters, trying to rouse the community to get involved. These lobbyists also report to politicians about the concerns and reactions they have gotten from community members. Indirect lobbying is also done through the media. Grassroots lobbyists write articles for newspapers and magazines and appear on talk shows to generate interest in and awareness of their issues.

Lobbyists tend to work long hours; working between 40 and 80 hours per week is the norm. When a bill is up for vote, lobbyists will usually work through at least one night. But the least attractive part of being a lobbyist may be the less-than-spotless reputation of the profession. While many of them are undoubtedly scrupulous, the staggering amounts some high-profile lobbyists can earn causes some degree of mistrust. The fact remains, however, that honest lobbyists are working to promote causes they believe are important and worthwhile.

Insider tips

Lobbying is a profession brimming with people who have changed careers. Working in a government or political office, especially as a congressional aide, takes you into the front lines, but it may also be useful to start out in a law or public relations firm. Many lobbyists also come from careers as legislators; former politicians often capitalize on their years of government service and their connections to old pals still in office. This is the "revolving door" that recent legislation has begun to regulate. Indeed, networking is the name of the game in lobbying, a profession in which people are hired as much for whom they know as for what they know. Someone who can schmooze at high levels will start his lobbying career from a high perch, while others face a long hard climb upward. Although there is no corporate hierarchy, this also means that there is no ceiling for individuals who do well.

Interview, Mary Gonsalves Kinney, Legislative Advocate, Platinum Advisors, LLC

How did you end up where you are now?

Starting at a very young age, I was always very interested in politics. Once I got to college I began taking all of the appropriate courses and then interned every summer in the state capitol and/or working on a campaign. Every school year I volunteered for my party doing voter registration. I spent a summer in DC as an intern with a pollster.

Once graduation neared, I knew I wanted to focus on settling down in a politically dense destination so I moved back to Sacramento to pursue a career in lobbying. I always knew I wanted to lobby, and being the impatient, stubborn person that I am, I decided that I would ignore common sense and skip working in the Building (the state legislature). I was going to get a job straight out of college as a lobbyist. Lucky for me, a lobbying firm took a chance and hired me on a three-month probationary basis. I survived and was hired full-time and took on some pretty hefty clients in my first year. I've worked for a couple of other firms before moving over to my current job. The rest is history. Wish I could tell you that it had more to do with "working my way up the ladder," but I was really blessed to have people who believed in me. I worked hard my whole life; I just didn't take the standard route to the bliss that is lobbying.

What do you actually do on the job?

Lobbying is definitely a seasonal sport. From January through late August, most lobbyists are busy harassing legislators for a vote. There are committee hearings (both policy and fiscal) and Floor votes (both the assembly and senate) and then you get to lobby the governor!

Our busiest time of the year is August. This is the last month to get a bill passed out of the legislature and signed into law by the governor. We call this month "hell month." It's a lot of last minute writing, negotiating, and hustling that requires late nights and early mornings. The fate of a bill can turn on a dime., often at the last hour of the last day of session. This requires a lot of last-minute negotiating of the language of certain bills, or "gutting and amending" as we call it in the biz. It only lasts a month, but it seems like forever and when it's over, most lobbyists would agree, the five month "recess" is much appreciated. Recess is not work-free, however. There's a lot of client management, informational hearings, preparation for the coming year, etc. that takes up the average lobbyist's time.

What are the rewards and the challenges of your job?

The reward of being a lobbyist is simple—delayed gratification. The legislative process is a long one and requires a lot of patience. Once the end is in sight, most lobbyists feel great about the time and effort they have put into their specific projects/clients and are looking forward to some sort of resolution/conclusion. No matter what the outcome, it is safe to say that you learn to appreciate the people behind the scenes (the staff and the analysts) and if fate will have it (a favorable legislature and/or governor) you feel *great* when your end goal is accomplished (i.e., your bill passes or fails, depending on your client's preference).

The biggest challenge is learning when to walk away or concede a point. Most lobbyists are aggressive and persistent—they have to be able to get anything done! It can be incredibly challenging to "negotiate" a deal with another interest group when you've worked so hard to get where you are on an issue. Sometimes, however, you have no choice. The end of the road has slapped you in the face, and it's time to surrender.

JOBS IN PUBLIC POLICY

Working in public policy is a natural fit and a logical career path for many history and political science students, and employers in the field are especially interested in hiring people from those majors. There are many ways to do policy work. The field is issue-driven and virtually every industry has policy-related jobs. As one policy analyst puts it, "I always refer back to my discovery of the Snack Food Association in Washington, DC. I know it's an industry group, but the optimistic side of me hopes that some Twinkie lover finally hooked up with her true calling."

Advocacy organizations, labor unions, and lobbyists work to influence and change policy. Think tanks conduct research and analysis on policy issues. Politicians are the policy-makers with legislative support agencies from all employment sectors doing the policy analysis. Public administrators implement policy. But there are also public affairs departments in most large for-profit companies and consulting firms with government contracts.

There is a wide variety of career paths available in public policy. But no matter what you do, strong writing skills are required. Creating persuasive and clear letters, analyses, and public policies requires the ability to critically read through a lot of source material and maintain sensitivity to different types of writing. A lot of policy work requires copious reading. As one public policy worker explains, "Monitoring newspaper stories and internet information composes a lot of my daily activity." You also need the ability to hit the ground running to quickly prepare "talking points" for your boss for a meeting that was scheduled at the last minute.

The policy research food chain

If you go to the websites of public policy institutions or job-posting sites, you may see the requirement of an advanced degree for research positions. Don't be discouraged. Certainly on the senior level policy candidates do need to have a master's or a doctorate degree to be competitive. But who do you think supports the research for those PhD and master's level policy analysts hired to manage a project? That would be people like you, recent graduates in history and political science who want to get a foot in the door. Called by a variety of names—research assistant, junior researcher, sometimes research associate—these entry-level positions perform data collection and data entry, logistical tasks, statistical analysis, report writing, and development of tables and graphs for related reports. An intermediate researcher would need to have demonstrated quantitative skills that enable her to proficiently collect and analyze data. She may also perform statistical analysis, interviewing, survey construction, and report writing, requiring advanced knowledge of quantitative and qualitative research methods.

PUBLIC POLICY JOBS

Senior Researcher/Policy Analyst	
Number of people in profession	155,000
Average hours per week	40
Average starting salary	$35,400
Average salary after 5 years	$54,900
Average salary after 10–15 years	$76,310

Life on the job

Senior policy analysts need to possess solid research skills in the areas of methodology, statistics, interpretation of results, and reviews of literature. Day-to-day activities may include overseeing multiple research projects, data analysis, and report writing. Most have a master's degree or higher in social science or public policy. Research directors are responsible for the day-to-day operations of research, project management, program development, data analysis, training, and report writing. Depending on the size of the organization, they may be responsible for overseeing multiple research projects, program implementation, and supervising assigned staff. Policy researchers can work for government, nonprofits, or in the private sector as consultants.

They may coordinate the work of other policy and communications staff and outside consultants. They represent the organization on relevant task forces and coalitions, and at collaborative meetings with partners, advocates, government officials, and other stakeholders. Day-to-day activities may include overseeing multiple research projects, data analysis, and report writing. Specific job duties may include securing sufficient funding for new projects to support the agency's research, training of staff, providing technical assistance for programs, speaking at professional conferences to advance the organization's mission or research initiatives, and publishing articles in peer review journals.

Insider tips

History and political science graduates working in public policy had this advice for you.

- Internships are vital during the school year and during summers and several believe that investing in a postbaccalaureate fellowship (see Chapter 2) offer great entrees into public policy.

- Knowledge of quantitative and qualitative research methods are a must and research-based experience is a real plus. Policy research may require demonstrated experience in statistical analysis software. Read job descriptions in the area of policy you want to get into—it's worth your time to get exposed to some of the software typically used.

- Don't be afraid to get a job waiting tables or working a bookstore while looking for a career job. It helps put things in perspective and can keep you financially afloat.

- Try to get as much experience as you can while you are in school. Editing, management, budgeting experience, etc. are particularly useful as they provide an excellent counterpoint to the analytical skills you develop over the course of earning a liberal arts degree.

- Don't be afraid to come into an organization laterally, like through administrative, entry-level management, or volunteer channels. The hardest thing is getting your foot in the door; once you are there it is just a matter of making yourself useful and demonstrating your competency. I would rather hire someone who knew my organization and whom I knew was an effective worker than someone from the outside.

- Talk to graduate students in your department about where research is taking place in your area of interest.

Interview: Scott Bruce, U.S. Branch Manager/Program Officer, The Nautilus Institute

How did you end up where you are now?

I graduated with a degree in history and with some management experience from having worked with my university's housing co-op where I wrote the budget for the organization and managed a couple of projects. I then got a part-time job as a research assistant for a book on Berkeley History by a member of the Berkeley Historical Association. I had excellent research skills as a history major so I performed very well in this role. The most useful skill I developed there was knowledge of how libraries and archives worked and what online document and photograph databases I could access.

From there I took a job as an office manager at the Nautilus Institute, a research institute specializing in Northeast Asian Foreign Policy Issues. I was hired because I had entry-level management experience and came with good recommendations from the work I had done during college. What made me appreciated was that I was organized, could track dates, and enthusiastically tackled any task put in front of me.

What do you actually do on the job?

My first real expansion of duties involved planning workshops that the institute hosted. This involved thinking though the logistics of hosting a workshop and getting all the materials and arrangements in place in a timely manner in preparation for these workshops. This also allowed me to travel to oversee the workshop while in process.

From this work Nautilus saw that I was good at managing my time, organized, and committed to the organization. My history degree and research experience with the Berkeley History Society demonstrated that I was an adept researcher. These attributes allowed me take over some research roles in addition to my managerial duties once those projects opened up and I eventually went full-time with the organization.

In 2004 our Executive Director left the U.S. to open our second office in Melbourne, Australia. Since I had skills and experience in managing staff, tracking budgets, and conducting large research projects with regular deadlines, I was chosen to take over the U.S. office and our remaining staff as U.S. Branch Manger and Program Officer.

I manage our office at the University of San Francisco and the three staff members there, along with the half-dozen independent contractors we have in the U.S. and the two to three interns we get every semester from the USF Master's in Asia Pacific Studies Program.

I also am responsible for the financial management of the San Francisco office of the organization as well as for some of the records for our office in Melbourne and Seoul.

I organize workshops in the U.S. and abroad and interact with scholars and policy-makers on behalf of the Nautilus Institute and USF. I also lead our research programs and edit or write our regular reports.

What are the rewards and the challenges of your job?

I get to learn something new about the world every day and travel to Asia and Oceania regularly for business. I get to be a junior expert in the field of international politics. I get to meet incredibly interesting and influential people in government and non-government circles all over the world.

Working with Asian issues is also difficult as you will almost inevitably need to pick up a second language. Finally, it can be very hard to develop good boundaries on your work. This is definitely not a 9-to-5 job. You need to keep up with events as they are occurring in real time. I spend a lot of my down time reading new research on the areas of my expertise and trying to write as much as I can. Most people around me are much older and have more experience that I do, and I know that it will be a long while before I get to their level.

That said, I find the challenges are far outmatched by the benefits. I am excited and energized by my job on a daily basis and can honestly say that, despite its frustrations, I really love what I do. If I won the lottery tomorrow I can say that I would keep doing exactly what I am doing for a living now. I would get a gigantic house and take much longer vacations but I wouldn't even think of quitting my job.

WORKING IN LAW

There are many history and political science graduates who go to law school, sit for the bar, and practice law. But if law school is not an option right now, there are many law-related career paths available to you. The legal field needs various professionals to keep the system moving: administrators, paralegals, and client advocates. There are opportunities in government agencies both locally—with district attorney and public defender's offices—and with a host of state and federal law-related agencies and commissions.

Nonprofits can offer exposure to other legal-related career paths from research with an international human rights organization to client advocacy at a family violence law center. Within the private sector, organizations from radio stations to biotech firms have legal affairs staff.

Interests (Languages + Law) = Intern, Hotline for Legal Intake Project

Qualifications

- Bilingual in Mandarin or Korean.
- Able to commit at least 12 hours a week per semester or 3 days a week during the summer.
- Able to read and write in language preferred but not required.

Responsibilities

- Conduct initial phone application and interview with prospective clients.
- Assess client's legal matters with the assistance and support of an attorney.
- Provide extensive counsel and advice, under the supervision of an attorney, to clients in their language.
- Provide clients with brief service, where appropriate, with assistance and support of an attorney.
- Provide accurate referrals to social services agencies for assistance with client's non-legal issues.
- Assist in the development of community education materials in language.

LEGAL JOB PROFILES

Paralegal

Number of people in profession 200,000

Average hours per week.........................40

Average starting salary...........................$30,020

Average salary after 5 years $37,950

Average salary after 10–15 years $48,760

Life on the job

Through a combination of education, training, and work experience, a paralegal performs "substantive" legal work and is "an integral part of the legal team," according to a vice president of a major firm. If you want to learn the nuts and bolts of the legal profession and understand the importance of careful and thorough research, then paralegal studies may be the right occupation for you. The paralegal (or legal assistant) profession is the ground floor to lawyering and often, every bit as important. In many ways, their duties include the same tasks that lawyers who assume responsibility for the legal work complete, but paralegals do not practice law and are prohibited from dispensing legal advice, trying a case in court, or accepting legal fees. Paralegals work hand in hand with lawyers, helping to prepare cases for trial. In their preparatory work, they uncover all the facts of the case, conduct research to highlight relevant case laws and court decisions, obtain affidavits, and assist with depositions and other materials relevant to cases.

A significant portion of a paralegal's work involves writing reports and drafting documents for litigation. After the initial fact-gathering stage, the paralegal prepares reports for use by the supervising attorney in deciding how the case should be litigated. Paralegals who work in areas other than litigation, such as patent and copyright law, real estate, and corporate law, also assist in the drafting of relevant documents—contracts, mortgages, estate planning, and separation agreements. Paralegals who work for government agencies maintain reference files, analyze material for internal use, and prepare information guides on the law. Those paralegals involved with community legal services help disadvantaged persons in need of legal aid. Much of their time is spent preparing and filing documents and doing research. Employee benefit plans, shareholder agreements, and stock options are the primary concern of the paralegal working for corporations.

The paralegal profession is a relatively new and rapidly expanding area. Previously, much of the groundwork now covered by the paralegal was part and parcel of being a lawyer. Now, lawyers can afford to focus more intently on the strategies of trying cases and resolving legal problems, thanks to the invaluable preparatory work of the paralegal.

An added benefit to working as a paralegal is to assess your interest in law school. One graduate working as a paralegal told us he changed his mind about applying to law school based on his paralegal experience: "After witnessing how attorneys work and what their work can involve, I decided that, at this time, it isn't the career path for me. Who knows, I may change my mind but I'm not strongly motivated to pursue a JD. I realize the lack of motivation would adversely affect my approach to my studies as a law student."

Computer technology will continue to play a significant role in the fact-finding and fact-gathering stages of most legal cases. Instead of poring over volumes of research material in law libraries, much of this information is easily accessible from online digitized law libraries and software programs. Of course the paralegal who specializes in a particular field and who is computer literate will have the added edge on advancement. Because of the continuous enactment of new legislation and revised interpretations of existing laws, the paralegal must keep constantly updated on every change, every proposal, and every nuance of the law.

Insider tips

Paralegals usually enter the profession after completing an American Bar Association (ABA)–approved training program. Beyond this, some firms hire liberal arts majors as paralegals directly after college and then train them on the job.

Here's some advice from your fellow history and political science majors working as paralegals:

- Network with paralegals to gather information. Do research on the different fields of the law, not just law firms but also corporations, government, and nonprofit organizations.

- Show evidence of the basic social science skills of research and writing. It's important to become a good and accurate writer. Gain undergraduate research experience with faculty.

- Take rhetoric classes or other classes on legal writing. Invest in a law-related or public interest internship.

- Consider temping. Many law firms use staffing service agencies to find paralegals.

Interview: Nestor Nunez

How did you end up working as a paralegal?

I didn't have a job when I got out of school, so I spent the next six months studying for the LSAT and working as a temp for a sole practitioner. After the LSAT I continued to temp at a few law firms until I ended up at my current firm about four years ago. I did a six-month stint working for the IP (intellectual property) group, and then returned a month later to work for the tax group. From there I was able to convert over to a permanent position because one of the case assistants left. After working there for a year and completing the study towards earning a paralegal certificate, I was promoted to paralegal.

What do you actually do on the job?

It varies, but with litigation there is a set pattern involved with taking a case all the way from inception to trial and possibly beyond. Along the way paralegals are heavily involved in the discovery process and fact gathering, preparing for hearings, depositions, and the trial itself, although many cases do end up settling.

What are the rewards and the challenges of your job?

The rewards of this position lie in the knowledge and satisfaction of completing challenging tasks that are critical to a case and working with a good team of people towards achieving a common goal. The challenges would be in prioritizing demands from various sources, multitasking and time management, and dealing with tough deadlines.

I think this is a good way to be involved with and to explore the legal field without going on to law school straight out of college. It provides the opportunity to work with attorneys and to explore a practice group or two. It provides hands-on, practical experience which clarifies the legal process and what it really involves.

Attorney

Number of people in profession	704,000
Average hours per week	50
Average starting salary	$60,000
Average salary after 5 years	$90,290
Average salary after 10–15 years	$145,600

Life on the job

There are four basic legal-practice settings. The majority of law school graduates begin their careers in private practice. Private practice involves working for a firm comprised of one or more attorneys. Large and medium-sized law firms tend to offer a variety of legal specialties within a general civil practice. Small firms and solo practitioners focus on either a general broad practice or a narrow specialty.

Public-interest lawyers work in several areas, including direct legal services, impact litigation (filing lawsuits to affect public policy), and public-interest private practice in which the firm is dedicated to a particular cause. People who enter public-interest law are usually dedicated to a particular cause or to public service.

Corporate lawyers ensure the legality of commercial transactions. They must have knowledge of statutory law and regulations passed by government agencies to help clients achieve their goals within the bounds of the law. To structure a business transaction legally, a corporate lawyer may need to research aspects of contract law, tax law, accounting, securities law, bankruptcy, intellectual property rights, licensing, zoning laws, and other regulations related to a specific area of business. The lawyer must ensure that a transaction does not conflict with local, state, or federal laws.

Trial lawyers represent clients involved in civil and criminal litigation cases. Criminal lawyers may represent plaintiffs or defendants. Civil litigators take the side of a party in a dispute in which no crime is involved. The trial lawyer's job is to persuade a jury of the facts in a case and to display them in a way that best supports their client's position. Each piece of evidence must be presented and disputed according to a complicated set of rules. On days out of court, trial lawyers review files and scheduling orders, contact witnesses, take depositions, and talk to clients. On court days, lawyers argue motions, meet with judges, prepare scheduling orders, select jurors, and argue cases. The preparation for a trial can take many months. Due to the tremendous cost of litigation, however, most cases settle before they ever reach trial. Trial law requires excellent analytical skills. Litigators use their knowledge of legal precedents to analyze the probable outcome of a case.

Local, state, and federal governments hire a large number of attorneys. Because of the diversity of agencies hiring attorneys, working in the government could mean practicing almost any kind of law. Examples of local government attorneys are district attorneys, public defenders, and county counsel. State lawyers may work for the attorney general or other administrative offices. Federal lawyers are hired in virtually every executive department or agency including the Department of Justice, the Environmental Protection Agency, and the Department of Transportation.

Law can be intellectually fascinating, and many attorneys take great satisfaction in the daily challenges. Detail mavens and big-picture thinkers alike find a friendly home in this profession. But the work is hard. Attorneys can work 18-hour days and spend up to 3,000 hours per year on cases. "On some level you have to like what you do because you're doing it all day long," mentioned one attorney we spoke with. Many lawyers are subordinate to senior associates and partners for the majority of their careers. Attorneys usually work at a number of firms before finding a position perfectly suited to them. Some specialized lawyers have restricted areas of responsibility. For example, district attorneys prosecute accused criminals, and probate lawyers plan and settle estates. The quality of life is low during the early to middle years, but many find the financial rewards too enticing to abandon. Those who wish to enter this field should have solid work habits, curious minds, and the ability to work with—and for—others.

Insider tips

Attorneys must have a law degree from an institution accredited by the American Bar Association. While in law school, students spend their summers working for potential employers, finding out what the working attorney's life is like, and discovering whether or not they want to work in a particular area. Before an attorney can practice in a given state, he must pass a state bar exam, a two-day written examination that tests the prospective attorney's knowledge of the specific laws of that state. Following passage of the written part of the test, many states require "character and fitness" oral examinations to test the ability of a person to practice law in a given state.

In law, the pressure starts early. Law school admissions are extremely competitive—the top 25 schools have an admission rate of about 10 percent. You can get tracked early: The kind of school you attend affects what kind of summer job opportunities you may have; this in turn affects the kind of permanent job you secure. The starting salary and kind of experience you have as a corporate lawyer can vary greatly depending on the size of the firm and geographic location. In a smaller firm, you will have more responsibility and more client contact early on, but the salaries can be tens of thousands of dollars lower than in a large firm. The content of your practice will bo difforont, too: A small town lawyor may take oaro of a houso olosing, drafting a will, and a divorce settlement in a day; big-city lawyers can spend months negotiating a single commercial transaction.

Mediator

Number of people in profession 11,000

Average hours per week.......................40

Average starting salary.........................N/A

Average salary 5 years ....N/A

Average salary after 10–15 years ....N/A

Life on the job

Historically, mediation has been used to settle many different types of disputes. Mediation was a solution sought after by warring Greek city-states. Catholic popes became mediators between European countries during the Renaissance. In the business realm, mediation has long been used as a source of conflict resolution. Since 1887, the American government has promoted arbitration and mediation for contractual disputes involving commerce.

Today, increasing numbers of colleges and universities offer degrees in dispute resolution and conflict management. The field is expected to grow faster than average for all occupations in the coming years. Lawyers, religious leaders, social workers, counselors, and educators are often called on to mediate. Judges and magistrates also play the role of mediator. Strong mediators have many possible professions open to them, including diplomat and politician.

Being a professional mediator is all about conflict resolution, and so the job demands a person with excellent reasoning, problem-solving, and peace-making abilities. When two parties have a dispute and wish to avoid the legal intricacies of litigation, they may call in a mediator to facilitate an equitable solution. Those who are suspicious of lawyers or attorneys might be more favorably inclined toward mediators, who more are often attributed with the qualities of wisdom, trustworthiness, and neutrality. Unlike lawyers and judges, who evaluate, assess, and decide for others, mediators help participating parties evaluate, assess, and decide for themselves. Parties wishing to avoid the delays, high costs, publicity, and ill will brought on by litigation look to mediators as a more peaceful, inexpensive, and expedient alternative.

Mediation is considered a form of Alternative Dispute Resolution (ADR). Although ADR sounds like a terrible syndrome, it's in fact a more Zen-like approach to conflict resolution, with mediators as the master practitioners. Corporations, government agencies, community organizations, schools, neighborhoods, and even families will turn to mediators when they seek mutually acceptable answers to their problems. Examples of conflicts they work to resolve include labor/management issues, health care disputes, environmental/public policy issues, and international conflicts.

Insider tips

The educational background of a professional mediator varies widely. A fair number in the field hold law degrees, while others may not even hold a bachelor's degree. Most important is an education in mediation, whether taken as part of an undergraduate degree or as individual training courses. University degrees in public policy, law, and related fields also provide helpful backgrounds. While few states require licenses or certification to practice mediation, most individuals in the profession have completed training and pledged to abide by certain ethical standards.

Here are some other tips from mediators we talked with.

- Get involved in student activities.
- Take courses in communication. Take any mediation or conflict resolution training that is available to you and try to link up with a community mediation program to get additional training and practice.
- Develop and practice the skills to train students and others.

Interview: Director for School Programs, Conflict Resolution Center

What do you do on the job?

I schedule student, staff and/or parent training at school sites on how to communicate effectively to solve problems. I contract with individual trainers who have the necessary skills and meet with school administrators with plans to create and maintain a safe school environment for all. My organization can provide neutral third-party assistance when necessary, including assistance with mediations at school sites and facilitation staff and or parent meetings, particularly if there are differences.

What are the rewards and challenges of your work?

It's fun and satisfying to work with students, staff, and parents. They all appreciate acquiring the skills to communicate more effectively. [The] greatest challenge for me was getting it all done in the time allotted. There are 23 school districts with over 120 schools in the county so there's far more work to be done.

CAREER OPTIONS IN NONPROFITS

Earlier in this chapter we looked at career opportunities in the broad areas of government, politics, public policy, and law. The business and communications fields we'll be looking at later in the chapter also offer opportunities in the nonprofit sector. Nonprofits have a central role in many places within many industries. In this section, we will be taking a look specifically at nonprofit career opportunities for history and political science majors.

What is a nonprofit?

Did you ever volunteer as a tutor or raise money for a homeless shelter for your student club? It's easy to think that your community service experience represents work in the nonprofit world or even assume that working for a nonprofit means working for free! However, the nonprofit world is an amazing network of organizations varying in size and mission and there are lots of nonprofit professionals out there making a good living doing personally rewarding work.

Nonprofits have been granted a tax-exempt status by the government and generally have a public service mission. If they do generate income—your university is a nonprofit and your tuition is income—it's typically reinvested in programs and services, whereas in the for-profit world income may be used for shareholder dividends or executive compensation. So where do nonprofits get their money? They are funded through government grants, public donations, fundraising activities, corporate gifts, or foundations.

Many history and political science graduates love their jobs with nonprofits. As one explains, "I enjoy the fact that I am working with people who have similar values. . . . I am learning skills that are really crucial in order to contribute to the growth and development of our nation's most underserved communities."

Finding your place within the nonprofit sector

You could approach the world of nonprofit jobs by looking either at the organization's mission or by considering the individual role you want to play within any organization, regardless of its mission.

Let's use the field of education as an example. Perhaps that tutoring job during college sparked an interest in the field of education. You could work in the public school system and teach (schools are nonprofits, too). If managing people or a project is something you find interesting, you could coordinate a tutoring program like the one you volunteered for as a student. Maybe you'd like to take a broader look at education. There are nonprofits with missions to educate the public or lobby legislators about the need for literacy and youth mentor programs. There are also research opportunities within education policy think tanks (see "Careers in Education" section later on in this chapter).

Maybe you don't have a favorite "cause" at the moment, but you love research and would like to keep doing it on some level. If you have documented research experience (and all history and political science students do) and some evidence of commitment to service, you will be of interest to a nonprofit research institution, regardless of the mission of the organization.

Now for a word about job titles within the nonprofit sector: This is definitely one place where you can't assume that a position as "administrative assistant" is beneath you. In some organizations, opportunities exist to assume a great deal of responsibility and move up fairly quickly into a coordinator or management position. "I was working at a nonprofit that trained and employed low-income youth in technology. For two months I hounded the manager in another program at my organization for an informational interview," one nonprofit professional told us. "Finally, she gave in and a couple of months later she offered me a job that they never needed to post. Now, three years later, I have taken over for my former boss." In other organizations the staff may be so small that there may not be room for advancement, and to move up the career ladder you must move to another organization. One nonprofit professional told us that when he graduated and started working in the nonprofit sector he was a bit envious of his friends going into the high-salaried financial services sector. "But now it seems many of them are now going through a 'quarter-life crisis' and are not very happy in their jobs."

The business side of nonprofits

A lot goes on behind the public image of nonprofits and the direct services they provide. There are nonprofit jobs available in finance, human resources, marketing, and information technology. One social service agency dedicated to helping people with addictions estimates that 75 percent of its positions involve direct service and 25 percent involve administrative duties including program coordination, human resources, fundraising, and fiscal management.

Another interesting niche within the nonprofit community is capacity building. Nonprofit consulting organizations provide consulting and technical assistance to nonprofits. With increased competition for foundation funding, nonprofits are held more accountable for their "bottom line," and these consulting firms provide training in a variety of areas including: effective financial systems, human resources practices, management, website development, and information technology.

Interview: Cristina Chan, Projects Director, CompassPoint Nonprofit Services

What do you do on the job?

CompassPoint Nonprofit Services is a consulting, research, and training organization providing nonprofits with management tools, strategies, and resources.

My work there can be divided into two areas: project management and publishing. In project management, I've been responsible for managing short- and long-term technical assistance initiatives through which foundations or government agencies fund CompassPoint to deliver capacity-building services (e.g., consulting or training) to their grantee or contractor agencies. Projects have included: services for HIV Prevention Organizations funded by the San Francisco Department of Public Health's AIDS Office; organizational assessment services for health organization grantees of the Sierra Health Foundation, capacity building for the Ford Foundation's Diversity in Media grantees, and a host of others.

Another line of projects in which I've been involved has been technology related—for instance, helping implement TrainingPoint, an online open curriculum portal, where nonprofit assistance providers can post and share their training curriculum. I've also served as the project manager for migrating online a directory of East Bay Funders created by Y and H Soda Foundation.

Publishing has been the other primary area of my work at CompassPoint. I serve as the editor of TalkingPoint, our newest e-newsletter, and served for seven years as the editor of *Food for Thought*, the first e-newsletter for nonprofit organizations.

What are the rewards and the challenges of your job?

I love the fact that I get to work on a wide variety of projects and with a wide variety of nonprofit agencies and funders. No two projects I work on are identical and I get to work with almost everyone on staff at one point or another; I learn something on every project I work on. One challenge of my job is accountability to multiple clients—e.g., I'm responsible and accountable not only to the leadership at CompassPoint, but also to the funders who support our services and programs and to the individual clients with whom we work on these projects.

Development Officer/Fund-raiser

Number of people in profession 300,000

Average hours per week 45

Average starting salary $40,000

Average salary after 5 years $50,000

Average salary after 10–15 years $68,000

Life on the job

Fund-raisers are employed by a broad range of hospitals, schools, religious and social service organizations, environmental and health-related organizations, arts organizations and museums, youth organizations, and retirement homes.

People who are successful at fund-raising develop large plans and are able to execute them down to the tiniest details. They also identify a target audience and tailor a unique appeal to that demographic. A fund-raiser should have excellent writing skills, a clear understanding of how and when to approach people, and an unbelievable sense of organization. Fund-raising on a large scale may entail up to seven different appeals to thousands of potential donors; fund-raisers without organizational skills quickly get dragged under by the tide of material that passes through their hands. Planning and attending meetings takes up the majority of the professional fund-raiser's day. Fund-raisers must remain on top of the concerns of potential donors, be responsive to the changing needs of their institution, and build up a successful system of reaching donors. Fund-raisers spend plenty of creative energy recreating campaigns to ensure success year after year.

While broad-based fund-raising (letter campaigns, high-profile events, and programs) are important for visibility, publicity, and support, the real work of high-level fund-raisers consists of presentations, education, and funds solicitation from their target market. Meeting others, teaching skills, and a touch of finesse are critical for a fund-raiser to be successful. Meetings with patrons, employees, and executives can take place after quitting time or late in the work day. "It takes a lot of your free time and great social ability to pull it off," mentioned one director of fund-raising for a private school. The ability to communicate the value and the need of your employer to others is required in this occupation and makes the difference between those who succeed and those who fail.

Insider tips

Aspiring fund-raisers need a gentle yet firm touch to communicate a platform and a position in writing and convince people to donate goods, services, and money. Entry-level applicants should be good with numbers, graphics, and design and have an excellent sense of timing, since fund-raising on an ongoing basis requires knowing when not to ask for donations as much as knowing when to ask. One other requirement for this job is the ability to withstand significant rejection. A fund-raiser should be able to bring together disparate elements within a community to reach their goals. Fund-raisers sometimes earn advanced degrees in nonprofit management, finance, marketing, or public relations.

Working for foundations: Grant-making, the other side of the fundraising picture

Foundations often provide technical assistance to applicants, review grant proposals, conduct site visits, and monitor the work of grant recipients, and there are many history and political science graduates working to support those efforts. One graduate working with a foundation providing grants to nonprofits has this to say: "The biggest challenge I face is demystifying the funder-grantee relationship. Historically, philanthropy has been a very inaccessible institution. I am very invested in my work and the communities and nonprofits we serve. They are the leaders doing the work in the community that is making a difference, and it is often difficult to build relationships with people who feel they have to always put their 'best foot forward' when trying to get their projects and programs funded."

Nonprofit Administrator

Number of people in profession 355,000

Average hours per week ....varies

Average salary $88,006

Average salary after 5 years ....varies

Average salary after 10–15 years ......varies

Life on the job

Whatever the mission of the nonprofit organization, the administrator's job calls for the management skills of a chief executive officer. Writing grant proposals and fund-raising take up more and more of the administrator's time as budget cuts flourish. The administrator must be prepared to delicately balance limited budgets with the compassion needed to provide basic care to the clients served and to preserve the general mission of the organization.

The responsibilities of the nonprofit administrator vary depending upon the size of the organization. Executive Directors (EDs) are often responsible for entire operations within a small organization, while within large nonprofits specialists run specific departments, such as the accounting, budgeting, human resources, policy analysis, finance, and marketing departments. ED's of both types are highly educated individuals responsible for overall policy directions and overseeing compliance with government agencies and regulations.

Program Managers have independent oversight over a particular program area within the nonprofit. Their responsibilities could include initiating new projects and managing their implementation. If the nonprofit relies on membership donations for funding (for example a museum or public broadcasting station), there is a need for a volunteer manager to bring members in, and keep them engaged and happy.

Insider tips

Here's some advice from history and political science majors working in nonprofits.

- Undergraduates should balance their classroom and volunteer experiences. Longevity of exposure is important—show that you have had an interest in the field you are hoping to work in through exposure that goes beyond one day of volunteering in the very recent past.

- Be willing to take an unpaid internship, even after you graduate. If necessary, couple it with a night job or other part-time job. The commitment you show will make you first in line when the non-profit gets new funding and can hire new staff.

- Learn how to coordinate and organize things on your own. Coordinating the recycling program in your unit or a one-day event are examples. Be able to show employers how you are different. Take into consideration your background, skills, education and be confident. Have the mindset that they should hire you over anyone else.

- Follow-up and persistence make a candidate stand out. In the interview, employers look for candidates who show a willingness to help out when needed, leadership skills, and an ability to take initiative.

- A master's degree in public administration or business administration may qualify graduates for entry into the higher levels of nonprofit administration. Graduates with a bachelor's degree often work in the field before starting a master's program. They advance by taking on more responsibilities and moving up and into such positions as associate director or program coordinator.

Interview, Tina Sang, Program Coordinator, Adolescent Health Working Group

What do you do on the job?

Most recently I had been coordinating all the administrative details necessary to put on a large conference to increase the medical community's awareness of adolescents and ADHD. This was attended by primary care providers, mental health care providers, school health providers, school counselors, parents, and youth.

My regular ongoing responsibilities are to research and help write a handbook to serve as a resource to primary care providers when they encounter issues related to mental health and substance use in teens. Our goal is to have primary care physicians ask these kinds of questions during a routine physical exam with a teenager.

What are the rewards and challenges?

It was hard to learn the ropes in the beginning. I read articles in medical journals to glean the important information and summarize it in one-page summaries for the handbook for healthcare providers. It was about a three-to-four month learning curve for me to become familiar enough with psychology and medical journals to understand what was important.

My job is incredibly rewarding. The nonprofit I work for is really small—an executive director (ED), four full-time staff, and two part-time volunteers. Our ED is a medical doctor who decided to become an activist. I really like the people I work with and the philosophy of the organization.

The downside is the funding situation. Private foundations fund our projects year by year and it's the projects that get funded, not the staff. So if new projects are innovative enough and get funded, then my job is good for another year but if not, I'll be out of a job.

Our executive director made the decision many years ago to work on projects that are not currently taken by other organizations. For that reason, we have had a steady stream of grants approved. Our director allocates as much funding from the grants as she can to pay for staff. Having a director with vision and good financial sense is a really important thing to look for when applying to nonprofit jobs.

Even with having to "chase down the money," I'd like to put in a plug for working for a nonprofit. It's a wonderful place for people to start because, especially in smaller nonprofits, they give you a lot of trust and assignments that researchers with graduate degrees would be doing if they could afford to hire them. Getting that level of responsibility really fosters confidence and I am proud to be a part of an organization that's doing great things.

WORKING IN MUSEUMS

Arts-related organizations and the movement to protect our nation's cultural and historical heritage are high public-policy priorities, according to the National Governor's Association 2004 Issue Brief. Even in the most successful new economies, "civic leaders are beginning to take stock of artistic and cultural assets, recognizing that they are essential to quality of life, which is necessary for sustained growth."[1] There are tons of career opportunities in arts and culture organizations, and many of them are particularly well suited to history and political science majors. As one history major told us, "I enjoy the public focus of museums and the role of the museum as a meeting place for the academy and the public. Before deciding to pursue work in museums and the public sector, I asked myself what motivated me the most in life. I realized I was an idea-driven person, and museums allowed me to grapple with ideas in a supportive, creative environment."

Museum education

Beyond the jobs of curator and librarian described below, museum education is another great option to look into. The education staff is the bridge between the public and the museum's exhibits and collections. The education officer is responsible for designing programs targeted to a number of different categories of visitor. This may include creating several types of tours, interactive education programs, as well as planning special events in conjunction with recent exhibits.

Recently many education departments have taken their programs out of the museum and into the schools in order to reach a broader audience. By creating materials that connect the museum's message with some element of a teacher's curriculum, both teachers and students have the opportunity for an enhanced lesson, and the museum can increase its visibility and entice more students to come through its doors. An education office will also usually be responsible for training and scheduling docents and volunteers.

1 Share the Arts: ArtsPerspective. Ohio Arts Council. National Governors Association Recognizes the Importance of the Arts.
www.oac.state.oh.us/news/artsperspective/archives/2001/apfall01/ap_4.htm

Interview, Anne Poubeau, Education Director, Old York Historical Society

What do you actually do on the job?

I am the education director of a history museum, so that means I do pretty much everything from teaching about eighteenth century life (in costume) to supervising volunteers and paid educators, designing school programs, and writing new interpretation for our nine historic buildings.

What are the rewards and the challenges of your job?

The rewards are definitely working with kids. I just started a new program for teenagers, a Junior Docent program. The pilot summer worked quite well and I felt very proud of the children. Some of them have come to the children's programs for the last six years and they are almost part of the museum staff.

The challenge is working hard for something you're passionate about and barely surviving from it. Supervising people is also another challenge for me; it's very hard to do it well without being "too mean" or "too nice."

Curator

Number of people in profession 22,000

Average hours per week 45

Average starting salary $26,400

Average salary after 5 years $35,270

Average salary after 10–15 years......$66,050

Life on the job

Curators administer the affairs of museums, zoos, aquariums, botanical gardens, nature centers, and historic sites. The head curator of the museum is usually called the museum director. Curators direct the acquisition, storage, and exhibition of collections, including negotiating and authorizing the purchase, sale, exchange, or loan of collections. They are also responsible for authenticating, evaluating, and categorizing the specimens in a collection. Curators oversee and help conduct the institution's research projects and related educational programs. Today, an increasing part of a curator's duties involves fund-raising and promotion, which may include the writing and reviewing of grant proposals, journal articles, and publicity materials, as well as attendance at meetings, conventions, and civic events.

Curators collect, exhibit, interpret, maintain, and protect objects of historical and aesthetic importance primarily in museums, libraries, and private collections. Curators are responsible for the safety and proper presentation of the works.

Curators' duties include creating exhibitions, acquiring works for the collection, meeting with and educating trustees, labeling exhibits, accurately and carefully keeping track of inventory, and, at times, overseeing research on collection pieces to make certain the integrity of the piece is maintained (such as dating tests for fossils or X-ray analysis of paintings to determine origin). The varied and wide-ranging duties require someone with a mind attuned to details.

Another facet of the curator's job is educating the public about the objects and publicizing their existence. Most literature one receives or audio tracks one listens to at a museum were written by a curator.

Grant writing is the third area of responsibility for most curators; much of this is done in consultation with collection managers and curatorial assistants. Curators should have excellent written communication skills.

Managing a large staff, including interns and volunteers, is the most unexpected side of the profession. Many curators find the classification and preservation skills they possess useless in coordinating the tasks of a full, dedicated staff. "You have to learn to delegate to people's levels of competence," mentioned one veteran curator, and others agreed. "Although you're in charge," said another, "you can't do it alone." Curators who can manage a staff and the details of their job are, for the most part, successful in and excited by their choice of career.

Both graduate education and practical experience are required for people who wish to become curators. Curators must have basic skills in aesthetic design, organizational behavior, business, fund-raising, and publicity. Many employers look favorably on foreign language skills as well. To become a collection manager or a curatorial assistant, a master's degree is often required. To become a curator at a national museum, a PhD is required, as is about five years of field experience. The market is competitive, and academic standards are very high. Nearly all curators find it helpful to engage in continuing education. Research and publication in academic journals are important for advancement in the field.

Insider tips

"Intern, volunteer, sign up to be a docent!" advises one graduate working in the field. The best way to determine whether a field is right for you is to immerse yourself in the environment as much as possible and, when there, explore as much as you can. Take advantage of the lower student membership rates for museums, professional societies, and organizations. This is an ideal way to stay on top of the important issues and trends in the field, and find internship and volunteer opportunities.

Museums rarely come to college campuses for recruiting, so landing that perfect job will be the result of diligent research and targeted application materials. Museums, and the responsibilities of positions within them, are so varied that a successful job search may depend on carefully and closely demonstrating how your particular skills and abilities fit the specific needs of the museum. Determining your ideal museum situation can help to guide your path from training to museum employment.

As a first-time job seeker you may initially need to pursue smaller-scale opportunities working part-time, as an intern, or as a volunteer for an organization. Or you may find yourself working several years in an entry-level position before gaining the skills and status to work up the ranks into higher paying positions with greater responsibilities.

Unlike many other fields, the qualifications for employment vary greatly among institutions, which make it difficult to generalize about methods of application. Small museums do not operate the same way a large one does. Interning will also help to distance you a bit from academia. The real world of museums is quite different. Get ready to dig in and your hands dirty!

Interests (Business + Arts) = Operations Manager, Large Metropolitan Museum

Qualifications

- The successful candidate will be a creative but analytical thinker, innovative but pragmatic.

- Possess a keen intellect and have a fundamental affinity for dealing with complex issues where many criteria matter but to varying degrees.

- An intuitive sense for the whole enterprise must be combined with a practical, project orientation.

- Excellent written and oral communication skills.

- Must be a facilitator who has excellent people-management skills and the ability to manage multiple projects simultaneously.

- Must be a problem-solver with the ability to be responsive to short-term concerns while developing long-range strategies.

- Requires three to six years of supervisory and process/project management experience in an institutional setting.

- Experience working in cultural or nonprofit organizations required.

- Basic knowledge and experience with accounting, purchasing, cost benefit analysis, and project control, human resource management in a medium-sized nonprofit or cultural institution is required.

Interests (History + Migration) = Immigration History Researcher, National Park Service

Qualifications

- Knowledge of, and interest in, related fields of history and issues related to immigration and migration.
- Resourcefulness in researching a variety of information sources and references.
- Ability to distill, summarize, and write text and gather and layout effective images to suit website format.
- Familiarity with websites and organizing and formatting content for websites.

Job Description

- Develop content to help populate and update the Immigration Museum website.
- Develop narrative content and images to be posted on the website regarding immigration, migration, and initial settlement of people along the Pacific Coast from aboriginal settlement up until present day.

Librarian

Number of people in profession 167,000

Average hours per week 40

Average starting salary...........................$33,560

Average salary after 5 years $43,090

Average salary after 10–15 years $54,250

Life on the job

Librarians comprise perhaps the most visible component of the information management community. They can be found in educational institutions, public libraries, historical societies, museums, state government, and business. Librarians catalogue and classify the different materials that enter the library; maintain a catalogue archive (electronic or paper); prepare search aids for the collection such as checklists and bibliographies; and offer general assistance to users. Almost without exception, professional librarian positions demand a Master of Library Science degree (MLS) from an institution accredited by the American Library Association. But several organizations and libraries do recruit persons holding college degrees as library assistants and aides.

Librarians are the custodians of our culture's retrievable media—books and audio and visual materials—and other data or physical objects that can be catalogued and stored. The modern librarian is the manager of an enormous warehouse, and people rely on him or her to help them navigate the increasingly voluminous world of data.

Research and computer skills are important; therefore, people who are generally less comfortable with computers find the transition to online archives much more difficult. Be prepared to work under real deadlines and significant pressure; individuals with corporate library jobs will find that although the salaries are higher, "if you can't do the job when they really need you, they'll show you the door." Librarians who specialize in medicine or law will find their professions to be more lucrative than general librarian jobs, but the books won't be the kind you take home and read for a little relaxation. For specialists especially, graduate studies prove invaluable for a successful transition to working life.

A librarian spends more than 60 percent of his or her day working with people, either library patrons or other staffers and back-office workers. Strong interpersonal skills are required for individuals who hope to succeed in this field. Librarians also work closely with their colleagues; they loan books, advise one another, and discuss daily work issues on a regular basis.

"I'm surrounded by books all day, and that's all I've ever wanted," reports one happy librarian. A librarian does far more than sit at the desk and check books in and out of the library. A large part of his or her job is research, and librarians love the sense of continuous education that comes with the job. Librarians are challenged daily to find creative ways of retrieving different information; and how well they can satisfy these requests determines their success and satisfaction in the profession.

Insider tips

A bachelor's degree is required, and a master's in library science is a plus; PhDs are becoming more common among professional librarians, as well. Solid knowledge of current events and contemporary themes is helpful. A sense of aesthetics helps, too; it is not unusual for a librarian to design a library exhibit. Individuals wishing to become school librarians must also complete any teaching certifications required.

What do you do on the job?

My department is in the business of lending and borrowing. In lending, where I work, we get around 300 requests a day from libraries all over the world to borrow materials from the libraries on this campus. These requests may come from scholars, graduate students, faculty, etc. on other campuses. My assistant and I download and sort out these requests daily. We review the requests guided by standard ILL policies, as well as our own departmental policies, and make the decision of whether to lend the material or not. There are several other tasks to the job, but this is the main function.

What are the rewards and challenges of your work?

I really appreciate the friendly and supportive colleagues that I work with. Getting to spend time every day in the great atmosphere my department head has created, and with a group of people whom I really enjoy being around, is essential. I also like seeing the requests coming in, particularly the dissertation requests from the history PhDs, and having access to almost all of the interesting materials stored on campus. I was a history major at Cal, and by working here, I feel like I am connected to all the scholarship that's going to come out of the history department.

Also, it's great to be immersed in a place where there are opportunities to be constantly thinking so my brain won't atrophy. I looked at other libraries for jobs but decided to stay on campus. This is a prestigious library, and I thrive on being surrounded by smart, challenging people.

WORKING IN EDUCATION: TEACHING, ADMINISTRATION, AND POLICY

Classroom teaching is clearly a viable option for history and political science students. But there are many other opportunities within the field of education that might interest you. Public and private schools employ lawyers, psychologists, counselors, principals/directors, administrators, and curriculum specialists, among others. One graduate explained the scope of his work as an after-school coordinator, working in the school system but not as a teacher: "I worked with 76 schools to implement after-school programs for diverse student populations. I wrote grants to state and federal education departments to fund the programs, trained program coordinators and school staff to implement programs, managed contracts with community-based organizations, and helped to draft educational policies at the local and state level."

"There is a growing movement of people entering education. I think it's great. Previously, many folks looked down upon the profession—admitting its value to society but 'something I would never do.' More and more folks are entering, and there seems to be a greater sense of urgency to reform schooling, which is leading to more opportunity to 'make a difference.' Since many teachers and administrators will be leaving in the next five years, it is a great opportunity to get some energetic and engaging new teachers into the profession!"

Political science major and social sciences teacher
Sean Delgado

Teacher

Number of people in profession 3,800,000

Average hours per week 45

Average starting salary...........................$29,850

Average salary after 5 years $39,810

Average salary after 10–15 years $62,890

"Be the best teacher you can be, and don't let the paperwork—or administrators—get you down!"

High school social studies teacher and political science graduate

Life on the job

The majority of teachers are employed by primary or secondary schools. Their focus is a specific subject or grade level. Before arriving at the classroom, teachers create lesson plans tailored to their students' levels of ability. At school, usually beginning at 8:00 A.M., teachers must begin the difficult task of generating interest in their often sleepy students. A good sense of humor and the ability to think like their students help teachers captivate their students' attention. Teachers have to generate interest in subjects that students often find tedious. Rousing them from their apathy and watching their curiosity grow is a giant reward of teaching. Teachers must have high expectations of their students and also be able to empathize with their concerns. They must be comfortable dealing with a spectrum of personality types and ability levels and must be capable of treating their students fairly.

About a fifth of the teacher's work week is devoted to their least favorite aspect of the profession—paperwork. Teachers have a block of time each day, called a professional period, to accomplish paper grading; however, all teachers report that this is not enough time. Teachers also perform administrative duties, such as spending one period assisting in the school library or monitoring students in the cafeteria. Teachers also need to be accessible to parents. Some teachers meet with parents once per term; others send progress reports home each month. Most schools require teachers to participate in extracurricular activities with students. A teacher may be an advisor to the school yearbook, direct the school play, or coach the chess team. Often they receive a stipend for leading the more time-consuming extracurricular activities. Teachers may also be required to act as chaperones at a certain number of after-school functions, such as dances and chorus concerts.

All good teachers agree that the main reason for entering this profession should be a desire to impart knowledge. Teachers must want to make a difference in the lives and futures of their students.

Insider tips

A college degree is required in this profession. You can receive your bachelor's degree in elementary or secondary education in five years. Prospective teachers take 24 to 36 credits in an area of specialization and 18 to 24 credits in teaching courses. They spend the fifth year student-teaching. Postgraduates can become teachers by returning to school for a master's degree in teaching. In addition, many states offer alternative teaching licenses (designed to help schools acquire a more diverse pool of applicants for teaching positions). The usual requirements are a bachelor's degree in the subject the candidate plans to teach, a passing score on state-required examinations, and completion of a teaching internship.

Prospective teachers are also advised to gain skills in communications, organization, and time management. Teachers can apply for teaching positions through their college's placement office or directly to their chosen school district.

Who was your favorite teacher in high school?

"I taught social studies, covering a variety of topics from history to economics. Social studies teachers are not in as great demand by school districts as science and math teachers, and Teach for America does not accept as many people now with my type of degree. I personally think this is a shame and would encourage any history or political science major who wants to teach to not be deterred by the more difficult job market because it is just such an important job. Math teachers are important, but nobody ever says a math teacher inspired them like they do their government teacher. It's true, think back to your favorite teacher, nine times out of ten, it was your history or government teacher."

PhD candidate Political Science UCLA
Ryan Enos

School Administrator

Number of people in profession	427,000
Average hours per week	45
Average starting, salary	$54,500
Average salary after 5 year	$66,500
Average salary after 10–15 years	$80,900

Life on the job

Administrators, unlike teachers, work a 12-month year. They are fairly busy for most of that time. Whether running a small, private day care center or an overcrowded public high school, an administrator's tasks are numerous and varied, ranging from curriculum development to student discipline. The most familiar school administrator is the principal. Assisting the principal are vice principals, whose duties tend to be more specialized and who have more responsibility for the day-to-day operation of the school than does the principal. In a central administration office, other specialists work with some or all the schools in a given district, overseeing particular programs, such as the evaluation of student academic achievement. Any one of these administrators may be responsible for infrastructure maintenance, the hiring and training of teachers, and student affairs.

School administration is a combination of intellectual work and grunt work. Organizational skills are key, as is the ability to operate within constantly tightening budgetary constraints. Since duties can range from hiring a basketball coach to providing AIDS education, administrators need to be versatile and flexible. An administrator must have a great deal of patience to deal with the enormous bureaucracy often associated with educational institutions. Finally, and perhaps most importantly, since administrators are responsible for the education of young people, a particular dedication to and an understanding of children's needs are essential.

Insider tips

Most beginning administrators have acquired related work experience—usually in teaching or management posts—and, as might be expected in an academic environment, they also have advanced degrees, including doctorates, in education, administration, or a combination of the two. Recently, some schools have begun to demand that their applicants have a Master of Business Administration degree. At the university level, deans are expected to bring a rich academic and professional background to their jobs. As with many educational jobs in the United States, school administrators must be certified, with exact requirements usually determined by the state government.

Interview, Daniel Luzer, Research Associate, Alliance for Excellence in Education

How did you end up where you are now?

I ended up at the Alliance for Excellent Education because I got an internship there a few months after graduating from college. I made it very clear in the course of the internship that I was interested in a permanent position and was taking the internship in an effort to secure permanent employment either at the Alliance or another policy organization.

I received a BA in government with a concentration in international relations from Cornell in January 2003 and moved to Washington, DC in July that year to look for a job in a nonprofit focused on public policy.

What do you do on the job?

I answer a lot of policy questions and do the background research (Does this program work? What's the research to support or that undermines this idea?) for my organization's projects and events. That's the interesting part of my job. The less interesting part involves a lot of "fill in the blank" stuff, e.g., how many states have a program and what the results have been. In terms of projects, there isn't really a typical week.

What are the rewards and challenges of your work?

The rewards of my job include meeting interesting people and getting a full understanding of policy and practice. The frustrating part is that policies are complicated in an incredibly frustrating way that often seems to defy logic.

CAREERS ON CAMPUS: FACULTY, ADMINISTRATION, AND STUDENT SERVICES

Your professors directly influence your life as a student, and you probably already have a strong impression of who they are and what they do. They have certainly made a serious and lifelong commitment to a focused field of research and scholarship. In Chapter 2, we discussed the road to becoming a professor in some detail. Here's another brief overview of the profession, along with an inside look at some other jobs that will keep you close to campus.

Interview, Joseph A. Rodriguez, Associate Professor, Department of History and Director, Urban Studies Programs, University of Wisconsin—Milwaukee

When did you decide to go for your advanced degree, and how was the graduate student experience for you?

I decided during my senior year. I did a summer in Washington, DC and worked in Sacramento in Governor Jerry Brown's office researching toxic substances. I was thinking about environmental law and took the LSAT, applied to Hastings School of Law and was accepted. I also applied to a couple of history master's degree programs.

During senior year at Cal I still thought I'd go to law school but I got in a summer pre-law program sponsored by Hastings and didn't like it. I ended up going to UC—Santa Cruz which had a new master's program in comparative history. I thought I would study Middle Eastern History and take Arabic but switched to U.S. history. The program was geared more toward Third World studies (lots of discussions and readings on peasant revolts), but luckily I found a couple of good Americanists, including James Borchert, who directed my master's paper.

It was mostly because of UC—Berkeley history professor Gunther Barth that I pursued history. I liked his classes on U.S. Urban History and the West and chose urban history as a specialty because of him. After getting the master's I decided to pursue the PhD at Berkeley.

My graduate experience was pretty good; I found a good mentor there. I received good support in the form of teaching assistantships and graduated without much debt. Intellectually I learned a lot from the professors and other grad students in history and in other fields. The grad students had a pick up basketball group that played twice a week that really helped break the isolation.

What are the rewards and challenges of life as a faculty member in the history department? How has that changed for you over the years?

I am lucky to be in a very collegial, friendly department. I enjoy teaching. The job is varied—some teaching, some administration, research, and writing. I enjoy Milwaukee and work in the community on projects like Arcadia Publishing, a local history publisher creating historical publications in small local niches. One challenge is that community-based projects don't get much recognition as "scholarly" activities. Another challenge is winters in Milwaukee, but I have learned to accept those!

Professor

Number of people in profession 1,600,000

Average hours per week..........................60

Average starting salary...........................$23,200

Average salary after 5 years $49,600

Average salary after 10–15 years $69,580

Things I was never told about being a member of the faculty

I'd never again have the time to read fiction.

I'd be so busy writing lectures, there's almost no time to do my research.

My impact on the world is shaping the way a generation thinks even though the teaching isn't rewarded and barely matters for tenure.

I'd really think about questions and answers to those questions undergraduates have, grappling with big issues with a sense of wonderment.

Dr. Ron Hassner, Assistant Professor, the Charles and Louise Travers Department of Political Science, UC—Berkeley

Life on the job

College professors organize and conduct the functions of higher education. They engage in a variety of activities, from managing research laboratories and supervising graduate student research to giving large undergraduate lectures and writing textbooks. With the exception of scheduled classes—which can consume as few as three hours a week in graduate universities or up to 12 to 16 hours per week for undergraduates—a professor's time is largely spent on research, preparing class material, meeting with students, or writing. This profession is thus best suited for motivated self-starters, and its highest rewards are given to individuals who can identify and explore original problems in their fields.

Tenured professors have relatively high job security and professional freedom. Once tenured, a professor can largely set his or her own responsibilities and decide to a large extent how to divide his or her time between teaching, writing, researching, and administration. However, tenure no longer means complete immunity; post-tenure review is now mandated at most universities, and individuals who fall behind on teaching and independent scholarship may not be so secure in their positions nowadays.

The most difficult years of being a professor are the early ones, during which there is great pressure to publish a significant body of work to establish the credentials that lead to tenure. However, the work of junior and senior faculty is quite similar, and the profession offers intellectual stimulation and freedom to all its members.

Insider tips

The path to becoming a tenured college professor is arduous. While a master's degree may be sufficient to qualify to teach in a two-year college or in some cases, as an adjunct, a doctoral degree is required to teach in four-year colleges and universities. PhDs generally take four to seven years to complete; after completing two to three years of course work, the graduate student will usually teach classes and write a dissertation (an original piece of research taking about three years to complete that is the most important element of the search for a first job as a professor). For the coveted tenure-track positions, virtually every successful job candidate now boasts at least one and usually two postdoctorate years, and these years are necessary to remain competitive, which means gathering a sufficient backlog of publications and writings. Personal relationships with faculty are also critical in the hunt for a first job, as teaching positions in many areas (particularly the humanities) can be scarce. While approximately 80 percent of college jobs are in four-year institutions, about a third of all college faculty are employed part-time or in non tenure-track positions, and this percentage has risen in recent years as colleges attempt to control costs.

Here's some advice given to us from graduate students in history and political science.

- I would say study what you find interesting for the BA.
- Realize that some fields require extensive foreign language training so take languages if you have an interest in those fields.
- Apply to PhD programs with a range of reputations. When applying mention the names of professors in your field with whom you'd like to work.
- Remember that funding is rather difficult to come by so you might have to live frugally for some years and it's easier to live on a budget in some cities than others.
- To increase your chances of landing a job post-dissertation, have some marketable skills (i.e., teach methods classes and quantitative history), be willing to teach anywhere in the country and to teach anything. Alternatively, a history BA should consider going into an interdisciplinary field like urban studies, which enables the student to teach, besides history, some sociology, geography, and political science, thus maximizing marketability, especially in smaller colleges that have "social science" departments.
- Read the *Chronicle of Higher Education* (http://chronicle.com), especially the forum section where graduate students give advice on writing the dissertation, finding a job, and being a younger faculty member.

- The most important thing, and something I did not do enough while an undergraduate, is to get to know your professors. They will write you the letters of recommendation that can make or break you. They can give you great advice about what graduate schools you should apply to. Some professors can be jerks, but I think the majority are not—I am always happy to talk to motivated, smart students about graduate school.

- Just know that the path to being a professor is very long and hard. Most people leave graduate school without their PhD. It takes so many hours of work, while you get paid a pittance, and as a grad student there is a lot of stress due to the uncertainty. I know people who finished, then went from one one-year position to another before finally getting a tenure-track position. Other people could not stand the hundreds of pages of reading every week, with 20-page papers in every class, and left. But if you're ready to persevere, the payoff is big (or at least it has been for me).

Cultural Resource Management

Cultural resource management is big business for the federal government, with resources like historic parks, battlefields, and archaeological sites falling under the jurisdiction of the National Park Service. Although the Park Service is known as the protector of natural landmarks such as Yosemite and the Grand Canyon, half of the 365 parks it protects are also historic and cultural sites, such as Alcatraz Island, the Gettysburg National Military Park, and the Lincoln Home National Historic Site in Springfield, Illinois.

Source: Careers in History, American Association of Historians

---

Interview: Gregory Weeks, Associate Professor, Department of Political Science, University of North Carolina

Had you always known you wanted to pursue your PhD and be a professor?

I was not sure what I wanted to do when I graduated from Cal. I sent off a few applications for graduate school, but was rightfully turned down, as I wasn't really sure what sort of research I might do or what my goals were. I went home to San Diego, and enrolled in a terminal political science MA while working part-time. There, I worked with a very well-known political scientist who focuses on Latin America (Brian Loveman) who had a huge influence on me. With his help, I focused my research and got into a very good PhD program (Chapel Hill).

What are the rewards and challenges of your job?

I love this job, and can't imagine doing anything else. You get to decide what kind of work to do, when to do it, and how to do it (especially after you get tenure, which I now have). There are demands on your time, of course, but largely you set your own schedule. It has been really nice while having two kids, so I am able to be very involved with my family.

There is also something very stimulating about going in front of a class and having a discussion. I get all sorts of new questions, and new ideas. At least for me, even a class (like Intro to Comparative Politics) that I teach every single semester, never really gets old because there are always new current events to discuss, and new ways for students to interpret things.

The primary challenge is the pressure to publish. This is where all success comes from—getting tenure and promotion, raises, etc. Another challenge is that even at good schools, you are not going to make a lot of money until you're pretty well advanced. Friends from Cal make more than me, but my job satisfaction is about as high as it can be which is important to me.

College Administrator/ Student Services Professional

Number of people in profession..............25,000

Average hours per week 50

Average starting salary ....$30,000 (varies)

Average salary after 5 years ....$64,640 (varies)

Average salary after 10–15 years ....$98,500 (varies)

Life on the job

Universities are just that: miniature universes. Most of their administrations involve all functions of a big corporation, even a small city, within the larger community in which they are located. A person can work for the same university for 20 years and have 20 different jobs during that time!

College administrators make recommendations about admissions; oversee the disbursement of university materials; plan curricula; oversee all budgets from payroll to maintenance of the physical plant; supervise personnel; keep track of university records (everything from student transcripts to library archives); and help students navigate the university bureaucracy for financial aid, housing, job placement, alumni development, and all the other services a college provides. Many administrators eventually specialize in one field, such as financial aid, in which responsibilities include the preparation and maintenance of financial records and student counseling about financial aid. Specialists in information management are responsible for coordinating and producing the majority of university publications. Administrators who specialize in student affairs (sometimes referred to as student services) deal with residence life, student activities, career services, athletic administration, service learning, health education, and counseling.

Communication skills are essential, as college administrator positions involve constant contact with students, parents, colleagues, members of other college offices, and sometimes even donors. Admissions officers, for example, need to be able to work effectively as members of a team, and have the capacity to manage multiple tasks simultaneously. Interacting with faculty, students, parents, and other university employees can be an exhilarating experience. One drawback, however, is that the job can also be stressful and demanding. As many colleges and universities face budget cuts, college administrators often find themselves taking on additional responsibilities in positions that already require a lot of multitasking. Nevertheless, most who are drawn to this position find that the rewards of working with students more than compensate for the stress.

Insider tips

While entry-level positions in financial aid offices, registrar's offices, and admissions and academic offices often require only a bachelor's degree, a PhD or an EdD is standard among those who hold influential positions in college administrations. Candidates for administrative positions should have good managerial instincts, strong interpersonal skills, and the ability to work effectively with faculty and students. People involved in the financial aspects of administration, including administering financial aid, should have significant knowledge of statistics and great mathematical skills. Computer proficiency is necessary at all levels.

Depending on the context of your campus job search, a master's degree can be helpful in making you more competitive. Even if an advanced degree isn't a requirement for the position, you should do whatever you can to enhance your marketability, such as completing relevant training courses or getting professional certifications in an area related to the job responsibilities.

Now that the job market is tougher than it was a few years ago, it might be useful to look into administrative assistant positions to get your foot in the door. It can be easier to market yourself and what you have to offer when your name or face is already known on campus.

As for the job-search process, take care in writing your objective—clarity is key. And be sure to submit a resume along with a cover letter for jobs you are interested in. If you think of your resume as being like your transcript, then your cover letter is like your personal statement. Both documents are helpful to campus employers in more fully evaluating your fit for the position.

Competition begins with the onset of a specialization. At upper levels, a graduate degree in education, business, student personnel administration, counseling, or information management is required. The hours increase, and administrators spend even more time away from the office at university events or other schools.

Interview, Leah Flanagan, Undergraduate Advisor, Department of History, UC—Berkeley

What do you actually do on your job?

I talk to students about their plans, mostly about which classes will fulfill the major, but also about other opportunities they should look into on campus, as well as some discussion about what happens after they graduate. I do a ton of filing and paperwork to keep track of grades and other administrative matters. I help students deal with problems in their lives, mostly minor, but some quite serious. I refer students to other sources of advice and help for various problems. I assist faculty with any issues concerning undergraduates, and make sure grades get posted. I staff the faculty committee in our department that deals with undergraduate issues. And I'm sure I'm forgetting quite a lot. That's just [what I have been doing] the past four days. Oh, I approve students to graduate as far as meeting the major requirements, and make a list of who is eligible for honors. And I know there's more.

What are the rewards and challenges of working in student services in higher education?

In this job I mostly want our majors to be comfortable, happy, and excited about learning, so that they can fulfill their potential in school. I want them to leave here and be ready to help improve things in the world around them for the rest of their lives. We have so many brilliant and energetic students, I'm sure they will go off to do amazing things. That idea is very rewarding. The tangible rewards are all the thank-you's and positive vibes I get every day. I love to find solutions to problems, or come up with new ideas that really light students up. It's not the money. I happen to love talking, listening, and helping people, so I have no idea why I didn't think of this as a career much sooner!

The challenges, aside from the frustrations of dealing with the awful bureaucracy of a huge public institution, are simply keeping up with the work, and maintaining the energy to get the boring parts of the job done.

CAREERS IN BUSINESS

Many history and political science graduates choose to enter the business sector. Certainly, the potential for lucrative pay is a big draw. Some popular career options in the business sector for history and political science majors—consulting, finance, and human resources manager—are described below.

Many consulting firms provide technical assistance, strategic planning advice, and risk assessment services and solutions to a broad spectrum of clients, ranging from the CEO's of *Fortune* 500 corporations, to lone politicians running for local government. For individuals interested in progressing along the corporate financial services track, there are many different jobs in the financial community, including positions as financial analysts, investment bankers, and financial planning consultants.

Financial analysts gather information, assemble spreadsheets, write reports, and review all pertinent nonlegal information about prospective deals. They examine the financial feasibility of a deal and prepare plans of action based on their analysis. Investment bankers advise their clients about high-level issues of financial organization. They manage the issuance of bonds, recommend and execute strategies for taking over and merging with other companies, and handle selling a company's stock to the public. Financial planning is the fastest growing segment of the industry. Increased activity by banks, brokerage houses, and mutual funds has prompted financial consultant companies to expand their financial planning services for both individuals and small businesses.

How to break into consulting and finance: Show an interest

The corporate recruiters we spoke with all told us the same thing: "We aren't looking for majors—we are looking for people." They are, in fact, interested in history and political science students and have hired students from those majors in the past. But initially, business and economics students may have an easier time explaining their interest in the profession. They at least have course work which demonstrates an interest in business.

Where is your evidence of your drive and passion for business? "You need to take charge of your business future by learning about it," explains one political science graduate working as a financial analyst. It's critical to demonstrate to corporate recruiters that you have a serious interest in the field and in what their company actually does. They need to see evidence of a set of skills relevant to their needs, and a clear indication that you have the ability to acquire additional skills while on the job or in their training program.

Susan Shald, director of talent sourcing at the Gallup Organizations, had this to say: "Each candidate at Gallup is looked at for the 'entire package' of skills they bring to the table. Sometimes this is experience, sometimes education. We are looking for individuals who have talent and desire regardless of their major. But if a student is applying for a role that seems to vary greatly from their major, they need to share with me why their individual passion is so great for this new role. Research the organization or career path and know what you want in the interview. At Gallup, for example, there is brand recognition among students for our public opinion survey arm, but many students don't realize that there are a wide range of positions within the organization and each role requires a different set of skills."

In addition to researching the organization beforehand, Shald recommends that students "Be passionate about your choice and let the employer know that you care about their goals and your future as it relates to those goals. Only apply for roles that you are truly interested in. Ask questions. If you are unsure of something or need help finding information please contact the recruiter to get all of your questions answered. Believe in yourself and be confident in your approach."

To sum up, business employers are looking for a lot of things besides college major when interviewing applicants for a position. To begin with, they look for interpersonal skills, multitasking capabilities, time management skills, and analytical/critical thinking abilities. They want people who are curious and continual learners. But they are also looking for evidence of quantitative analysis skills and a real comfort with numbers. While liberal arts majors typically don't have to take a lot of math courses in college, there is still a way for you to demonstrate your quantitative proficiency to employees.

Reality check: Do the numbers.

It's great that as a history or political science major you have demonstrated your ability to consider an abstract question, take on a position, and defend that position with rigorous reasoning and examples. To make yourself even more irresistible to the corporate recruiter, it's critical to show evidence of your understanding of quantitative analysis and comfort with numbers. If you have taken a research design, research methods, statistics, or calculus course, that's good information to put in the "related course work" section of your resume to show that you can run the numbers when you need to.

There are other ways to show evidence of your quantitative ability. If you examine your course work, student jobs, and extracurricular activities with an eye on the numbers, there is probably proof that you can crunch them when the time comes.

Resume entries of a quantitative kind

Treasurer, My Student Club

- Managed budget of $3000.
- Prepared bi-weekly status reports.
- Approved and monitored all expenditures.

Cashier, Drugstore

- Operated cash register.
- Monitored and stocked a wide variety of inventory.
- Responsible for daily deposit count.

Teller, Local Bank

- Handled deposits and withdrawal transactions.
- Organized and filed new account signature cards.
- Responsibly handled large amounts of cash.

Administrative Assistant, My campus work-study job

- Generated purchase orders for all procurement requests up to $1,500.
- Processed and organized travel vouchers, deposits, and check requests.
- Contacted vendors for invoices and receipts to validate charges.
- Audited monthly payroll ledger.

Course work that's considered evidence of quantitative skills

- Basic Social Statistics
- Business and Economic Statistics
- Research Methods
- Quantitative and Qualitative Analysis
- Demographic Techniques and Analysis
- College Algebra
- Calculus
- College Math

Management Consultant

Number of people in profession	577,000
Average hours per week	60
Average starting salary	$61,496
Average salary after 5 years	$78,932
Average salary after 10–15 years	$112,716

Life on the job

Companies, focused on improving efficiency and profitability, hire management consultants to identify problems and recommend solutions. Consultants' objectives can be limited to analyzing such issues as shipping functions, and then streamlining procedures. Alternatively, their goals may be broadly defined and include reorganizing a multinational corporation to take advantage of the synergies that developed when it acquired new businesses. "Sometimes you're asked to solve a particular problem, and you find that the problem is just a symptom of another problem, so you need to spend a lot of time at the beginning identifying where to start and what you need to do," said one consultant. The need to spend time at the beginning doing research, identifying areas of concern, and mapping out how the different areas of a business affect one another is often a difficult sell to clients who want immediate results. "No one wants to hear that you've got to look at five years of data—they want you to tell them how to fix things today," wrote another. Management consultants have to be accomplished analysts, attentive listeners, and firm but tactful communicators. They are thinkers and problem solvers who know how to convince others that change is needed.

Though even starting management consultants make good money (and income rises considerably with experience), as a management consultant you must be willing to sacrifice time from your personal life. Sixty-hour workweeks are part of the training and education process and travel and time spent on-site at clients' offices can be considerable. Consultants must get used to leaving home on Sunday for a business trip and not returning until Thursday or Friday. Satisfaction is generally high in this career, despite its demands.

Insider tips

Most major employers run their own programs to train junior consultants in accounting, internal policy, research techniques, and how to work as part of a close-knit, hardworking team. But very little guidance is available on the job, so you need to demonstrate academic, work, or entrepreneurial experience that shows yourself to be a self-starter and dedicated to excellence in whatever you do.

Seek out a mentor in the field who can give you informal insider advice about the work and what's expected. Join a business club on campus to show your interest in the field, and get some face time with recruiters who may attend student-run events while on campus. Remember to do your research on the field and the company. There are a lot of firms out there and you need to figure out the differences in what they do before you complete an interview. Recruiters need to evaluate your personality—this is crucial in the decision-making process—so take every opportunity to meet them in person. As one consulting recruiter put it: "When you are in front of the hiring manager, be clear that that's the job you want. Be able to tell them why, that you have done your research, and are excited about the opportunity."

Interviews will most likely involve case questions in which you are given a business problem and need to think through the problem by applying analytical methods used in the industry. Be prepared and practice working through several cases so that your natural intelligence and ability to "think out of the box" will be evident. Getting the right answer is often less important than demonstrating a creative, analytical thought process. History and political science students are great problem solvers and this industry wants to see how you think, so with some exposure to practice cases beforehand, you could really impress the interviewer. Several of the major consulting firms have sample cases on their websites for your review.

Interview, Corey Robbins, Associate, Deloitte Consulting

What do you do?

I have been on a variety of internal and client engagements over the past year. One particularly interesting one was for a very large high-tech manufacturer in Silicon Valley. Our team was tasked with developing a five-year roadmap that would outline a best-in-class "opportunity-to-order" process for the client's business-to-business sales. Once the best-in-class process was defined, the roadmap would give the client a five-year plan to get there.

The project was focused on understanding the pain points of various stakeholders in the organization with the current process and needs and requirements to support future business growth. Based on this information, we were able to use Deloitte's expertise to design a customized best-in-class vision for the client. As a member of the team, I was mainly involved with interviewing key client managers, capturing key facts/metrics related to current and future state needs, and assisting with the business case development behind the team's best-in-class recommendation.

What are the challenges and rewards of your work?

At a large firm like Deloitte Consulting, there are many talented practitioners who are involved in a variety of interesting projects. A challenge at any consulting firm is to get yourself connected with these practitioners. When I initially joined the company this was difficult because I did not have an internal network, and the business analyst training program was intense. Now that I have been at Deloitte for over a year, I am expected to design and execute on my own career path. To do this, I continue to reach out and make connections with people working on projects in which I am interested. Consultants do not have a boss in the classic sense. While there are senior practitioners who I report to when I am staffed on a project, there is not one person who is continually responsible for my work and development between projects. If you want a job where you have a very structured organization with a lot of direction, consulting isn't the field for you.

Besides the flexibility and breadth of opportunities, the rewards for me are that I work with phenomenal people in different settings and with different clients. The job is constantly changing. At Deloitte we have a Business Analyst Rotational Program; I will change clients/locations at least every six months. Moving around that way is great because it [gives] me the chance to learn about different industries and to work with various functions (e.g., marketing, finance) of world-class organizations.

Life on the job

Most analyst jobs are with banks or financial consulting firms, which means working in a corporate environment in which suiting-up daily is the norm. Analysts must be prepared to travel, if necessary, to close a deal. Those who wish to rise in the industry should note the necessity of significant "face time," attending social events and conferences and spending downtime with people in the profession, which can be expensive; this social circle tends to be marked by expensive clothing, hobbies, habits, and diversions.

Analysts sacrifice a lot of control over their personal lives during their first few years, but only a few other entry-level positions provide the possibility of such a large payoff come year-end. Many employers use bonuses—equal to or double the beginning analyst's salary—to attract and retain intelligent personnel. Successful financial analysts become senior financial analysts or associates after three to four years of hard work at a firm. Analysts with strong client contacts and immaculate reputations start their own financial consulting firms. Many of them work as analysts for about three years and then return to school or move on to other positions in banking.

Financial analysts work long hours, and deadlines are strict. The occasional 15-hour day is mitigated by the high degree of responsibility these analysts are given. Beyond this, the long hours breed a close kinship. Analysts are extremely supportive of one another, and this makes the demanding work schedule a bit more bearable. Most people become financial analysts because they feel it is the best way to immerse themselves in the world of finance and a great way to earn a lot of money. They're right on both counts, but be aware that the immersion is complete and somewhat exclusive, and although people earn a lot of money, few analysts have the free time to spend it.

Insider tips

Entry-level positions are highly competitive. To become a financial analyst you need to have a strong sense of purpose that your future lies in the financial world. Some history and political science graduates may have that kind of drive for the field. Worried that you don't have an accounting degree? As one graduate working in finance told us, "Some liberal arts students sweat a lot about the financial analysis skills like accounting and finance. It isn't rocket science. A couple of night classes can teach you the basics. You can learn the rest on the job. In my opinion, running of the numbers is the easy part. The judgment necessary to interpret the input and output of a financial model and the leadership skills to inspire people to achieve numerical goals set forth in a financial model are much more important."

Interview: Jill Hitchcock, Recruiter and Group Vice President, Fisher Investments

Any general tips for resume writing or preparing for interviews for your company or field?

We are interested in candidates who have demonstrated prior success, whether that be in their area of study, student organizations, or athletics. Therefore, we encourage candidates to construct a resume that clearly shows how they have spent their college years. The resume should be clear and easy to read so it's easy for the interviewer to pick out the important points. Students should not cram their resumes full of insignificant details or minor activities. We would prefer a candidate who was very involved in only one activity but made a significant impact to a candidate who had superficial involvement in many activities but didn't leave their mark anywhere.

Students should read about our company before interviewing with us so they have a general understanding of our business. They should also come prepared to discuss their experiences in detail, including being prepared with examples of challenges and successes. Successful candidates should be able to convey their interest, drive, and motivation to the interviewer.

Investment Banker

Number of people in profession:	40,000
Average hours per week	70
Average starting salary	$143,000
Average salary after 5 years	$321,000
Average salary after 10–15 years	$1,070,000

Life on the job

The work of an investment banker involves a large amount of financial analysis, so completing additional course work in finance and economics may be necessary. Personal and strategic skills are also vital to investment bankers because they serve as strategists for their clients, helping them both develop and implement their financial plans. At the profession's highest level, investment bankers serve as crucial figures in the shaping of the American and world economies, managing mergers of multibillion-dollar corporations and handling the privatization of government assets around the world.

All this is time-consuming, and investment bankers work long hours. Seventy-plus-hour work weeks are common, and all-night sessions before deals close are the rule rather than the exception. Still, the work is extremely interesting, and those who stay in the profession report high levels of job satisfaction. Investment bankers spend large amounts of time traveling to pitch ideas to prospective and current clients or to examine the facilities of companies being purchased by their clients. In the office, they spend their time developing strategies to pitch to clients, preparing financial analyses and documents, or working with the sales forces of their banks to sell the bonds and stocks that are created by the investment banking department's activities.

Entry-level jobs in analyst programs are available to college graduates who want exposure to the profession. Analysts perform much of the grunt work required in preparing financial proposals, although they often travel to sit in on meetings with clients and sessions in which senior bankers pitch ideas to prospective customers. After two years, analysts usually move on, either to business school or to another profession, though a few are offered jobs as associates—the position that investment banks offer to MBA holders. In many banks, this is as far as one can rise without an MBA, though there are exceptions; a few prominent bankers never went to business school.

Insider tips

One I-Banking recruiter had this to say: "People who look up alumni and make contact with them, attend presentations, read the *Wall Street Journal*, watch the markets, are involved in investment or other business-related clubs on campus, or possibly even invest in their own portfolio are the ones who show the necessary dedication to really get noticed in an interview." The critical-thinking and reading skills of a liberal arts background can also come in handy. As our recruiter explains, "The drive and motivation to succeed can be shown regardless of the major, and these are the things they can't teach you. But to get your foot in the door, you need to show serious evidence that you are interested in business and follow that world."

Financial Planner

Number of people in profession: ....N/A

Average hours per week: 50

Average starting salary: $20,000

Average salary after 5 years: $40,000

Average salary after 10–15 years: $90,000

Life on the job

Financial planners determine how their clients can achieve their lifelong financial goals through the management of their financial resources. They examine the financial history—and current financial situation—of their client's assets and suggest exactly what steps the client needs to take in the future to meet his or her goals. Although other professional financial advisors usually focus on one area of a client's financial life, the broad-based approach to financial advice that financial planners offer distinguishes them from the rest of the profession. In this sense, financial planners are jacks of all trades, but they do not work alone. Financial planners will inevitably meet with the client's other advisors—attorneys, accountants, trust officers, investment bankers—to fully understand their client's financial goals. (The last thing a financial planner wants to do is map out a plan that conflicts with investments that the client has already made with their bankers.) It is a research-intensive profession, as well as a stressful one: You are making recommendations about how people should spend, invest, and save their money. It is a very corporate profession as well, and you will be expected to look and play the part.

Although many financial planners are asked to devise comprehensive plans for their clients, some people hire planners to handle a specific interest and financial goal, such as planning for retirement, buying a home, or investing an inheritance. A financial planner will conduct questionnaires and personal interviews, detailing the client's financial objectives, current incomes, investments, risk tolerance, expenses, tax returns, insurance coverage, retirement programs, estate plans, and other pertinent information to put together a plan that meets the client's specific financial agenda. The plan itself is a set of recommendations and strategies for clients to use or ignore as they see fit, and financial planners should be ready to answer challenging questions about the integrity of the plan they map out. Because of this, financial planners must constantly update their plans and watch the market for trends that will affect their recommendations.

According to the Institute of Certified Financial Planners, planners spend the majority of their time advising clients on investment planning, retirement planning, tax planning, estate planning, and risk management. All of these areas require different types of financial understanding, and planners are generally expected to be knowledgeable about asset management, employee benefits, estate planning, insurance, investments, and retirement funds. On top of all of this required knowledge, a financial planner must also have good interpersonal skills since establishing a client-planner relationship is essential to a planner's professional success. It also helps to be a great presenter since even the best financial plan, if presented poorly to a client, can destroy the client's trust.

Insider tips

A degree in history or political science is a fine starting point, but in addition you'll need to have some evidence of quantitative aptitude. Education alone is not going to give potential clients the peace of mind they need to turn over their finances. On the issue of trust, it is prudent to note that no federal agency regulates financial planners. There is regulation on the state level, but only in some states. Because of this, most financial planners choose to become certified by the Certified Financial Planners (CFP) Board. The CFP Board is an independent professional regulatory organization that extends licenses to those planners who pass the CFP certification examination.

Human Resources Manager

Number of people in profession: 219,000

Average hours per week: 50

Average starting salary: $43,200

Average salary after 5 years: $65,000

Average salary after 10–15 years: $87,600

Life on the job

America's transition from an agricultural to an industrial society created the need for talented, creative workers and a need to manage these human resources. Companies wanted to have more control over hiring, salary structure, and resource allocation.

Human resources managers handle personnel decisions, including hiring, position assignment, training, benefits, and compensation. Their decisions are subject to some oversight, but company executives recognize their experience and skill in assessing personnel and rely heavily on their recommendations. Although physical resources—capital, building, equipment—are important, most companies realize that the quality and quantity of their output is directly related to the quality and commitment of their personnel. Human resources professionals make sure that appropriate matches are made between support staff and producers, between assistants and managers, and between coworkers to enhance productivity, support the company's business strategy and long-term goals, and provide a satisfying work experience for all employees.

A human resources professional in a smaller firm is a jack-of-all-trades who is involved in hiring, resource allocation, compensation, benefits, and compliance with laws and regulations affecting employees and the workplace and safety and health issues. This multiplicity of tasks requires individuals with strong organizational skills who can quickly shift from project to project and topic to topic without becoming overwhelmed. Strong interpersonal skills are crucial for managers at small firms. These managers spend much of their day handling questions, attending budgeting and strategic planning meetings, and interviewing prospective employees. The rest of the time, they take care of paperwork and talk on the telephone with service providers (insurance, health care, bank officers, etc.). At larger firms, human resources managers often specialize in one area. Compensation analysts work with department managers to determine pay scales and bonus structures. Hiring specialists (also known as recruiters) place ads in appropriate publications, review resumes, and interview candidates for employment. Allocation managers match assistants, support staff, and other employees with departments that have specific needs.

The most difficult feature of the human resources professional's job is handling the dirty work involved in the staffing of a company: dealing with understaffing, refereeing disputes between two mismatched personalities, firing employees, informing employees of small (or nonexistent) bonuses, maintaining an ethical culture, and reprimanding irresponsible employees. Performing these tasks can be disheartening for human resources managers who are supposed to support and assist employees, and many human resources managers feel that employees dislike or fear them because of this role.

Insider tips

There are entry-level administrative support positions that history and political science majors might need to consider to get their foot in the door. Master's degrees in human resource management, industrial relations, organizational development, organizational behavior, and business administration are also considered worthwhile. Each company has its own internal protocols, and most new hires are trained in them when they begin. A human resources manager must have strong interpersonal skills, and many employers conduct multiple interviews that test a candidate's ability to relate to a diverse group of people.

Entry-Level Position in Human Resources = Administrative Assistant

Responsibilities

- Manage calendars, schedule meetings, reserve conference rooms, and make travel arrangements.
- Process invoices and expense reports.
- Screen and direct telephone calls and visitors.
- Compose, edit, and proofread correspondence and reports.
- Process personnel action notices.
- Complete special projects as assigned (i.e., ordering department gifts; organizing department functions; maintaining monthly reports and spreadsheets; meeting planning; drafting meeting minutes, etc.).

Qualifications

- Proficiency with Microsoft Office applications (e.g., Word, Excel, PowerPoint).
- Excellent verbal and written communication skills.
- Must demonstrate high level of knowledge, good judgment, and confidentiality and discretion in handling communications with all levels of internal and external clients.
- Excellent organizational skills with the ability to prioritize and handle multiple projects in a fast-paced environment.

CAREERS IN MEDIA AND COMMUNICATIONS

Media-related careers appeal to many students of history or political science. The work of public relations and marketing professionals is to understand clients' needs and develop strategies to effectively reach and influence customers regarding the organization's goods, services, or ideas. Public affairs is related to public relations, but rather than influencing the general public, public affairs professionals seek to influence the political climate and elected officials on behalf of the organization/causes they represent. Within government there are PR specialists who keep the public informed about the activities of agencies and officials. A press secretary for a member of Congress makes sure constituents are aware of the representative's accomplishments. A publicist gets press coverage for his or her client and is often the intermediary between the high-profile personality and members of the media. All these communications professionals need the ability to create and cultivate media and press relationships.

Public Relations Specialist

Number of people in profession 203,000

Average hours per week 45

Average starting salary $34,038

Average salary after 5 years $77,400

Average salary after 10–15 years $128,200

Life on the job

Public relations, like the title implies, is about managing the public's perception of clients. Public relations specialists—also referred to as *communications specialists* and *media specialists*, among other titles—serve as advocates for businesses or nonprofit entities to build and maintain positive relationships with the public. As managers recognize the importance of good public relations to the success of their organizations, they increasingly rely on public relations specialists for advice on the strategy and policy of such programs.

Public relations specialists work to maintain good working relationships with the community and with the media. They create and maintain a network of designated contacts and internal "clients" within the organization with whom PR must interact on a regular basis to get information and serve the communications needs of their organization. Their job is to get the organization's "story" to the public. To do this, they prepare and disseminate information about the organization through newspapers, periodicals, television, radio, and other forms of media.

Public relations specialists also arrange and conduct programs—speaking engagements, social events, programs, and conventions—to keep the organization in the public eye. In addition, they are responsible for preparing annual reports and writing proposals for various projects.

A publicist gets press coverage for his or her client. The publicist is often the intermediary between a high-profile personality and members of the media. He or she usually wants his or her client to receive positive acclaim, but as the old adage goes "the only bad publicity is no publicity." Politicians and captains of industry require a little more specific spin on their press—they want to be seen as forward-looking and confident—but other professions are less picky, as in the case of the rock star who reveals the sordid details of his or her nightlife to cultivate a rough image. Publicists also perform damage control, and attempt to counteract any undesirable press coverage the client receives. This position as the "last line of defense" is what distinguishes the adequate publicist from the extraordinary one. Good publicists can transform scandal into opportunity and create valuable name recognition for their clients.

Insider tips

In public relations firms, a beginner might be hired as a research assistant or account coordinator and be promoted to account executive, senior account executive, account manager, and eventually vice president.

Many colleges help students secure part-time internships in public relations that provide valuable experience and training. Writing for a school publication or television or radio station provides valuable experience and material for one's portfolio. People who choose public relations as a career need an outgoing personality, self-confidence, and an understanding of human psychology.

Public Relations Intern

Job Description

- Assist the Public Relations Director in all activities.
- Assist in the writing of calendars, media advisories, and press releases.
- Staff high-profile events by assisting with media check-in.
- Conduct internet research to identify and contact possible program attendees.
- Help to update and maintain press lists and media coverage tracking.
- Assist with compiling press clippings and monitoring media for press coverage.
- Interact with TV, print, and radio to gain coverage for organization's programs.
- Assist with other duties as assigned.

Qualifications

- Exceptional writer.
- Excellent communication skills and quick learner.
- Attention to detail.
- Interest in public affairs.

Edward L. Bernays: The Father of Public Relations

When Bernays took on Diaghilev's Ballet Russes American tour in 1915, he wrote, "I was given a job about which I knew nothing. In fact, I was positively uninterested in the dance." He wasn't alone. Americans thought male dancers were deviants, and of limited interest.

Bernays began to connect ballet to something people understood and enjoyed. First, as a novelty, a unifying of several art forms; second, its appeal to special groups; third, its direct impact on American life, on design and color in American products; and fourth, its personalities.

Beginning with newspapers, Bernays developed a four-page newsletter for editorial writers, local managers, and others, containing photographs and stories of dancers, costumes, and composers. Articles were targeted to his four themes and audiences. For example, the "women's pages" received articles on costumes, fabric, and fashion design; the Sunday supplements received full-color photos.

Magazine coverage, timed to appear just before the ballet opened, was his next approach. Bernays tailored his stories to his editors. When *Ladies' Home Journal* said that they couldn't show photographs of dancers with skirts above the knees, he had artists retouch photos to bring down the hem. His ability to understand editors' needs resulted in wide coverage on that front.

Bernays created an 81-page user-friendly publicity guide for advance men to use on the tour. When a national story about the Ballet Russes appeared, advance men could tailor it for local coverage. The guide contained mimeographed pages, bios on the dancers, short notes and fillers, and even a question-and-answer page that asked, "Are American men ashamed to be graceful?"

He persuaded American manufacturers to make products inspired by the color and design of the sets and costumes, and national stores to advertise them. These styles became so popular that Fifth Avenue stores sold these products without prompting from Bernays. Bernays used overseas media reviews to heighten anticipation for the dancers. When they arrived at the docks in New York, a crowd was waiting. Bernays then took photos of the eager crowds and placed them in Sunday magazines throughout the country. The ballet was sold out before the opening. The ballet toured American cities; demand had already dictated a second tour, and little girls were dreaming of becoming ballerinas. Bernays had remolded biases to get his story told. The American view of ballet and dance was changed forever.

Source: The Museum of Public Relations, PRmuseum.com

Consumer advocacy nonprofits: Monitoring fairness in marketing and advertising

Summer Internship, Consumer Advocacy Group

Job Description

- Draft congressional testimony and consumer-education correspondence.
- Prepare lobbying documents.
- Research issues and provide office support as needed.

Qualifications

- Excellent writing, editing, and research skills.
- Strong interpersonal, organizational, and communications skills.
- Ability to work with a wide range of people, work well under pressure, adapt to changing situations on a daily basis, solve problems, and work independently.
- Familiarity with legal, public policy, congressional, and public interest issues.

Market Researcher

Number of people in profession 72,400

Average hours per week 45

Average starting salary............................$38,100

Average salary after 5 years $59,800

Average salary after 10–15 years $93,300

Life on the job

Market research as a distinct profession emerged out of the multiple-product nature of large companies. In the 1950s, many successful organizations began to analyze who their customers were and what other products they might be interested in buying. As advertising and marketing techniques became more sophisticated, so did market research techniques. Today, market researchers prepare studies and surveys, analyze demographic information and purchasing histories, review the factors that affect product demand, and make recommendations to manufacturing and sales forces about the market for their product. This multifaceted job requires financial, statistical, scientific, and aesthetic skills, as well as common sense.

Market researchers work on projects that proceed in stages. At the beginning of a project, a market researcher may spend three weeks with other market researchers designing a survey and testing it on small samples of their intended population. In later stages, they may define demographics, distribute the survey, and collect and assemble data. In the final stages, they may analyze survey responses to uncover consumer preferences or needs that have not yet been identified. Like all scientific experiments, "The assumptions we make are key. If we don't get those clear at the beginning, it's going to affect our entire study," one market researcher told us. Those people who specialize in public opinion surveys are particularly careful about how they phrase their questions, as a single misplaced modifier can dramatically affect the meaning of a question and, likewise, its responses.

New technology continues to redefine the role of the market researcher, as computers expedite, expand, and sometimes even replace their functions. But thanks in part to an increasingly competitive economy, the outlook of the market research profession looks bright, with the field expected to grow faster than average over the next five years.

Insider tips

Invest in a statistics or research methods course. Work experience that demonstrates a creative intellect and the ability to work on teams is also well regarded. Prospective market researchers should be aware that early jobs in the field entail plenty of menial work—copying, proofreading, inputting data, and the like. Individuals who are willing to carry out these entry-level tasks go on to fill positions of responsibility. Graduate degrees in marketing, business, or statistics are becoming more common among individuals in management positions.

Interests (Government + Market Research) = Social Science Statistician, U.S. Bureau of the Census

Statisticians are responsible for designing, managing, and analyzing national and international surveys and studies that supply the official population and housing statistics that Congress, state and local government, other federal agencies, and businesses need on various topics such as:

- Population size and distribution
- Income and poverty
- Employment and unemployment
- Family and fertility
- Health and disability
- Housing and neighborhood characteristics

WORKING IN JOURNALISM

History and political science majors are found in many roles within the world of media. One graduate working in broadcast journalism told us: "In television it is more important to be able to tell a good story and be aware of our cultural history as a whole than to have a great deal of technical ability. The entertainment industry is in dire need, in my opinion, of people who can envision what a good story is and how to tell it in interesting ways."

Below is a quick look at jobs in the journalism industry. Radio stations need someone to be responsible for the on-air programming, and that someone is the radio producer. Television producers make sure television shows run smoothly and take responsibility for everything from coordinating writers and performers/correspondents to overseeing the fact-checking of credit names and titles. Television reporters gather information, investigate leads, and write and report stories live or tape their news reports—sometimes called "packages"—for a later broadcast. There are many types of print journalists, from the local beat newspaper reporter to the foreign correspondent, the magazine feature writer to the freelance book reviewer.

Most people who want a career in broadcasting gain experience by working at college radio stations or through internships at professional stations. Interns are often unpaid, but the hands-on training they earn can be invaluable. Some individuals start out as production assistants, helping the producer create the programming. They also provide clerical and research assistance. Radio producers just starting out usually find a job at smaller stations serving smaller markets. Competition for positions in large metropolitan areas is strong. The chance for advancement is small unless employees change employers. Relocation to communities in other parts of the country is frequently necessary.

Television Producer

Number of people in profession..............42,000

Average hours per week.........................55

Average starting salary $22,500

Average salary after 5 years $42,900

Average salary after 10–15 years $93,900

Life on the job

Having complete responsibility for all facets of on-air production can be a very stressful job, and above all the successful television producer has to be organized. He or she must be able to communicate clearly and succinctly with everyone on and off the set, from actors to directors to writers to technical crew, and have a gift for thinking on his or her feet to come up with creative ideas under extraordinary time pressure. Television producers report high excitement and job satisfaction—they are implementers and problem-solvers who are project-oriented and love to see tangible results.

The public perception of the television industry is one full of high-profile personalities, and while it helps for the television producer to act as a dynamic, motivating force, nearly everything a producer does is known only to individuals involved with the show itself. A good producer should have enough of an ego to make important decisions and defend them, but should not be afraid of drudge work. Writing script may even be a part of the television producer's last-minute job. Most producers rise in the ranks from production assistant positions, so they know what it takes to get a show from concept to broadcast. Producers ultimately take credit for a successful broadcast but also have to take the blame for anything that goes wrong on their watch.

For individuals who can master it, television production is an exciting, difficult job that can be quite financially rewarding. History major and ABC producer Charlie Herman talked to us about the need to "be at the right place at the right time." He explains: "I worked for a while in advertising after I graduated and then quit to move to Paris. Because I spoke French, I got hired by ABC as a driver during the bicentennial celebration of D-Day. I met people in the organization and went to Washington, DC. Because of my production background and how I could put together stories, I moved up through the ranks. My current position is producer of the business beat with ABC. I oversee day-to-day operations of that area where stories range from housing to energy to the market, to spending to savings and retirement."

Entry-level positions, such as production assistant jobs, may include duties as mundane as proofreading copy for typos and making sure lunch reservations are made. College internships are heavily sought-after because they provide an appreciable advantage in securing that first job as production assistant. Aggressive pursuit and completion of more and more demanding tasks distinguishes the production assistant who rises in rank from one who does not.

Interests (Business + Journalism) = Advertising Sales Manager, Independent Daily Newspaper

Job Description

- Report directly to the display advertising manager.
- Responsible for coaching, training, and managing a sales team.
- Lead the cross-selling of advertising in print and on the web.
- Set sales goals, developing new revenue, foster exceptional customer service and meet revenue goals.
- Provide motivation, hands on leadership, fresh ideas, and a "can do" attitude.

Qualifications

- Strong organizational and communication skills.
- Ability to work well with others, and work in a fast-paced, deadline-oriented environment.
- Media sales experience a plus.
- Requires a demonstrated familiarity with the Internet and the ability to think strategically and identify opportunities.

The Origins of Mass Communications

Mass communication began with the fifteenth-century invention of the Gutenberg printing press. The business of selling printed news evolved over the next 250 years in Western Europe. Newspapers sprouted up throughout the colonies, and the first newspaper with original local news and commentary in Boston was *The New England Courant*, started by none other than James Franklin, the brother of Benjamin Franklin. The more famous Franklin would go on to buy his own newspaper, *The Pennsylvania Gazette*, in 1729. Henry Luce launched the first weekly news magazine in the United States, *Time* magazine, on March 3, 1923. To create value, it not only reported the news, but also analyzed it. Readers praised the magazine, and *Time* spawned numerous imitations, both in print and, later, on television.

Journalist

Number of people in profession: 70,000

Average hours per week: 55

Average starting salary: $28,100

Average salary after 5 years: $44,600

Average salary after 10–15 years:...... $69,300

Life on the job

It is difficult to pin down the daily routine of an average journalist. Journalists interview sources and review records to assemble, collect, and report information and explore the implications of the facts. They must be able to report quickly and accurately and time pressure is one of the most distinguishing features of this job. Journalists must maintain a point of view while remaining objective about their subjects, which can be difficult. Interpersonal skills, excellent writing skills, and a reporter's instinct (the ability to accurately assess the significance of obscure and incomplete information) are essential for success.

The uncertainty of the daily routine makes it difficult to incorporate family, hobbies, and any regularly scheduled plans; but those who detest the predictability of nine-to-five jobs are attracted to journalism because no day is a carbon copy of the day before. Long hours and chronic deadline pressure can be significantly negative factors. When an editor calls you in on a breaking story, you have to be prepared to drop everything; when you're on deadline, you can get crazed trying to write a complicated story in half the time you need. This ball and chain to the office leads many to resent, and eventually reject, the reporter's life. Journalists who are protective of their prose rarely last in this profession, since articles are often edited for publication without their consultation. More than 40 million people read newspapers in the United States each day, and more than 50 million people read magazines each week. The opportunity for your writing to reach a large audience is tempting indeed, and many find the initial low pay, uncertain and occasionally dangerous conditions, and chaotic schedule a fair trade-off to be allowed to do what they do. In fact, many seem drawn by the excitement and challenge of these very conditions.

Insider tips

More than a few distinguished journalism careers have begun at the school or local magazine or newspaper, before ever progressing on to a large metropolitan publication. Building a collection of clippings (samples of your work cut from the newspapers in which they were published) is key to being able to make this transition successfully.

Bone up on your proofreading skills before applying for any job. Skills required of journalists include: good grammar and spelling, extensive vocabulary, curiosity, ability to respond well under pressure and meet deadlines, ability to write under duress, and diverse background and life experiences.

If you enjoy research and investigation, starting in the field as a fact-checker may be your ticket to working for a large magazine or news organization. Fact-checkers verify the accuracy of text written by reporters. They research information and statements of fact through print and internet-based resources in addition to phone interviews. Don't expect much pay when you're first starting out. It's all about the experience you gain and the people you will meet. The big bucks will come later, after you win that Pulitzer.

CAREERS IN BOOK PUBLISHING

Book publishing is an extraordinarily large industry, and those who (successfully) enter the profession have no illusions that what they do is merely artistic in nature. "You've got to keep things on schedule. You've got to make them pay for themselves, or you're out of business," said one publishing professional, adding that "publishing" is a term that can encompass many positions within a publishing house.

The most high-profile job is that of editor, or someone who works with authors to produce a quality product. Many other positions are available for those interested in the industry, including managing editors responsible for controlling production flow; publicity managers; promotions specialists; subsidiary rights managers; production managers; and salespeople. These occupations are critical to the successful functioning of a publishing house. Those who want to pursue a career in this industry should examine their own skills in light of the variety of opportunities available for ambitious and creative individuals who find the prospect of working with books exciting.

Managing editors are the traffic controllers of the publishing industry. They track production schedules and budgets, allocate personnel, and control the flow of material between departments. A large publishing house can have hundreds of projects running simultaneously, and the managing editor needs to be attentive to detail and be able to anticipate problems before they occur. Publicity, promotions, and sales positions reward creative and outgoing personalities. Successful professionals in this industry utilize their interpersonal skills to drum up consumer interest and encourage sales by bookstores. Salespeople spend significant amounts of time on the road meeting with bookstore buyers and managers. Subsidiary rights departments are usually divided into two arms: domestic and international. The most lucrative rights for works of fiction—movie rights—are usually negotiated only by senior personnel experienced in negotiating with production companies. It requires putting in long hours to rise from assistant and administrative positions to positions of responsibility. For all but the highest up, salaries remain relatively low in this profession.

People in the publishing industry are quick to note that contacts are crucial. Those who want to advance pursue new opportunities zealously, and any advantage one can gain over other candidates is fair game. Far from cutthroat, however, many people in this profession enjoy support from their associates and coworkers. Publishing is a financially tough life, but it's ideal for those who are dedicated to books and who want to spend their days with like-minded people.

Aspiring book-publishing professionals should be persistent and willing to do anything to get started in the field. Editorial or publishing experience in college literary magazines, newspapers, or journals is advantageous for applicants. Those who wish to advance in this profession should understand that work may occasionally take up all of their free time.

Editor

Number of people in profession: 130,000

Average hours per week: 40

Average starting salary: $30,770

Average salary after 5 years: $41,170

Average salary after 10–15 years: $58,930

Life on the job

For people who love the written word and know they have the ability to plan, organize, and see printed material through its several stages of production, editing may be the ideal job. A critical link between authors and the reading public, editors control the quality and nature of printed material, working with authors on rewrites; correcting grammar; and smoothing out inconsistencies. Editors have significant input in the final product. They analyze work for quality of content, grammatical correctness, and stylistic consistency. This requires patience, thoroughness, and an ability to keep in mind both small details and the big picture simultaneously. Editors must be able to work closely with writers, diagnose problems, and offer advice on how to avoid them in the future. This requires a keen, analytical mind and a gentle touch.

An editor frequently meets with others who are also working on a publication, including artists, typesetters, layout personnel, marketing directors, and production managers. In most areas of publishing, the success or failure of a product relies on continuous and open communication among different departments; a snag in any area may throw off the scheduling of another. As links between departments, editors must be able to handle personality issues diplomatically; be comfortable with the rigorous scheduling and economics of publishing; and coordinate and communicate their requirements clearly and effectively.

Editorial positions are available in many types of companies, from established publishing houses to online service companies. A magazine editor has a different schedule and handles matters distinct from those of a books acquisitions editor or a newspaper editor. Interests, opportunities, and luck lead editors to an area of specialization. People who wish to progress in this field nearly always read manu-scripts in their spare time or stay late to do extra work. Competence is rewarded, and lateral and upward mobility within large houses is common.

An editor in the Web world has a very different job than one in a traditional print position. The online world is one of interactivity, which may involve creating single-loop feedbacks such as real-time polls, or developing community-oriented content—information that is taken from people responding to a site. While print media are geared toward the masses, interactive content relies on an understanding of the one-to-one nature of the Web. "In most traditional media, once you've written a piece, it's done," notes one writer. In contrast, many online writing projects are never really fin-ished, especially as far as website content is concerned. "Expect to update, revise, expand, or tweak existing written materials not just occasionally, but continuously," she notes.

A Web editor develops the content or editorial plan of a website, working with a team that may include a creative director, a writer, a designer, and an information architect. Web editors at different types of companies have varying responsibilities. Someone at iVillage.com, for instance, may deal with large amounts of content and update the site on a daily basis. An editor at an online magazine could be brought in to match the site's particular style or to provide an original voice. If you work for a web developer that produces original content for different companies, your work will be more project-oriented. You will develop material for a range of clients, as well as ensure that the information is accurate and conveys the true voice and tone for the site. The web editor's work encompasses a broad spectrum of writing and can run the gamut from short articles to product descriptions. Copyediting and proofreading may also be part of a web editor's job.

Insider tips

A history of editorial positions on college newspapers or literary magazines is important. Most employers require potential editors to take word-processing and proofreading tests before extending an offer, so it's a good idea to be familiar with standard word-processing programs and proofreading symbols. Familiarity with desktop publishing and design programs is also extremely helpful. Some find it beneficial to take a six-week publishing seminar to enhance their resumes, but no employer requires it. Because of the relative paucity of entry-level editorial positions, many people enter publishing firms, magazines, and newspapers in advertising, mar-keting, or promotion departments, and parlay these jobs into editorial positions.

Community newspapers, literary magazines, and college publications often supply valuable—yet often unpaid—opportunities to hone your writing skills; and magazines and newspapers offer internships for students. Though postgraduation jobs aren't guaranteed for interns, offers for competent candidates are likely, and the industry experience and contacts you will gain are invaluable assets for a position in any sec-tor of the publishing world.

The Chicago Manual of Style, a handbook for editorial professionals around the world, is perhaps the most essential reference for anyone who works with words. When the University of Chicago Press first opened in 1891, professors who were planning to publish manuscripts brought their work directly to the compositors at the press; the compositors would then attempt to decipher and consistently typeset the manuscripts before passing on these newer versions to proofreaders. To remedy the problems that this process had the potential to create, the compositors teamed up with a proofreader to make a single list of the most common errors they were coming across. This meeting marked the birth of the manual. The list turned into a pamphlet, which grew into a book; and more than a hundred years later, it's still the reference source that sits on the desks of those whose business revolves around the written word.

Equally influential in the history of editing in America, Maxwell Perkins used connections to get his foot in the door of the *New York Times* in 1907. After covering his share of entry-level emergencies (police reports, fires, and disasters), Perkins applied for a job with Charles Scribner's Sons in 1909 and was granted an interview a year later. Working his way out of advertising, Perkins moved up to the editorial floor and made his first discovery in 1919: a Princeton dropout named F. Scott Fitzgerald. Other breakthrough writers soon followed: Ezra Pound, Ernest Hemingway, Thomas Wolfe, and Marjorie Kinnan Rawlings.

CHAPTER 4

Choosing a Path: Identifying the Jobs that are Right for You

WHERE HAVE I HEARD *THAT* BEFORE?

You've tried to be good-natured about it for a long time, but admit it—you're getting a little tired of having the same conversation over and over again. You know, the one in which a distant relative or long-lost friend congratulates you on your recent graduation and asks what you studied. You tell them you majored in history or political science, and they immediately want to know what on earth you're going to do with your degree. You can detect a bit of cynicism in their tone—as though they don't quite believe you'll be able to be a fully functioning, self-supporting, tax-paying member of society just because you didn't major in accounting or "pre"-something. Sure, the cynicism is wrapped in good intentions and support, but it's still there. And if you say you don't have a job lined up just yet, they try to buoy your spirits by saying something like, "Well, I guess you could always *teach* or something."

If teaching actually *is* among the options you're considering, then a comment such as this probably won't bother you. But if you have a different path in mind, or you haven't fully explored your choices yet, the implication—however subtle—that your career options are limited can be annoying. What's worse, it can be contagious—if you have this conversation frequently enough, anxiety can creep in no matter how passionately you believed in your academic choices.

You'll need to dismiss the notion that it will be harder to find a job with a degree in history or political science than it would be with any other field of study under your belt. Sure, you won't necessarily be pursuing the same types of positions as your more vocationally minded classmates, but that doesn't mean you're any less marketable or qualified for the jobs that interest you—once you've determined what those are.

But maybe you already know that you have literally thousands of career options to choose from (at the very least, you know about the ones we've described in Chapter 3). Perhaps your anxiety stems from not knowing which of these options you should pursue. Maybe all you know at this stage is that you'd like to secure a solid, respectable job—one that will make the best use of the skills and passions that you've cultivated in school, one that will convince Mom and Dad that paying your tuition was a worthwhile investment, one that doesn't require you to wear a hairnet or break the law. But of the jobs that fit those criteria, how on earth are you going to choose the one that's right for you? Don't worry—that's what this chapter is all about.

First things first: Distinguishing jobs from careers

Before we go any further we should define both "career" and "job," because the two terms are not interchangeable. Most people who are just getting started tend to think of themselves as ensconced in a career only when they have a steady, full-time job with an ample paycheck and a respectable title in an organization, or at least in an industry or field, in which they intend to stay for the foreseeable future. But that's not necessarily the case; you can still work toward your professional goals even if you know the position you're currently in, or the one you're about to take, won't last indefinitely.

What's more, you can still build a career even if the job that pays your bills isn't the one from which you derive the most professional satisfaction, or the one that provides the most opportunities for advancement. A career encompasses a lot more than any one full- or part-time job; rather, a career is *all* the things you're doing at any given point to advance your professional goals. You might work as a waiter while doing internships or volunteer work related to your long-term career aspirations. In other words, your career *includes* your current job, but that's not all it includes.

Taking that idea one step further, we should point out that you as a person are defined by much more than your job *or* your career. Your hobbies, personal interests, involvement in the community, relationships with friends and family—all of these things are just as important as your vocation when it comes to defining who you are. Obviously, satisfying and meaningful work that makes full use of your skills, abilities, and interests is important (otherwise, we wouldn't be writing a book about it), but any specific job or career-related decision only makes sense if it's consistent with all of the other areas of your life that are important to you.

Granted, it's hard to avoid being identified by the job you do or the occupational field you're a part of. Whether you're applying for a credit card, renewing a passport, or making small talk at a cocktail party, everybody wants to know what you do. We obviously do a lot of things in life, but what most people care about is what we do for a living.

This cultural norm can be a real pain for people who get their intrinsic rewards from pursuits other than the activity that brings them their paycheck. We all know the type—wannabe actors schlepping trays of food, cab drivers writing the next Great American Novel between fares, and personal assistants who get their kicks from the hobbies they pursue on the weekends.

Add to this list those whose jobs are just stepping stones to long-term career goals—e.g., recent grads in the mailroom on the slow road to CEO, aspiring attorneys copyediting while in law school. The jobs recent grads hold don't always hold their full interest or attention. Education usually pays off down the road, but, initially, you may find yourself with a job title and job duties you'd rather not be identified with.

Even if it doesn't exactly fulfill all of your professional goals, however, your first job shouldn't trigger a massive identity crisis—nor should your second or third job, for that matter. Most career experts agree that careers evolve over time, and they rarely progress in a linear way. Few people experience a professional epiphany at the age of 18 or 22 or 26, figuring out exactly what they want to do and sticking to it for the rest of their lives. Most people end up trying several different jobs—often in a number of different fields—before they decide what fits, and that's okay. At this stage, you are gathering information, investigating various options, and gradually refining your career goals as you find out more.

Over time, you'll start building on the themes and patterns you might already see emerging—a commitment to social service, a love of learning, an entrepreneurial streak. Your professional priorities and values might change, and your personal circumstances might change as well. When you move from one job to another to accommodate these changes, you carve out a career for yourself. You may decide to move after you've worked in a particular position for some time. Maybe you'll decide that you need to be closer to your family, or maybe you'll want to start one of your own. Perhaps you'll decide to return to school, and your graduate studies will spark an entirely new realm of intellectual and professional interests. Whatever the reason for the change in your personal circumstances, it's not uncommon for jobs to change along with them. And no matter what's driving the change, your experience from your past job (or jobs) will probably influence what you do next. Let's say you loved the intellectual challenges your first job provided, but wished the work had been more team-driven. Chances are, when you look for your second job, you'll be looking for positions that are decidedly more collaborative. Your second job will tell you even more about yourself and the specific things that float your professional boat, and you'll apply that knowledge and experience when looking for job number three. This process—the process of continually revising your goals, priorities, and values—is what allows your career to evolve over time.

So while you probably won't be able to map out the exact progression of your entire career right now, the good news is that you don't have to. Instead, you can focus on specific experiences that in one way or another weave together your interests, skills, and values.

Narrowing the field of options

Now that we've finished our pep talk, it's time to start thinking about what specific jobs make the most sense for you. As you may already know, there are countless personality tests and skills inventory tests out there intended to help you determine what type of work you're best suited for. But, at the end of the day, deciding what career you're going to pursue all boils down to something far less scientific and formulaic and far more instinctive: What do you like? What do you do well? And what do you care about? The answers to these questions correspond to the categories "interests, skills, and values," which are often seen as the ABCs of career choice. By contemplating these questions, you're also addressing the question: "Who am I and in which environments will I thrive?" The key to finding a job you like is figuring out a way to balance your skills, interests, and values in a satisfactory way.

- Your **interests** are those things you enjoy doing, discussing, or daydreaming about. They include hobbies, sports, academic subjects, work activities, topics you read about, and anything else you like. They might be lifelong passions or just passing fancies. Your job is to decide which interests need to be part of your work life. You might major in art history but then work as a banker, reserving your art appreciation for museum visits on the weekends. Or you might have an interest so strong it must be a part of your daily work life.

- The category of **skills** encompasses three main areas: learned skills (tangible things we've learned how to do, such as using a computer or writing a newspaper article); innate skills (aptitudes or talents); and personality skills (such as being hardworking, detail-oriented, or creative). Deciding which skills you enjoy using is important in defining a career focus and in finding a job you enjoy; as you'll read in Chapter 5, your resume, cover letter, and interviews are all opportunities to tell a prospective employer what specific skills and abilities make you a perfect fit for a job. If you trumpet skills you don't particularly enjoy using, it's entirely possible you'll land in a position you don't like very much.

- **Values** are things that are important to you. You probably already have a good idea of what personal values—e.g., honesty, integrity, loyalty, self-reliance—you hold most dear. For the purposes of this guide, however, we're referring to *professional* values specifically. Identifying your professional values helps you answer the question of what's really important to you in a particular position or work environment. The more closely your job—and your work environment—is aligned with your professional values, the greater the chances you'll be fully engaged and invested in your career at any given time. So what are examples of professional values? Here's a list—by no means exhaustive—to get you started:

  - Advancement opportunities
  - Autonomy
  - Availability of training/development programs
  - "Brand equity" (Will people immediately recognize the name of the employer that I'm working for?)
  - Compensation package (base salary, benefits)
  - Contribution to society
  - Creativity
  - Direct contact with customers and clients
  - Diversity of daily tasks/responsibilities
  - Intellectual stimulation
  - Job security
  - Meritocracy (Are the right people promoted? Does exceptional performance get rewarded?)
  - Quality of colleagues (colleagues that are friendly, supportive, and social)
  - Quality of direct manager
  - Quality of formal/informal mentoring
  - Prestige of the organization/occupation
  - Predictability (in terms of hours, required travel, etc.)

- Relatively low stress level
- Work/life balance

What's your MVV (Most Valuable Value)?

The relative importance we place on each of the values above tends to change over time, reflecting not only changing professional priorities, but changes in our personal circumstances as well. There might be times in your career when making money is your top priority; as your career progresses, things like intellectual engagement or a sense of working toward the greater good might become more important to you. And what's more, if you're still in college or have only recently graduated, you might not really know what relative value you place on the factors listed above; in most cases, it takes actually working in positions that represent different sets of pros and cons before you really have a sense of what's important to you. You may accept your first job out of college thinking that a better-than-average base salary and ample advancement opportunities are the most important things to you, only to discover that intellectual stimulation and colleagues that you can relate to are far more important, even if attaining these things means earning a lower salary.

Figuring out how you assign importance to these factors is a highly personal process—and you probably won't assess individual jobs or careers in the same way (or using the same criteria) that friends or peers would. For example, imagine what would happen if you printed out the list of values we provided above and distributed it to 20 of your closest friends and acquaintances. Let's say you asked each person to go through the list and assign a number between 1 and 10 to each value, where 1 meant that they assigned little importance to that factor, and 10 meant that it was a professional "deal-breaker." Chances are good that even among 20 people—a relatively small sample size—no two people would submit identical assessments. If you asked the same 20 people to complete the same exercise even two years later, their responses probably wouldn't be identical the second time around.

Lauren, who double-majored in history and French at a New England liberal arts college, accepted a job with a small corporate research firm after graduation. Three years later, she went back to school to earn her MBA. After her first year of business school, when her family and friends asked her what career she was likely to pursue after graduation, she admitted that she still wasn't sure. "All I know is that I have to work for a company whose name people will recognize," she said. "When people asked me where I worked before business school and I told them, I always had to explain what kind of company it was. I'm tired of that. It's important to me that the next company I work for has instant name recognition." Not everyone assigns the same level of importance to brand equity—in fact, some people might consider Lauren's perspective a little bit shallow. But values aren't normative—in other words, there are no right or wrong answers when it comes to deciding what's important to you in a job. But you do need to give some thought to what's important to you in order to find a job in which you'll thrive.

At the end of the day, jobs (even the best, most desirable jobs) represent a set of trade-offs. Especially in the early days of your career, it may be difficult to get everything on your personal and professional wish list. Even so, the process of assessing (and continually reassessing) your priorities will enable you to figure out which trade-offs you're willing to make and which things are too important to give up.

Major breakthrough

If you're getting stuck when it comes to figuring out your skills, interests, and values, spend some time thinking about what you've studied. Your major can tell you a great deal about the type of work you're likely to enjoy. Think of it this way: Many career experts say that the first step in determining your professional destiny is asking yourself what kind of work you'd do for free. In other words, if money weren't an issue, how would you spend your time? The rationale, of course, is that if you're truly passionate about the work you're doing, then you're far more likely to excel and advance in your career.

In a way, your major *does* represent the type of work you'd do for free. Not only were you not paid to study what you did, but chances are you actually paid (in one way or another) for the privilege of studying it. And if you're lucky, you had the freedom to decide what you wanted to study without spending too much energy on the myriad practical considerations that come with choosing a job. You didn't have to factor in compensation or benefits or promotion potential or the part of the country in which you wanted to live: You probably chose a major that you liked—or at least one that you thought you might like when you chose it.

Take some time to revisit the reasons you chose your major: What attracted you to your field of study, and what made it compelling enough to stick with? What made it rewarding for you? What made you glad you did it? What specific aspect of your major did you connect with the most? For example, did you enjoy the fact that it was research-intensive? Or that it involved a lot of writing? Did you appreciate that most of the work you did was independent versus collaborative (or was it the other way around)? Did your classes inspire intellectual debate and discussion that kept you engaged in the material? What specific classes did you find the most rewarding, and what about those classes floated your intellectual boat? How has your major—and the specific skills you developed while you studied it—contributed to success in other arenas? If you switched majors somewhere along the line (and many, many people do) think about what prompted you to switch gears.

Getting to the heart of what drew you to a specific major can tell you a lot about the type of work you'd find satisfying, and, conversely, the type of work that'd be a round hole to your square peg. Consider the specific jobs we outlined in the previous section: A lobbyist, a political aide, and a foreign-exchange trader might all have undergraduate history degrees in common, but it's very likely each one would have a different answer when asked what made their course of study so appealing and so valuable.

Balancing priorities

Once you've identified your interests, skills, and values, you need to weigh your priorities. It isn't always easy: Sometimes two or more of these things seem to work against each other. Let's say you took an oil painting class as an elective while you were an undergraduate. The class was completely unrelated to your major, but it inspired a genuine interest in oil painting—and in the arts more generally. You've decided oil painting is something you want to pursue one way or another. However, when you look at the list of work-related values outlined above, you realize that job security and making a lot of money are important to you. The starving-artist route is probably not for you, then, so you'll need to land a job that's more stable and more lucrative—maybe something on the business side of an arts-related organization. Or you may decide to keep your art interest "pure" by painting in your spare time and working a job unrelated to the arts in order to make money. (As we said at the outset of this chapter, the job that pays your rent doesn't have to satisfy all of your interests, skills, and values on its own.) However you go about it, you'll need to decide what your priorities are before you can pursue a job that meets your needs. Here are some of the ways in which entry-level job-seekers state their priorities.

- A foot in the door in an industry or sector in which I have a focused interest
- Any old job I have the ability to do and at least a basic interest in that will provide some professional experience and allow me to establish a work routine
- A job that will reasonably fit my interests, skills, and values but will more importantly allow me to live where I want and give me the amount of money I need to gain financial independence
- A job that bridges the gap to a new career field

These are all perfectly legitimate ways to frame your short-term career goals so that you can conduct a targeted, focused job search. In fact, they can be especially useful when looking for your first job, as many recent grads haven't figured out their long-term goals yet and need a framework to figure out which jobs to pursue. The key, however, is to continually ask yourself whether the jobs you're applying for are consistent with your priorities—and to ask questions that will enable you to determine if your expectations about the job are realistic.

"Foot-in-door disease"

Many smart and talented folks with liberal arts degrees convince themselves to take jobs they don't really want because they want to get a foot in the door at an organization or in an industry in which they are particularly interested. There's nothing inherently wrong with this approach—as long as it's well-informed and realistic.

Imagine, for example, your dream is to write for *Rolling Stone* magazine. Also imagine you are the most astute proofreader in the Western hemisphere—you can spot a wayward semicolon a mile away. Unfortunately, you enjoy proofreading about as much as you enjoy listening to chalk screech on a blackboard.

By stressing your exceptional proofreading skills on your resume, you could probably land a job at one magazine or another—as a proofreader. "That's okay," you say to yourself, "I'll have my foot in the door and eventually prove myself to be the great feature writer I know I am." Who could argue with the logic of this approach? By and large, organizations prefer to hire from within, so doesn't it stand to reason that you'll be able to work your way up fairly easily once people have gotten to know you and like you?

Well, maybe—but maybe not. First of all, you've got to ask yourself how long you can stare at columns of text looking for bad kerns and misplaced modifiers before you want to drive a number-two pencil into your skull. What toll will all the dreaded proofreading take on your mind, body, and spirit? And do proofreaders at *Rolling Stone* have even the slimmest chance of being promoted? Only you can answer these questions, but, in general, it's probably a bad idea to take a job you loathe because you suspect it might evolve into something else down the line. It might very well blossom into something better, but it also might not.

Employees in virtually every industry can get typecast in the same way that actors and actresses do. You might very well be *Rolling Stone's* next great features writer—heck, you might already be able to write better stories than the person who currently inhabits that role—but if your boss sees you as a proofreader and nothing else, your chances for advancement could be slim. In fact, your proficiency in a role (even one you don't like) might paradoxically keep you from moving up. Your manager might decide that you are such a great proofreader he couldn't bear to hire someone else to replace you if you were promoted to features writer. That's why it's so important to talk to industry insiders in order to make informed choices about your career. During your informational interviews (which we'll cover in Chapter 5), be sure to ask about career advancement opportunities, promotion potential for specific roles, and the organization's philosophy and approach when it comes to developing its existing staff. After all of your conversations, you may very well decide that the foot-in-door approach makes the most sense, and that's okay. But you don't want to get your foot in the door only to find out that the rest of you will not be allowed in, nor do you want to get your foot in a door that you should have left closed to begin with.

GETTING FOCUSED

As we suggested at the beginning of this chapter, landing a job doesn't mean you've got your entire career mapped out. It also doesn't mean that you don't have to be focused during your job search; in fact, one of the easiest ways to sabotage your search is to come across as unfocused. These concepts aren't as contradictory as they may seem. You can be crystal clear that a job you're applying for is right on target for you at the present time, even if you're a little fuzzy on your long-range goals. Your cover letters, interviews, and follow-up correspondence—basically every moment of contact with prospective employers—must convey that you have a focus and have arrived at that area of focus in a careful, thoughtful way. (We'll talk more about how to package your qualifications and career goals in the following chapter). But before you can convince anyone else that you should be hired, you have to figure out for yourself why any given job would be right for you and why you should be hired.

It helps to have a framework for thinking about the universe of job opportunities available to you. Every position you will consider can be defined on three distinct levels: the industry or field (e.g., publishing, finance, education, government), the function or role you'd be fulfilling (e.g., writer, editor, account manager, analyst), and the particular company or organization you'd be working for. The function represents the core of what you do; the industry you're working in and the company you're working for provide context. For example, you could be an editor in any number of organizations representing a range of industries. But the same function (editing) would be an entirely different experience at a *Fortune* 500 company that makes semiconductors than it would be at a consumer magazine. A role that's fascinating and rewarding in one industry might be utterly unbearable in another one.

While the same function can be very different depending on the industry you're working in, the reverse is also true: The same industry (e.g., advertising, government) can offer wildly different experiences depending on the function you have. Every field is highly complex and encompasses a variety of subfields and job titles. Each of these, in turn, requires different skills, credentials, and personality traits. In advertising, for example, there is a world of difference between the work an account executive does and the work a copywriter does. They are two different animals who happen to inhabit the same zoo. If you've identified the career field that interests you most, you've made a good start. And if you know the function you'd like to fulfill at your job (e.g., network administration), even if you don't yet know the industry or field you'd like to target in your search, you've also made some progress. But to make a compelling case to potential employers, you'll need to do legwork to fill in the missing piece. By "legwork," we mean research—checking out all available resources, online and otherwise—that will provide more information on specific fields and functions.

Chapter 3 of this book is a great place to start your research, and the Bureau of Labor Statistics—part of the U.S. Department of Labor—offers excellent career profiles of thousands of specific occupations. Whether you want more information on being a pathologist or a poultry farmer (seriously), the Occupational Outlook Handbook available on the Bureau's website (BLS.gov) will tell you about the training and education needed, average salaries, expected job prospects, job responsibilities, and other job-related details. You can also check out the websites of professional and industry associations (a simple internet search will turn up a lot of them). When it comes to research, there's really no substitute for good old-fashioned informational interviewing (a process that we'll describe in detail in the next chapter). If you need help, enlist the help of the career-planning office—their resources should be available to you whether you're a current student or an alum.

Practical matters

Balancing your interests, skills, and values is definitely an important part of the job-search process. It's an important part of life, for that matter—and it requires an enormous amount of introspection and emotional energy (if it didn't, networks like the WB wouldn't have any programming). There are also, however, significant practical implications you shouldn't disregard as you evaluate specific jobs. We've outlined a few of them below.

How much do I need to be paid?

A lot of people would like to think that, if given the choice, they'd rather make less money and do something they really care about than earn more money to do something they despise. Then many of these people go to law school, move to Manhattan, or take on a mortgage. The truth is, we'd all like to think that the most important factor determining our choice of profession is the ability to pursue our life's passion—to do work that's consistent with the very core of our being, that makes a difference in the world, or that makes the best possible use of our unique talents. However, unless you happen to be Oprah Winfrey, it can be difficult to balance these needs with the more immediate need to keep a roof over our heads, eat, pay off student debt, and eventually pay for junior's college education.

The truth can be a bitter pill to swallow. On average, graduates with undergraduate liberal arts degrees do indeed earn lower salaries right out of the gate than their counterparts in other disciplines. According to the National Association of Colleges and Employers (NACE), the average starting salary for class of 2006 graduates with liberal arts degrees is just under $31,000 a year. (By way of comparison, starting salaries for accounting undergraduates start at about $46,200, while finance/economics majors earn about $45,200 their first year out).[1] Gulp.

We're not going to lie to you: Living on $31,000 a year will mean living pretty modestly, especially if you have your heart set on living in a notoriously expensive metropolitan area (depending on the industry you choose, you may find you have to live in such an area in order to pursue the most attractive opportunities). Every year, Mercer Human Resource Consulting ranks cities across the

---

1 National Association of Colleges and Employers. "High Starting Salaries Show Competition Heating Up for New Grads." April 6, 2006.
www.naceweb.org/press/display.asp?year=2006&prid=233.

globe according to their cost of living. In 2006, New York City, Los Angeles, San Francisco, Chicago, and Miami ranked as the most expensive cities in the United States.[2] If you're unsure how big-city living might affect your pocketbook, online tools such as Salary.com's Cost-of-Living Wizard enable you to figure out what you'd need to earn in one city to maintain the same standard of living you would in another.

Salary.com, along with SalaryExpert.com and the U.S. Department of Labor website (BLS.gov), also provides salary information across various industries, functions, and geographic areas. Keep in mind that the salary ranges these sites provide are necessarily quite broad; you'll need to supplement this information with your own research. Occasionally, you'll be able to glean at least some salary information by browsing the postings on job websites, but, more often, you'll need to rely on insiders to give you a meaningful and realistic range. (You'll learn how to ask for salary information tactfully in Chapter 5, under informational interviewing).

Of course, all of the salary information in the world won't do you any good unless you know how much money you really need to keep you going. Though financial planners use slightly different formulae to help people devise their monthly budgets, the following guidelines will give you a rough idea of how to allocate your net monthly income:

- **35 percent toward housing.** This means your rent or mortgage, utilities, and the costs of any home repairs or improvements.

- **15 percent toward repaying debt.** This includes debt of both the student and credit-card variety.

- **15 percent toward transportation.** These costs include car payments, car insurance, parking, fuel, and cab, train, or subway fares.

- **10 percent toward savings and investments.** You are saving something, aren't you?

- **25 percent toward everything else.** This means you've got one-quarter of your take-home pay to cover everything else: vacations, food, dry cleaning, clothing, recreation. Anything that you spend money on that doesn't fall into one of the aforementioned categories has to be accounted for here.

2 Mercer Human Resource Consulting. "Worldwide Cost of Living Survey 2006—City Rankings." June 26, 2006.
www.mercerhr.com/pressrelease/details.jhtml/dynamic/idContent/1142150.

Once you've crunched the numbers, ask yourself if they paint a realistic picture: As we've said before, your salary won't go quite as far if you live in a famously expensive city such as New York or San Francisco, and you'll have even less wiggle room if you're staring down the barrel of substantial debt incurred during college or grad school. Keep in mind, though, that starting salaries are just that—starting salaries. Through job research, you'll (hopefully) find out how quickly and how often you can expect your salary to bump up, either through performance-based pay increases, annual bonus eligibility, or an annual inflation-based adjustment.

There's location, location, location . . .

It's an age-old dilemma (or at least it's been a sub-plot of many sitcoms and motion pictures): Is it worth moving to a new city— perhaps one you've never wanted to visit, let alone live in—for the job opportunity of a lifetime? Though you're unlikely to face such a dramatic decision in the early stages of your career, giving some serious thought to where you'd like to live is important nonetheless. As you consider your options, be sure to ask yourself if the jobs/careers you're considering are available in that locale. Some industries have high concentrations of jobs in particular geographic areas. Finance jobs, for example, are predominantly in New York, Chicago, and San Francisco; technology jobs are clustered in Boston, Seattle, and Silicon Valley; publishing jobs are chiefly in New York; most entertainment jobs are in Los Angeles; and numerous government jobs are in Washington, DC.

There are other factors to consider when deciding where you'll hang your hat: Are the job opportunities in your field of interest on the rise or at least stable for now? Are there interesting, varied places to hang out, like coffee houses, art galleries or museums, and movie theaters? Are there places you could take classes, such as colleges or universities, learning centers, or public libraries? Do there seem to be people you can relate to on an intellectual, artistic, recreational, spiritual, or other level that is important to you? What's the housing like? Is it plentiful, desirable, and affordable? How about the public transportation system? Do you need a car? Can you park a car if you need or want one? Do friends and family live there (or at least close by)? Is that important to you? How about your significant other? Speaking of significant others, if you don't have one but want one, does the city have a vibrant singles scene? Or is it a popular place for families to settle down and plant their roots? Consider these and any other questions that might be relevant to your situation: The extent to which you like where you're living plays a much bigger role in determining your overall happiness than you might think— it might be as important (if not more important) than the work you're doing.

. . . And there's relocation

So you've considered the list above and you've found a city that meets all your criteria. Congratulations! You've figured out exactly where you'd like to live—that's a huge weight lifted off your shoulders. Now, do you want to live there forever? Or just the next few years? It helps to have at least an idea of how you'd answer that question, because your response might help you determine how attractive a particular job opportunity is for you. Just as professional priorities often change over the course of a career, so to do geographic priorities. Some careers can be pursued in just about any area of the country. If you're thinking about a career in social work, health care, elementary education, or family counseling (just to name a few), then you probably have more flexibility when it comes to geographic location than you would if you wanted to pursue a career in magazine publishing or the federal government—sectors in which job opportunities are highly concentrated in discrete geographic areas.

As an example, let's say that you've zeroed in on magazine publishing as a career field you might like to pursue. You know there are literally hundreds of magazines whose editorial offices reside in the New York metropolitan area, which is good news, as the city's energy and diversity—along with the sheer number of cultural and recreational opportunities it offers—have always seemed appealing to you. But while you'd love to live in the Big Apple for a few years, you sense it's not a place where you'd like to settle for the long term. Maybe you don't want to rent for the next ten years. Maybe you can't stand the thought of choosing between a long commute and a tiny living space. Or maybe the West Coast has always held a special place in your heart because that's where most of your family and friends reside. If you decide to move to another part of the country, can you parlay the skills you've developed in magazine publishing into another position in an unrelated field? While there are opportunities in magazine publishing on the West Coast, there are considerably fewer of them than there are in New York. If you do find a great editorial job with a West Coast magazine, what will happen if the company downsizes in three years, forcing you to look for other opportunities? Or what if you decide—for whatever reason—that the job or the company no longer satisfies your personal or professional goals? Are you comfortable knowing that there are considerably fewer places to approach for jobs if you decide to jump ship?

Keep in mind that even if your industry isn't highly concentrated in a specific geographic area, the organization that you're considering might offer more opportunities in a specific location (usually its headquarters city) than it does elsewhere. Let's say you've identified a great opportunity in the New York office of a Cincinnati-based consumer products company. If staying in Manhattan for the foreseeable future is among your top priorities, be sure to ask whether career advancement is likely to require a tour-of-duty at company headquarters before you sign on the dotted line.

Leaving on a jet plane . . . don't know when I'll be back again

If you ask people whether or not they like to travel, most would probably say yes. (We haven't done any scientific research to corroborate this point, mind you, but we think it's a pretty safe assumption to make). Most people think they like to travel, just as most people think they have a good sense of humor: It's rare you'll find somebody who admits to being either a homebody or a drip. If you like to travel and are looking for jobs that will enable you to hop around the globe (or at least the country), at least keep this in mind: Business travel and personal travel are two entirely different animals. Think about the last flight you took: Were there long security lines, interminable flight delays, hours spent in the middle seat directly in front of a screaming baby? Without a vacation on the other side of these annoyances, they can sap your strength—it takes a person with unique energy and stamina to excel at a job that requires frequent travel. If you think a jet-setting professional life means you'll get to see lots of interesting places and rack up hundreds of thousands of frequent-flyer miles, remember these things too: If you're traveling for business, chances are you'll visit lots of interesting cities, but you'll probably only see the insides of those cities' hotels and conference rooms (along with whatever scenery happens to reside between the airport and your hotel). And if it's the frequent-flyer miles you're after, remember it's pretty hard to redeem those these days anyway. You can always buy a plane ticket and visit interesting places on your own time.

Making the most of your job, once you've gotten it

It's comforting to know no career decision is ever final, and that it's perfectly acceptable (even expected) for personal and professional priorities to change, and for jobs to change along with them. This knowledge, however, can to a chronic case of "What's next?" disease. Even if you haven't experienced this yourself yet, you might have heard other people express this type of mindset. They tell you they've gotten a new job, and the first thing they mention is how great their new role will look on their resume. Wouldn't it be nice if you could just take a breather and relax for a minute?

Well, the truth of the matter is it's never a bad idea to be thinking ahead to the next position or company or rung on the career ladder—in fact, it's often what keeps your battery charged in your current role so you remain interested, engaged, and productive. While it's never advisable to announce to the world you've got one foot out the door, it's absolutely advisable to pave the way to future career opportunities by distinguishing yourself in whatever job you've got at the moment. Here are a few specific ways to make the most of your current job.

Find a mentor.

Regardless of the industry, organization, or functional area you're currently in, identifying and enlisting the help of a mentor is one of the single best ways to make the most of your current job. Mentors are a valuable resource no matter how high up the organizational ladder you are, but they're especially valuable early in your career, when the learning curve is the steepest.

A good mentor plays multiple roles when it comes to your career development. First of all, she's a sounding board—someone who will listen to your specific challenges, goals, or aspirations and provide an informed, objective perspective. She's also a valuable insider—someone who can give you the inside scoop on who the real decision-makers are in your department, what it's like to work with (or for) certain people, and what it takes to succeed in your current position, ace your performance review, make a lateral or geographic transfer within your company, or get a raise. In certain situations, your mentor can become your strongest and most vocal advocate—someone who will speak up on your behalf when your performance is being evaluated (formally or informally), or when you're being considered for a promotion or important assignment. Your mentor can also assume the role of professional matchmaker, introducing you to the other people at the company whom you need to know—either because they're in a position to help you achieve your career goals, or because they share your personal and professional interests. Finally, your mentor can be the best kind of critic—one who's honest, direct, and willing to give you constructive feedback and advice with only your best interests in mind. In short, she's indispensable.

Many organizations have formal mentoring programs in place, where senior-level employees are paired with more junior-level employees to help integrate young professionals into the company and provide them with ongoing career guidance and feedback. Whether your employer offers a formal program like this or not, take the time to identify a mentor—and solicit this person's advice and assistance from the outset. (We talk about networking in the following chapter and one of its key tenets applies here too: By and large, people like to share their experiences and wisdom for the benefit of people who value their advice, so don't be shy when it comes to asking for help). You needn't formalize the relationship with matching t-shirts, monthly lunches, or even an official "mentor" designation. The important thing is to identify someone you trust—and someone whose professional achievement you'd like to emulate—who's willing to share their expertise with you over an occasional lunch, coffee, or happy-hour cocktail.

Remember, too, that your mentoring relationship doesn't have to be an exclusive one. In fact, there may be multiple people from whom you would like to seek advice and guidance and who you think will be of assistance in your career; when it comes to mentoring, the more the merrier. Long-distance relationships work, too; while at least one of your mentors should be someone you see in the office every day, your personal advisory board might also include people outside your office, organization, or industry. As long as someone has valuable advice to share and is willing to share it with you, you owe it to yourself to bring them on board.

Kick it up a notch.

David Bach, a former financial planner who became a speaker and best-selling author, says that in order to get more out of your job, you've simply got to put more into it. Bach offers the following picture of a typical day at the office for many people: "Get into the office around 9:00 A.M. (never early). Have coffee, check in with friends, talk about last night's episode of *Survivor*. Around 10:00 A.M., start to answer voicemail and e-mail. Fiddle around until 11:00 A.M. Work hard for a half hour because it's lunchtime. Get ready for lunch. Go to lunch. Get back at 1:00 P.M., tired from the big meal. Return some calls, maybe go to a few useless meetings, answer some e-mails. Around 4:00 P.M., start winding down and prepare for another busy day tomorrow." Most people achieve the highest levels of productivity, he says, right before they go on vacation—when they realize they have a lot to do in a very short period of time. In "pre-vacation mode," people show up early, make to-do lists, work quickly and efficiently, and then— with everything done and dusted—leave.[3] This general idea could just as easily be dubbed "pre-finals mode" or "pre-term-paper mode": The point is, you tend to get a lot more done during crunch-time than you do when things aren't quite as urgent.

3 David Bach. *Smart Women Finish Rich*. New York: Broadway Books, 1999. 271–72.

Bach's advice for consistently achieving this level of productivity is simple: Start working every day as though it's the day before you go on vacation. Get to the office early, work hard, get your work done, and then get out of there. Chances are, your efforts will get noticed—in a very positive way. You'll build a reputation as the "go-to" guy (or girl): the person who can be relied upon to show up on time and get things done in a professional, organized, and efficient way. Whether you plan to stay in your current job for the foreseeable future or not, that's a good reputation to have.[4]

Remember that attitude is everything.

We know where you're coming from: A few months ago, you were listening to a series of commencement speakers who implored you to take your hard-earned diploma and use it to make the world a better place. They got you all hyped up to go out and be wildly successful—either by earning buckets of money, building homeless shelters in your neighborhood, or curing one of the world's major communicable diseases. Those speeches may seem kind of remote if you just spent the last half hour at the Xerox machine mastering the fine art of double-sided, collated copying. But no matter how much you achieved during your academic career, you need to be careful not to fall into a familiar trap: becoming bored and disenchanted with your job, growing increasingly resentful about it, and eventually becoming an underachiever.

The truth of the matter is this: Even though you worked hard in school (and just as hard to get a job), early jobs can be a little bit anticlimactic. If you end up feeling this way about your first job, know that you're not alone—surgeons, lawyers, investment bankers, and countless other highly educated people also start out at the bottom of their respective totem poles, doing mundane things they weren't necessarily dreaming about as they slogged through all those extra years of school.

If you're bored or otherwise dissatisfied with an early job, consider channeling all of your energy—perhaps that intellectual energy your current job doesn't require—toward expanding the scope of your job, or pursuing on-the-job training that will keep you engaged. Remember, you're not going to get promoted into a more rewarding role unless you excel at your current one, so it may be in your best interest to grin and bear it—at least for 6 to 12 months (according to many career counselors, that's the amount of time it takes to give a job a fair shake). If your

4 Ibid.

dissatisfaction comes from not having enough to do, there is an up side: Less-than-challenging jobs usually leave plenty of time for other pursuits, both during the work day and outside of office hours. So whether you take an evening class at a local university or attend networking events sponsored by industry or professional associations, make sure to spend your extra time wisely. Distinguish yourself in your current role by adopting a positive attitude and looking for processes to overhaul or improve.

For some people, having enough to do isn't the issue; instead, the work they're doing—while more than enough to fill the day—just isn't as fulfilling or as satisfying as they had hoped it would be. In situations such as these, focusing on an element of the work that is in some way rewarding—even if the position's responsibilities are mundane—is crucial. If there's another position within the organization that seems to be more aligned with your interests and goals, find out whether it's a position you could be working toward while still fulfilling your current responsibilities. It may mean adding an extra project to an already full plate, but the extra hours you put in might (paradoxically) re-energize you if you're consciously working toward a goal. The same is true for job-related training: If your company offers internal training programs (or tuition reimbursement for job-related courses at local colleges and universities), consider taking one. If you already feel maxed out, taking on extra commitments may not initially seem to make much sense, but trust us: If side projects or courses keep you engaged and invested in your career, you'll have a much better shot at landing a more fulfilling and interesting job down the line—whether it's within your current organization or outside of it.

Along those lines, if you work at a larger company there may be opportunities to serve on a cross-functional team or committee; by getting yourself onto one, you'll have the opportunity to meet people in other departments. From there, you can learn more about your employer, establish a professional network, and build a cadre of mentors (who might eventually be in a position to help you land a job elsewhere in the company later on). Actively seek opportunities to create demand for yourself—if you set a goal to become the person everyone wants on his team, you'll have a better shot at actually getting onto someone else's team.

No matter how much or how little work your current position requires, go out of your way to ask for constructive feedback. Your organization may offer formal performance reviews already (if it does offer such assessments, ask for informal feedback in between reviews). If it doesn't, make it a point to ask what you're doing well and what aspects of your work performance could use improvement.

Know when it's time to move on.

As we said at the outset of this chapter, first jobs often mean taking on responsibilities—and job titles—you'd rather not be associated with or don't make full use of your skills, talents, or education. So if you find yourself in an entry-level job you dislike, how do you know whether it's just part of the inevitable dues-paying process, or whether your dissatisfaction stems from a more fundamental mismatch between you and the career, organization, or position? A recent article on CareerJournal.com (the *Wall Street Journal*'s career-planning website) offers the following advice: Take a look at the responsibilities of more senior colleagues at the organization. Do their jobs seem appealing to you? If so, enduring your current position for a little while might enable you to land a more rewarding role down the line. But if the senior jobs also seem awful—or if they seem palatable, but hardly worth tolerating a job (or series of jobs) you don't like in the interim, that's a sure sign you may want to consider other options. After all, there's nothing to be gained from paying your dues if getting promoted only means another job you'd despise. And speaking of promotion, remember our earlier advice: Consider whether entry-level personnel are typically promoted at your current organization—and, if so, how long it takes—before you stick it out in hopes of advancement down the line.[5]

5 Erin White. "First-Job Blues: Adjust or Move On?" *Wall Street Journal Online.* July 26, 2006. www.collegejournal.com/columnists/thejungle/20060726-jungle.html.

CHAPTER 5

Landing the Job: Networking, Resumes, and Interviews

NETWORKING

No man is an island—especially if he's looking for a job

Without question, the universe of liberal arts majors includes its fair share of unassuming, introverted folk. You probably already know whether or not you fall into this camp: You'd rather have dinner with one or two close friends than go to a party and face a room full of strangers (and if you're persuaded to go to a party, you'll spend the next day on the couch, recovering—alone). On an airplane, you fasten your iPod before your seatbelt—just so the person next to you knows you don't want to chat. If a college professor ever gave you the choice between an individual paper and a group presentation, you didn't think twice about going solo. And when people tell you that you need to network to land a job, they might as well be telling you that you have to stand on a street corner wearing a cow costume and a sandwich board, pointing passersby to the sale at Lou's Land of Leather. It just seems too vulnerable, too desperate to even consider.

Even if you're not a card-carrying member of the introvert society, the notion that you'll have to network as part of your job search might not sound that appealing—or maybe you just don't know exactly how to go about it. Either way, you shouldn't worry: For all of the negative connotations associated with the term, networking doesn't require you to interact with people in a way that's contrived or insincere. And it doesn't just take place on golf courses and at cocktail parties—or in nondescript hotel ballrooms during designated networking events. It's not a process that's only effective for job-seekers aggressive enough to approach virtual strangers, give a 30-second summary of their professional accomplishments and aspirations, and ask for help finding a job. The people you'll approach as you build your own network will not—contrary to popular belief—assume you're a pathetic freak motivated solely by self-interest or desperation.

For the networking-phobic, it often helps if you think of networking as research, rather than as a job-hunting tactic. It's a process that allows you to leverage the richest source of information at your disposal: other people. At its most powerful, networking actually helps you decide which careers, industries, and organizations are interesting to you (and on the flip side, it can help you weed out the ones that aren't as appealing). It can also help you figure out what you'll need to do to get started, and eventually help to frame your candidacy once you've gotten your foot in the door for a specific position.

In the following pages, we'll explain what effective networking is—and what it isn't. We'll tell you how to use the contacts you already have to begin building an extensive and powerful network that will give you a leg-up when it's time to apply for the job you want. We'll tell you about the various ways you can network—from the casual power brunch to more structured informational interviews, and we'll provide guidance on the types of questions you can ask to make sure you get the most out of your conversations. Finally, we'll give you a list of do's and don'ts for networking so your experiences put you in the best possible position to land the job you want.

Hide and go seek: The hidden job market

If you hang around career counselors for any amount of time, you'll probably hear them emphasize the importance of the so-called "hidden job market"—the one you'll need to tap into to land the perfect job. The term itself implies a little more mystery and intrigue than it probably should; in reality, the "hidden job market" simply refers to the universe of available jobs that are not formally advertised. When it comes to quantifying the size of this market, different experts cite wildly disparate percentages: Some say the hidden job market represents about 60 percent of all available jobs, while other sources estimate it's closer to 95 percent. Whatever the actual percentage is, it's too big a number to ignore. If you want your job search to be successful—and by successful we mean that you not only land a great job, but that it doesn't take you longer to find it than it took to complete your degree in the first place—you cannot rely on job boards and company websites alone. You have to find out about jobs before the rest of the world does.

The hidden job market doesn't exist solely to make your life—and the lives of millions of job-seekers like you—more difficult. It arises because positions are often filled before they're ever advertised formally. Once a company identifies a staffing need, it can be weeks—even months—before the position is formally announced. It's not as though Willy Wonka just woke up one morning and decided that he needed a successor to his chocolate throne, posted an ad on Monster.com later that afternoon, and then had Charlie and the other four candidates at the factory for interviews the next day. It was a much more time-intensive ordeal than that: He was probably mulling on it for some time, realizing he wasn't getting any younger and that he couldn't run the factory himself for much longer. Once he decided he needed to hire someone, he had to orchestrate the whole Golden Ticket process—and you can bet he had to get all those Oompa Loompas to approve of it. If someone would have told Willy about a good candidate before he kicked off the Golden Ticket campaign, you can bet he would have orchestrated his series of tests for *that person* first.

The real-life hiring process is also fairly slow-moving. Once a hiring manager decides he needs to create a new role—or find a new person for an existing role—he usually has to obtain approval from the higher-ups first. All along, he's thinking of potential candidates he already knows who might fill the position: people who already work at the company full-time, as well as any freelance, contract, or part-time workers who have expressed an interest in a full-time position. Once he gets approval, he may have to post the job internally first to comply with company policy. While the job is posted internally, the hiring manager is probably asking current employees if they know of anyone who'd be a good fit for the role. (This is where networking comes in—you need to be one of the people at the top of current employees' minds when they hear about the position!) If the well of internal candidates and employee referrals runs dry, then the position is usually posted externally—on the company's website, and/or on job websites like Monster, Hotjobs, and Craigslist.

If the job does end up seeing the light of day, you've got another obstacle to confront: Setting yourself apart from the literally hundreds of other candidates who have also seen the very same job posting and are furiously updating resumes and crafting cover letters at the same time you are. Even if you did nothing all day but hit "refresh" on your internet browser to be sure that you're the very first one to submit your application for any new job that strikes your fancy, you'd still be one in a crowd of hundreds of applicants. Some hiring managers confess they simply just can't weed through the volume of applications the more popular job boards generate: If they get 200 resumes for a single position, they might look at the first 20 that come in, and then pick the best five to invite in for an interview.

All of this might seem miserably unfair to you; after all, if you have all of the experience and education the job posting outlines and you just happen to be the twenty-first person in line, why should you be out of contention? Unfortunately, the job-search process—like life—often falls short of a pure meritocracy. Hiring managers aren't lazy, but they are often overworked and eager to bring in a qualified candidate who will fit into the organization's culture as quickly as possible. In many cases, they know any number of people could do the job—even if they don't have all of the requisite experience when they walk in the door. Still, the more time hiring managers spend reviewing resumes, and the more time they spend interviewing candidates, the less time they spend on their core responsibilities, and the harder their existing teams must work because they're short-staffed.

When you build a network of contacts that can tell you about openings (and potential openings) before they hit the company's website or external job boards, you will have far more success than you would if you went it alone. This is true for two reasons: first, you'll be competing with a far smaller number of applicants if you express your interest before the job is even posted externally. Why would you want to compete against 200 other candidates when you can compete against a handful—or none at all? Secondly, people in a position to hire prefer to bring in candidates who have been referred to them by existing employees—always. When you think about it, this makes perfect sense. Existing employees know what a firm's culture is really like better than anyone else, and they usually have a good sense of what people are likely to fit in—and thrive—in that environment. If you approach an organization through an existing employee, you've essentially made it through the first stage of the screening process. If you're basically qualified, generally likeable, and hardworking, the hiring manager would far rather hire you—or at least interview you—than sit down with a pile of 200 resumes. Wouldn't you?

Think of it this way: When you need a book to read on the beach during your summer vacation, do you go to Barnes & Noble and read the synopsis on the back of every book in the store before you made your selection? Or do you ask friends and family if they've read any good books lately and choose among those based on what sounds the most interesting? Chances are, you do the latter, and it's not because you think there aren't any other books out there that would make a great beach-read. You do it because considering every possible option out there wouldn't be a good investment of your time, so you rely on other people to help you narrow your options down. It's the same with hiring decisions, and it's why networking is so critical to a successful job search.

Networking "Yes, buts"

To help you overcome any anxiety you might have about networking, we've outlined the most common misconceptions about the process. We call these networking urban myths the "Yes, buts," and they're usually invoked by job-seekers who are reluctant to network. When we tell these folks how important networking is to the success of their search, they usually begin their objections by saying "Yes, but . . . ." The most pernicious "Yes, buts" keep some people from networking effectively, and they prevent other people from networking at all. To help you separate networking fact from fiction, we've outlined the nine most common "Yes, buts" below, along with an explanation of why each one should be banished from your internal job-hunting dialogue—forever.

"Yes, but networking seems like a forced and unnatural way to deal with people."

Networking is essentially talking with other people and getting their opinions in order to make an informed decision about something. Chances are, you've done this already—have you ever asked someone else what they thought of a particular book or movie, or if they knew of a good dentist or tailor? Did that seem unnatural? Did people seem annoyed that you asked for their advice? Remember, these scenarios aren't that different from asking for career advice. You're probably better at it than you think, and people will probably be much more eager to give it than you ever expected.

"Yes, but I've never been very good at schmoozing. And networking is just a more sophisticated term for schmoozing, right?"

Wrong. Networking sometimes involves schmoozing, but the two aren't synonymous. Think of schmoozing as the art of small talk: Without question, establishing a relationship with someone new requires some degree of small talk. But networking is more than working the room at a cocktail party. No matter how casual or informal the setting, networking has two very specific purposes: learning as much as possible about appealing career options, and telling other people what you're looking for so they can point you in the right direction.

"Yes, but networking feels insincere and manipulative to me. People won't want to help me if they feel like I'm using them to get something."

By and large, people like to be helpful by sharing their experiences and expertise. Unless you give people the impression you don't value their perspectives or respect their time, chances are they will be happy to help you if they can. In his essay, "Life Without Principle," Henry David Thoreau said: "The greatest compliment that was ever paid me was when one asked me what I thought, and attended to my answer." This probably rings true for you, too. Think back to the last time someone asked what you thought about a class or a professor: Did you feel used? Or were you flattered someone valued your opinion enough to ask?

"Yes, but I hate asking for favors. What could I possibly offer them in return?"

There's nothing inherently wrong with asking for help. What's more, enlisting the help of others during your job search effectively makes other people stakeholders in your success. Once someone provides you with guidance in your job search, they're personally invested in you and therefore want to see you do well. And often times, this investment isn't just metaphorical: many organizations use referral programs to encourage existing employees to bring in talent from the outside. In these situations, your contacts have more than just the warm fuzzies to gain if all goes well and you're hired.

"Yes, but what if I don't know that many people? I'd have to approach complete strangers and ask them to talk to me."

Networking does not involve approaching strangers in the vain hope that one, one day, may be able to help you land a job. In fact, it actually starts with the people who know you best: your family, close friends, professors and teachers, and current and former colleagues. Consider these—and anyone else you interact with on a regular basis—your own personal A-listers. The people your A-listers know are your secondary contacts. You might know some of them—if only tangentially—but you probably won't know most of them. It's often your secondary contacts who can put you in touch with people close to decision-makers. It doesn't really matter if you've got legions of close friends and professional contacts who know you well; all that matters is whether someone on your A-list knows one or two people who can help you set things in motion. While you're getting word out to your A-list about your job search, don't forget to ask them what's new in their professional lives too: Talking to people you already know (e.g., family, friends, classmates) about what they do can be an incredibly valuable tool—one most people don't use enough.

"Yes, but networking means that I'll have to ask people that I barely know for jobs—and then 'sell them' on my skills and abilities."

If you're approaching it the right way, you won't be doing either of these things during a networking conversation. Networking is not about asking for a job—it's about getting advice from people who are in a position to provide it. Asking the right questions— and actively listening to the answers—is more important at this stage than selling your skills and abilities. A wise woman (advice guru Dr. Joyce Brothers) once said that "listening, not imitation, may be the sincerest form of flattery." Author Dale Carnegie—who literally wrote the book on winning friends and influencing people—once said you'll make more friends in two months by becoming interested in other people than you will in two years trying to get other people interested in you. Their advice rings true when it comes to networking: Your focus should be learning and listening, not talking and selling. And who knows: Maybe you'll make a friend or two along the way.

"Yes, but I'm an introvert. Only extroverted people are effective networkers."

This "Yes, but" is a corollary to the previous one, so our response will sound familiar if you've been paying attention. But we'll risk being repetitive in order to make this point clear: The ability to listen to (and remember) what people say is critical to building relationships. At its core, that's all networking is: building relationships. If anything, introverts might have a slight edge over extroverts when it comes to networking conversations and informational interviews, because introverts are often better listeners than more gregarious folk. As we said before, asking someone for their opinion and making it clear you value what they have to say is critical to getting them on your side. Finally, if you really pay attention to what they have to say—and manage to retain it—you'll reap benefits during the interview stage. As you read in Chapter 4, the ability to demonstrate a solid understanding of a given job, and a sincere interest in the organization it's with, often distinguishes a successful candidate from the rest of the pack.

"Yes, but I'm very qualified for the positions I'm applying for. My credentials and past performance will speak for themselves and distinguish me from the crowd. I don't need no *stinking* networking."

We hate to be the ones to break it to you, but the real world—and this includes the job market—is far from a pure meritocracy. As a student, you're generally rewarded for what you know and how well you do your work. Sadly, there aren't many jobs where you can succeed by the sweat of your brow and the ingenuity of your ideas alone: With few exceptions, attaining professional success requires you to develop meaningful connections with other people. The importance of personal relationships applies to the job search as well. Remember that old cliché, "It's not what you know, it's whom you know"? Well, it's partly true—in reality, it's what you know and whom you know. As we mentioned earlier in the chapter, an impeccable academic record and stellar professional achievements won't mean anything if your resume never gets read.

"Yes, but networking involves being aggressive and pushy. I'm neither of those things."

Contrary to popular belief, networking is actually more effective if you're not aggressive or pushy. In fact, one of the most common mistakes gung-ho networkers make is advancing their own career agendas too early in the process, which doesn't win them many friends or professional allies. Again, it's important to keep the bigger picture in mind and keep your expectations realistic. Think of networking as groundwork for a job search that will yield results later down the line. No matter how badly you want someone to pass along your resume or act as an internal reference for that dream job you've learned about, you will get much more from your conversations if you really, genuinely approach them as opportunities to learn. Your contacts aren't a means to an end; they're more like a personal "board of directors" whose experiences and perspectives you value. If this type of thinking governs your interactions with other people, you won't be aggressive or pushy—and you won't be perceived that way, either.

Start spreading the news . . .

When it comes to true love, people often say it only finds you when you're not looking for it. Does this maxim apply to finding the perfect job as well as the perfect mate? Sadly, no—not for most people. But that's not to say you can't end up finding out about a great job in the course of a conversation that was never intended to have anything to do with your job search. That was the case with Alison, a 24-year-old consultant who ended up unintentionally networking when she just wanted to hear a familiar voice. "I had just moved to London from New York, and not only was I having a hard time with my job search, but I was incredibly homesick," she explains. "So I called a friend of mine back home, and I was just telling him how cold and rainy it was in London. He mentioned that a friend of his had worked in London for a few years and had experienced a similar thing. Anyway, I found out that the company his friend had worked for when he was overseas was one that I had interviewed with when I was a senior in college. I didn't know that the company even had an office in the U.K., but it turned out that my friend sent my resume to his friend, who in turn forwarded it to my current manager. I got an informational interview at first, then a job interview, and eventually the job."

The moral of the story? Jobs won't usually find you when you're least expecting them to, but romance and job-searching are similar in a different way: You're probably not going to get very far in either endeavor if you never leave your house, or if you never let people know you're in the market. In fact, one of the most obvious mistakes people make when they're networking is focusing on the people they don't know and completely overlooking the people they do.

Spreading the word involves talking to the people on your A-list: family members, close friends, current and former colleagues, classmates, teammates, professors, teachers—anyone who knows you well and interacts with you regularly. (As a general rule, anyone who couldn't pick you out of a police lineup does not belong on your A-list.) Not only should you make sure these folks know you're looking for a job, but you should let them know—with as much specificity as possible—what you're looking for. If you don't know exactly what you want to do, don't worry: The important thing is you've let people know you're in the market. Unless they know you're actively looking, even your close family and friends won't be able to help you. Remember: your job search might very well be at the top of your priority list, but it's not necessarily on anyone else's radar screen. We're not suggesting you send out a formal press release to inform your friends and loved ones you're looking for a job, but it's important to get the word out. That way, when an A-lister or secondary contact gets wind of a great opportunity, you'll be among the first to hear about it.

Don't look a gift networking contact in the mouth

You've been there, we've been there: You talk about your career aspirations during Thanksgiving dinner. The next thing you know, you're getting regular phone calls from your mother, who's suddenly playing the role of Yenta the Matchmaker in the off-Broadway musical, *Your Job Search*. You said you wanted to be a writer? Well, your cousin Mary-Beth is a medical journalist who made six figures last year interviewing doctors and publishing articles on public health issues. She says you can call her and she'd be happy to talk to you. Fast-forward to a few weeks later: Have you called your cousin Mary-Beth yet? She's expecting your call.

While it's tempting to roll your eyes and move on to other things, it's probably not a bad idea to call your cousin Mary-Beth, even if you're not entirely sure medical journalism is your calling. At the end of the day, effective networkers leverage the resources and the contacts they're given. If someone else is willing to make an introduction or otherwise break the ice for you, then what are you waiting for? Yes, it might seem awkward at first, but chances are you'll be glad you talked to her. Maybe she has some interesting things to say about pursuing writing as a livelihood. Or maybe she has some tips for becoming a great interviewer. You just never know. Motivating yourself to network when you have the opportunity is a lot like motivating yourself to go to the gym: You may dread it with every fiber of your being, but, once you do it, you feel so much better about yourself and the world in general. Networking releases the same sort of endorphins. Will a single conversation with your cousin land you a job? Probably not (in much the same way that 20 minutes on the treadmill probably won't reshape your body), but at least you're doing something, right?

It's a marathon, not a sprint

Keeping with our physical fitness metaphor, we should point out that networking muscles are built over time, not overnight. Some hard-core networking books will tell you to aim for five new networking contacts per day—only you will know whether that's a realistic target for you or not. If you try to do too much too soon, you probably won't stick with it. And networking really is the job-search equivalent of a long-term fitness plan: Unless you can really make it part of your lifestyle, it's not going to do you any good. So don't start out with Atkins when you know South Beach will probably work better in the long run. Don't start by going to impersonal networking events or job fairs. Send an e-mail to one person—just one—who you've been thinking about but haven't contacted recently. Don't ask for anything. Don't tell him you're looking for a job. Just check in, see how he's doing, and ask what's going on in his life. Take the time to acknowledge people's birthdays and anniversaries, and send an e-mail congratulating them when they graduate from school, get engaged, or reach other milestones. If the reason networking makes you uneasy is because you feel like you're getting in touch with people only when you need something, there are really only two ways to avoid that problem: Not asking for help when you need it, or being in touch more consistently so that asking for help is just a natural extension of the relationship you already have. Guess which strategy we endorse?

'Tis the season . . . for continued networking

Of course, going the extra mile to keep in touch with your A-listers is one thing, but what about the folks you know less well—the ones that you've met through referrals, informational interviews, and networking events? You can't possibly be expected to remember and acknowledge their birthdays and anniversaries (unless you want people to think that you're stalking them), right? That's right, but you can take a moment to give them a shout during the holidays—it's a thoughtful, proactive gesture that will keep these relationships current without giving anyone the impression they might need a restraining order down the line. Taking the time to maintain professional relationships means you won't have to feel awkward when you have to call a contact out of the blue about a job opportunity or ask for a reference.

To get started, dig up all those business cards you collected over the course of interviews, summer internships, job fairs, and—if you've already done some structured networking at this stage—power brunches and lunches, formal networking events, and informational interviews. Buy a pack of generic holiday cards and write short notes to your contacts wishing them a happy holiday season and offering a brief update on your professional status. Keep your tone positive, genuine, and subtle. For example, if you're still in the market for a job, your card might look something like this.

Dear Carrie,

It was great meeting you earlier this year at the Women in the Arts luncheon. Since then, I've had the opportunity to meet with some great folks about my interest in becoming a columnist with a daily newspaper, and while I'm still looking for the right opportunity, I feel excited about the many prospects. I hope all is well and that you're enjoying a wonderful holiday season. I hope to speak with you again soon.

All the best,
Joanna Jones

Or, if you're employed but want to keep your list of contacts current, something like this would work.

> Dear Samantha,
>
> I know it's been awhile since we last spoke, but I wanted to send a quick note to wish you and your family a wonderful holiday season. Things are going well for me at Smith Public Relations, and I've had the opportunity to work on some exciting new projects. I hope all is going well with you, and that the new year brings you continued success. Let's stay in touch.
>
> All the best,
>
> Robert Yule

While the holidays are one obvious opportunity to send cards or notes like the ones above, keeping in touch doesn't have to take place between Thanksgiving and New Year's Day. The important thing is not the specific holiday or the time of year, but the fact you're reaching out and keeping yourself visible. In fact, if there's one drawback to sending cards around the holiday season, it's that people receive so many cards yours may not stand out as much as it otherwise would. You can send out Thanksgiving cards, which makes it fairly likely yours will be the first holiday card your contacts will receive. Some people even send out networking cards around the Easter holiday (if you go this route, be sure each recipient observes the holiday). Even if there's not a bona-fide Hallmark holiday on the calendar for months, there are other good reasons to stay in touch—if you see an article or news clipping you think would be of interest to someone in your circle, send it to them and let them know you're thinking of them. No matter what occasion you choose, be sure to enclose a business card with your correspondence, or write your e-mail address and contact phone number beneath your signature.

INFORMATIONAL INTERVIEWS

So what exactly do you do once you've tapped your network and identified individuals who might be able to help you with your search? In a nutshell, you ask them to share their experiences, perspectives, career advice, and professional wisdom with you—regardless of whether they have the faintest idea who you are. Officially, this is called informational interviewing, and it's the best way to glean valuable job advice from the people you've met through your networking efforts.

An informational interview is any conversation where the primary objective is finding out about a particular field, company, or job opportunity. Informational interviews are not job interviews (and you shouldn't approach them with the expectation they'll lead to one). Instead, informational interviews are targeted conversations with people who currently work in the industry or field that you're interested in. Targeted doesn't necessarily mean formal: Oftentimes, you'll be able to glean just as much information over a casual brunch with someone you already know as you would during a more structured meeting in an office setting with someone you've never met. But no matter how formal or casual, all informational interviews are the perfect forum for:

- **Learning about a particular organization**—how the company distinguishes itself from its competitors in the industry and how it distinguishes itself among other employers in the same field; its hiring process; its values and culture.

- **Learning about a specific job/position**—what educational background or work experience is required; which personality traits or working styles are particularly well-suited for the role; what the day-to-day responsibilities are; how the role fits into the organization's broader mission; what challenges and rewards are inherent to the job; what career development opportunities are typically available.

- **Getting advice on your job search**—how your background and credentials might be viewed by hiring personnel in a particular industry or at a specific company; what factors interviewers are most likely to focus on during the recruiting process; what "barriers to entry" might exist that you didn't know about before (skills tests, writing samples, background checks, etc.); what successful candidates at a specific company have in common; which other individuals might be willing to speak with you.

- **Learning about potential job opportunities**—how a particular company fills job openings; whether there are industry-specific job boards or websites employers rely on when they have openings to fill; whether there are any industry-wide trends or company-specific developments that might affect hiring (mergers, acquisitions, restructurings, lateral movement, etc.); the most effective ways to find out about positions that have not yet been publicized.

On the approach

In order to snag informational interviews with the people who are best suited to give you advice, the way you ask is everything: Your request should be polite, concise, honest, and un-intrusive. While there are definitely situations where it's more appropriate to lob in a telephone call, asking for an informational interview is one task best accomplished over e-mail. You can rest assured you won't catch your contact just as she's rushing into a meeting or out the door for a dentist appointment, and you've left the ball in her court without making her feel awkward about it if she can't accommodate your request. Over e-mail, you can take the time necessary to make sure the tone of your request is appropriate: assertive yet respectful, specific yet flexible, complimentary but never cloying. You provide all of the nitty-gritty details (who you are, how you know who she is, and what you want from her) in a single, seamless paragraph. Here's an example of an e-mail requesting an informational interview:

Dear Ms. Walker,

My name is Karen McCarthy, and I'm a recent graduate of New York University here in Manhattan. I was referred to you by a friend of mine, Scott Davis, who worked with you last summer at the *Village Voice*. I am currently considering a career in newspaper journalism, and part of my research process involves speaking to people currently working in the field who are willing to share their perspectives and experiences with me. Scott mentioned that you have a very interesting professional background, and that you would certainly have some unique insights into the skills and experiences I should be building in order to launch a successful career in the industry. If you have a half hour to spare in the next week or two, I would love to meet with you in person. If an in-person meeting isn't possible, maybe we could schedule a brief telephone conversation at a time that makes sense for you; I'm obviously happy to work around your schedule.

Thanks so much in advance for your help, and I hope to hear from you soon!

Kind regards,

Karen McCarthy

Take what you can get

There will be times when a networking contact lets you know right off the bat that he can't meet with you in person or (for whatever reason) can't help you along in the hiring process. But if your contact is willing to share advice via e-mail or over the phone, don't discount the value of a dialogue just because it's not what you initially asked for. You can still learn a lot from these "virtual" meetings, and saying "thank you," by the way, is still in order.

The "Power Brunch"

You may have heard of a "power lunch" before, but the term "power brunch" might be an unfamiliar concept. A "power brunch" is the most casual version of an informational interview, and—especially if you're a novice networker—it's a great way to start getting the word out about your interest in a particular industry and getting advice about packaging yourself for maximum success. If you're a reluctant networker, the power brunch is the perfect way to start out; after a few weekend meals over omelets and cappuccinos, you'll definitely be more comfortable with the idea of asking for help when it comes to finding the perfect job.

Not only does the power brunch enable you to practice your informational interview skills, but you'll probably learn a lot more than you would in a more structured setting. To a greater extent than e-mail, telephone calls, or even office visits, power brunches create a relaxed environment that promotes candor; after all, you're presenting yourself as a trusted confidante rather than a jobseeker on the prowl for insider information. While the focus of a power lunch is selling yourself, there's no such pressure when it comes to the power brunch: Here, the focus isn't on you, but on the person you've invited. Your brunch guest might give you valuable information on breaking into the industry you want (including referrals to other contacts in your target industry), general advice on pursuing opportunities in a specific field, or insider tips on positions that haven't yet been advertised. Compared to weekday lunches—which can often be hurried and seem formal—power brunches are just more fun. You can show up in jeans and linger over a mimosa if the conversation takes off or if you just want to catch up after you've talked shop.

The people you'll most likely invite to a power brunch are actually the people you already know best: the "A-list" we described earlier in this chapter. As we've said before, many people focus all their networking efforts on people they don't yet know, while they overlook the valuable perspectives and advice of the people they already know. After a few power brunches, you'll see there's good reason not to let this group go unnoticed. Remember, your A-list includes friends, family members, roommates, neighbors, teachers, professors, advisors, colleagues past and present—anyone you already interact with on a regular basis. To set up a power brunch, you needn't send a formal, polished e-mail like the one you'd send to someone who didn't know you from Adam: Simply call a friend or family member whom you haven't talked to in a while who's doing something cool.

The "Power Lunch"

With a few power brunches under your belt, you'll graduate to the power lunch—many times, a power lunch will involve someone a brunch date referred you to. The power lunch gives you the advantages of an in-person meeting: You get to observe the other person's body language (which will help you gauge how comfortable they are giving you the inside scoop), and develop the type of rapport only a face-to-face meeting can establish. However, because most power lunches involve contacts you don't know quite as well—and contacts slightly closer to the hiring process—the power lunch isn't quite as candid or relaxed. Though you still aren't expected to treat it as a job interview, you are expected to be professional—that means showing up on time, making sure your lunch sticks to the time you've allotted for it, and thanking your lunch partner profusely for taking time out of his busy schedule to meet with you.

Don't sweat the small talk: Specific questions to ask during informational interviews

Whether an informational interview takes place over the phone or happy-hour cocktails, you should prepare for it by developing a specific idea of what you hope to learn. Of course, the types of questions you'll ask will depend on what stage of the job-research process you're at. If you're just trying to get a sense of what a career in academia might entail versus a career in the private sector, you won't ask the same questions as someone who wants to find out what it's like to work as a research assistant for a specific university professor. The research you've done up until this point (whether online, at your career-planning office, or through other informational interviews) should also help you decide which questions to pose. Have one or two primary objectives in mind at the beginning of the conversation (whether it's finding out about a specific company's culture or figuring out what technical skills a particular job requires) and let that shape the direction the interview takes. If you get stuck, here are a few topics you might want to cover during your conversations, along with a few sample questions in each category.

- **Educational background:** I was wondering if you could tell me a little bit about your background—what did you study in college? Did you go to graduate school? Is your educational background typical of someone in your position? Are there aspects of the job that make particularly good use of the skills you developed as a history/political science major?

- **Job-search tactics:** As you prepared for your interviews, how did you go about conducting research on specific organizations? What strategies did you find most helpful? Looking back at your interviews with this organization, were there specific things about your background and experience that your interviewers were especially interested in discussing? What surprised you (if anything) about the hiring process at your company? Is it fairly common for employers in the industry to give any job-specific tests or assessments to evaluate your suitability for the position?

- **Career path:** How did you decide to go into this particular field? What other industries were you considering (if any), and why did you choose your specific organization? How did you arrive in the specific area/department you're currently working in? How do you see your career at Company XYZ evolving? What types of advancement opportunities are available to you? Are lateral moves—either within the company or from one company to another—fairly common? Is it realistic to expect that if I start out in an entry-level role, I'll be able to move up within the organization? How does your organization approach developing its staff and promoting from within?

- **Day-to-day responsibilities:** What do you do on a daily basis? Can you describe what a typical day/week is like? Could you describe for me some recent projects you've worked on and your specific role in those projects? How do your specific responsibilities fit into the bigger picture of what your department does? How does your department fit into the larger organization?

- **Fit with the job:** What do you think it takes for someone to be good at this job, and what do you think it takes for someone to really enjoy it? What have you found to be the most frustrating and the most rewarding aspects of the job? What do you wish you had known about the job before you started it? Does the job frequently require travel, relocation, or long hours? Are people in these positions supervised closely, or are they expected to work independently, with little managerial oversight? Would you describe the job as highly collaborative or not?

- **Fit with the organization/industry:** Now that you're at Company XYZ, what has surprised you about working there? About the industry in general? How would you describe your firm's culture? What do you think is different/better about working there than anywhere else? Are there any factors specific to your experience that might influence your answer? What do you think your firm takes particular pride in?

- **Advice for you:** In general, what advice would you give someone hoping to break into this field? Based on your experience, what advice would you give someone looking to explore career opportunities at your firm? Are there specific areas of the company that seem particularly well-suited for someone with my education, experience, and background? Can you recommend other people—either inside or outside of Company XYZ—who might also be willing to share their perspectives of working in the industry? Are there any industry-specific resources (websites, trade journals) that might be helpful to someone researching the industry? Which professional associations are linked to the field and what types of activities do they sponsor? Are there any with which I can be involved right away?

Unless your contact answers your questions with monosyllabic, one-word answers, you probably won't be able to get through all of these questions in a single informational interview, so keep your one or two primary goals in mind throughout the conversation. Regardless of how many or how few questions you ask, you should definitely be conscious of your contact's time; these individuals are not your personal career consultants, nor should you feel as though you can enlist them to support your case with recruiters. Never ask for more than a half-hour of your contact's time; if she's willing to give you 45 minutes, that's great—but be careful not to overstay your welcome. And no matter what, be sure to acknowledge that your contact has sacrificed precious free time to speak to you, and always thank her profusely for helping you out.

Compare apples to apples

If possible, speak with contacts whose backgrounds are similar to yours in some way, whether it's their educational background, previous work or internship experience, specific professional interests, geographic location, or even outside interests or hobbies. This is helpful for a couple of reasons: The more you have in common with a person, the more relevant their job-hunting experiences are likely to be to you. Also, if you're interviewing someone you haven't met before, you'll both feel more comfortable if you can find some common ground to get the conversation started—and keep it going. It's human nature, really: As a general rule, we're more comfortable with people who are like us. The more your contact can relate to you, the more comfortable—and therefore candid—they'll be when it comes to sharing the secrets of their success. Tap into your school's alumni directory and extend an introduction to alums who work in the fields that interest you. If you're a member of any social or networking clubs, ask around to see if anyone knows of a butcher, baker, candlestick-maker, or anyone who fits the career profile you're hoping to build for yourself. If there are websites or resources you regularly consult as you're doing research on your target fields, keep an eye out for specific articles that capture your interest, and contact the authors to see if they're willing to speak with you further about the topic.

Practice makes perfect

Like any other skill you're just starting to learn, informational interviewing requires time and practice if you want to become particularly good at it. The more people you talk to, the more natural the process will seem, and the less you'll feel like a seventh-grader working on a research project for your social-studies class. While conversations with people you've never met might initially make you nervous, you'll eventually find you look forward to them (yes, we promise). But no matter how adept you become at informational interviewing, keep the following rules of the road in mind so your conversations continue to be productive:

Take the road less traveled.

Your conversations with people who aren't directly involved with recruiting might prove the most valuable. If you keep your informational interviews separate from any formal application process, you can be reasonably sure the questions you ask won't have a direct influence on a subsequent hiring decision. You'll be more comfortable asking questions you wouldn't necessarily bring up in an evaluative setting, and you'll probably get more valuable answers than you would get from a recruiter or HR contact; these folks are generally too close to the recruiting process to give you an objective perspective, and, because they're generalists, they won't necessarily be able to provide a lot of detailed information about what it's like to work in any one specific position.

Asking contacts outside the regular recruiting process for the real scoop, however, doesn't mean you can say or do anything unprofessional—just because the details of your conversation won't necessarily get back to decision-makers doesn't mean it's outside the realm of possibility. No matter how informal the setting, you should still approach your informational interviews with professionalism.

Avoid the resume "balk."

Unless your contact has specifically asked you for a copy of your resume, don't fork one over during an informational interview. If someone has agreed to speak with you on a purely informational basis and you hand her your resume, you're essentially changing the direction of the conversation with little or no warning. In other words, you're committing the job-hunting equivalent of a "balk" in baseball (if you're unfamiliar with the term, here's the 411: In baseball, a pitcher must come to a full stop before he pitches, and, once he starts, he's got to follow through or it doesn't count. A violation of this rule is called a "balk"). You owe it to the people who've granted you informational interviews to give them fair warning, too. If you've told someone that you want to speak with them to learn more about a specific industry or job, you can't switch the rules halfway through the game by asking someone to submit your resume on your behalf. At best, your contact might not know quite how to react or what to do with it. At worst, she might question your sincerity and credibility. Of course, you are welcome to submit your resume if your contact asks for it in advance of your conversation—or during it. Have a few copies ready just in case, but don't go until you've gotten the green light.

The favor of your reply is requested.

Whenever someone takes time out to help you with your job search without any expectation of getting something in return, a formal thank-you is in order. Not only is it good manners, but leaving someone with a favorable impression of you makes good business sense, too. A thoughtful e-mail is sufficient, but a hand-written note makes a bigger impact—and not just because it takes a little more time and effort. "I send hand-written thank-you notes because my contacts won't wonder whether they're expected to respond," explains Carrie, a 26-year old assistant editor. "An e-mailed thank-you note might leave the recipient wondering, 'should I send a response to say good luck? Or should I offer to keep them posted on job opportunities?' A hand-written, mailed thank-you note lets you just say 'thank you' without giving the impression that you might expect something else down the line." We think Emily Post—and your mom—would probably agree.

Mind your manners when it comes to money.

When you bring up the issue of money, you always run the risk of getting someone's knickers in a twist over it, and it's no different when it comes to researching jobs and careers. We all know that it's considered impolite to talk about money in virtually any situation, but shouldn't it be fair game as you investigate which career options make the most sense for you? It should, but it isn't. Most people (including us!) will tell you that in the context of a formal job interview, you shouldn't talk about compensation until you're offered a job. But in order to negotiate effectively, you need to have a realistic salary range for comparable positions in mind. Salary surveys and databases are a start, but because the ranges they provide are broad, it's best to have a firsthand source to help you manage your expectations.

But how do you ask about money so early in the process? Very carefully. Perhaps more than any other topic of conversation you'll navigate during the informational interview, the money discussion is a little bit of a dance; the way it unfolds depends entirely on how well you read your partner.

Some people—God bless them—will come right out and tell you how much they make in their current position, or how much they made when they started out in their profession. In that case, they've opened the Pandora's Box of compensation issues for you, and it's reasonable to ask whether or not the figure they've cited is realistic for the type of position you're considering. Unfortunately, most people you'll speak with probably won't volunteer this level of detail. If this is the case, you'll have to gauge how the conversation is going and how receptive your contact is likely to be if asked to provide salary information. If you save the money talk for last (and we recommend that you do), you'll have time to figure this out. If the person is reticent when it comes to discussing his company's interview philosophy, then chances are he's not going to be eager to show you a copy of his W-2. Rely on your intuition and common sense when deciding whether to broach the topic.

If you decide to ask, keep in mind that the less direct your questions, the less threatening they're likely to be. You can always cite the salary ranges your initial research has revealed and see if you get a nibble: Your contact might advise you whether your expectations should lean toward the high or low end of the range. If you haven't been able to pin down any sort of range for the job, you can see if they'll be willing to provide one. Again, the way you ask the question is critical: Saying "I'm in the beginning of my job search, and I have no idea what sort of salary range is realistic for entry-level jobs in this field" is very different from asking "Do you mind if I ask you what you make?" Asking open-ended questions that leave room for discretion are preferable to questions that require a single numerical answer. Such questions give your contact an escape route if he or she feels uncomfortable.

While we're on the subject of discomfort, we should emphasize the importance of recognizing it during the interview. If you sense your contact is starting to bristle when the subject of money comes up, there's absolutely nothing to be gained by being persistent—and there's an awful lot to lose.

If your informational interview ends and you're no further along when it comes to salary information, remember you can consult other sources besides the salary databases we mentioned earlier: professional associations, staffing companies, temp agencies, and headhunters can often provide salary data. Scour online job postings for similar positions and look for ones that specify salary. If you're still in school, remember that your career-planning office will probably be able to help you hone in on a reasonable range—even if they don't have firsthand knowledge of the position or industry, they're generally more adept at tapping into other resources, including alumni and recruiters who interview on campus.

Know when to say "when"

We can't overemphasize the importance of not becoming "that guy" or "that girl" in the eyes of your networking contacts: The one who won't stop calling or e-mailing to check on the status of available jobs. Wake up and smell the hummus, folks: Your networking contacts are not your personal career gurus. Nine times out of ten, they don't know about every current job opening their organization has posted, and they surely don't know about all of the ones that are still in the pipeline. Usually, they have little to no influence over hiring decisions. Even if they did, they can't work miracles if you don't have the requisite skills, training, or experience for a given job. If they barely know you, you shouldn't expect that they'll be eager to provide a personal endorsement of your candidacy, so don't ask them to do it. Regardless of whether they're eligible for a referral bonus if you end up getting hired, they're not on your payroll: They have their own jobs, too.

Not only can dogged persistence backfire when it comes to your own job search, but it has the potential to create bad networking karma all around. "When I first graduated from college, I designated myself as a career mentor on my university's alumni database, which meant that current students and other alumni were welcome to contact me for career advice," says Matthew, a 28-year old analyst at a government agency. "But I got so many e-mails and calls from people who didn't really want advice; they just wanted me to help them get a job. A lot of them just wouldn't quit, even if I told them that my involvement in the process was limited. Eventually, it got old and I took myself off of the list."

Unfortunately, many job-seekers end up misusing and abusing the opportunities that informational interviews provide. While people generally enjoy lending their advice and expertise, even the most generous, well-intentioned person will start to lose patience with someone who takes advantage of his time or just won't back off. Think about it this way: Did you ever like a song the first time you heard it on the radio, but come to despise it after a while because all the stations played it ad nauseam? When it comes to your networking contacts, know when to pipe down.

Don't be a one-trick pony.

As with any single component of the job-hunting process, you can't rely on networking prowess alone to get the job you want. We said that the most impressive resume wouldn't do any good if no one ever read it, and we meant it. But the inverse is also true: No matter how savvy a networker you are (or eventually become), you won't get the job if you can't convince the person or people in a position to hire you that you'd be good at it. However, information is power: Networking allows you to figure out what you want to do in the first place, what opportunities might be available that fit your criteria, and what you need to know about a specific organization before you interview there. You can use what you've learned by networking to make your resumes, cover letters, and other application materials more targeted and effective. So while networking is an important piece of the puzzle, it's just that: one piece. You have to make sure everything else fits into place, too.

RESUMES, COVER LETTERS, AND INTERVIEWS

What have I done to deserve this?

Now that your job search is underway, you may find a lot of unsolicited (but well-intentioned) advice coming your way. All of a sudden, it seems as though everyone is an expert when it comes to searching for—and getting—the perfect job. If you haven't already heard every job-hunting cliché in the book, just give it time. Chances are good someone will tell you "it's not what you know but who you know," "it's all about eye contact and a firm handshake," and "getting your foot in the door is what really matters—after all, you can always work your way up." With all of the unsolicited guidance coming your way, it can be difficult to distinguish tried-and-true job-hunting advice from old wives' tales perpetuated solely to put anxious minds like yours at ease.

In the following pages, we'll help you separate myth from fact when it comes to landing the job you want. If there's one thing we hope you'll learn from this chapter, it's that hiring processes at most organizations are much more an art than a science. When you're in the market for a job, you'd like to think employers' decision-making processes are—if not completely scientific—at least rational, predictable, and based predominantly on candidates' relative merits. But as a candidate for a given position, you're essentially marketing a product (that product is you, of course), and human beings aren't always rational and predictable when it comes to deciding what to buy. It's not enough to develop the product (by completing your degree, gaining work experience, joining professional associations, volunteering in the community, and so on)—you have to pay attention to the packaging, too. In the context of a job search, cover letters, resumes, and interviews are all part of the packaging: Once you've taken the time to figure out exactly what you have to offer a potential employer, you've got to present your qualifications in a compelling, convincing way. This section will teach you how to do just that.

It had to be you: What employers look for

Before you can figure out how to present yourself—your achievements, qualifications, and experience—to a prospective employer, you need to know which specific attributes organizations will be looking for as they evaluate your candidacy. It stands to reason that every industry (and every company, and every function or group within that company, for that matter) uses its own unique set of criteria to inform its recruiting process and hiring decisions. Nonetheless, employers across industries mention the same qualities over and over again. According to a recent study by the National Association of Colleges and Employers (NACE), an organization that publishes research on recruiting and employment issues for college graduates, employers consider the following skills and personal attributes most important to their evaluation of a job candidate:

Skill/Personal Attribute	Importance
Communication skills	4.7
Honesty/integrity	4.7
Teamwork skills	4.6
Strong work ethic	4.5
Analytical skills	4.4
Flexibility/adaptability	4.4
Interpersonal skills	4.4
Motivation/initiative	4.4
Computer skills	4.3
Attention to detail	4.1
Organizational skills	4.1
Leadership skills	4.0
Self-confidence	4.0

(5-point scale where 1=Not at all important and 5=Extremely important)

Source: "Employers Rate the Importance of Candidate Qualities/Skills." *Job Outlook 2006*. National Association of Colleges and Employers. NACEweb.org.

If the list of attributes above seems like a lot to remember, take heart. We're not suggesting you commit it to memory, or that you convince a prospective employer you possess every single one of these traits. Instead, the list is intended to reassure you that the skills you developed as you worked toward your degree are highly relevant in the job market. In fact, many of the skills that were most critical to your success as a student are the ones employers prize most highly. Consider the list above a starting point for taking inventory of your own capabilities and strengths.

In the following pages, we'll help you turn the skills you've developed pursuing your degree into a compelling, marketable package you'll present to prospective employers during your search. Though we address the resume, cover letter, and interview separately, keep in mind that each of these is part of a single process—a process that offers numerous opportunities to demonstrate exactly what you have to offer.

RESUMES AND COVER LETTERS

If it hasn't happened to you already, it will probably happen to you soon: You've successfully landed a "power brunch" with a friend of a friend who has the job of your dreams. The two of you have hit it off, and after a few cappuccinos she's giving you the inside scoop on what it's like to work in the industry—what it takes to be successful, what recruiters look for when they're scouting new talent, and how she landed her job in the first place. The more detail she gives you about her work, the more convinced you are you've found your professional Holy Grail. And it gets better . . . there's an opening in her department that would be perfect for you! And she's offered to pass along your resume! Just e-mail it to her, she says, and she'll deliver it to the right person, along with a personal endorsement of your candidacy.

You think about it for a moment: You know you must have a resume somewhere. You can remember writing one, but it's been awhile since you've updated it. You're eager to strike while the iron is hot, though; if your new best brunch buddy has offered to hand-deliver your resume to the recruiting contact at her company, you'd better fire one off to her as soon as possible, right?

Well, yes—as long as it's error-free, easy to understand, tailored (to one extent or another) to the job for which you are applying, and accompanied by a concise, well-written cover letter. If it's lacking in any of these areas, it will be worth taking the extra time to get it in tip-top shape before hitting the "send" button and setting your application in motion.

How resumes and cover letters are used

In virtually every industry and organization, employers use resumes as a way to assess which candidates should be considered for an available position. There is no way around it: You absolutely must have one; without it you will not pass "Go," you will not collect $200, and—until someone comes up with a more reliable, efficient way to screen applicants—you will not get a job. When it comes to effective resumes, there's no single magic formula that guarantees success in every circumstance. However, the best resumes have a few things in common: they are concise, results-oriented, and clearly presented. Most importantly, good resumes convince hiring personnel to interview well-qualified candidates. *The primary purpose of a resume is getting an interview. A resume alone will not land you a job offer.*

Once you've been invited to interview, your resume will shape your subsequent conversations with recruiters, hiring managers, and other employees at the company. Every person you speak with during the interview process will likely have a copy of your resume, and each person will probably look for gaps, weaknesses, and inconsistencies that they'll expect you to address during your conversation. Once you've left the office, your resume helps your interviewer (or interviewers) remember you and serves as the basis for the discussion of your candidacy.

Cover letters can play a less significant role. In general, they aren't read with the same level of scrutiny resumes are; sometimes they're read, more often they're skimmed, and, occasionally, they aren't reviewed at all. Nonetheless, you can't take any chances with your cover letter. There are many recruiters and hiring managers who will look to the cover letters when faced with several applicants who have similar resumes. You'll need to craft a cover letter that effectively introduces your resume, explains your interest in the specific position and the company, and highlights exactly what you can contribute to the role. Don't write one cover letter for several different jobs; make sure every cover letter you send out is job specific.

Together, your resume and cover letter introduce your qualifications to recruiters and hiring managers. Remember the list of attributes we mentioned at the beginning of the chapter? The person reviewing your resume and cover letter will have these qualities in mind and will be actively looking for evidence you've demonstrated them in the past. To give you an idea of how this works, we've listed a few of the key success factors below, along with the questions recruiters will most likely be asking themselves as they review your application materials.

- **Communication skills.** Is your resume well-written? Is your cover letter (or cover message) thoughtfully prepared, tactfully worded, and customized to the position for which you are applying? Does your correspondence strike the appropriate balance between confidence and deference? Are your resume and cover letter both flawless, or are they riddled with typos and grammatical errors?

- **Teamwork, interpersonal, and leadership skills.** Have your prior work experiences, academic pursuits, and extracurricular activities required you to work in teams? Do your extracurricular activities and outside interests require a high degree of interpersonal interaction? Does your resume include evidence of your leadership ability? Do any of your credentials suggest you are adept at motivating and persuading others?

- **Strong work ethic, motivation, and initiative.** Does your resume show you've successfully juggled multiple priorities? Are you actively involved in extracurricular activities (or, if you've already graduated, do you consistently pursue interests outside of work)? Does your resume list achievements that suggest you're both self-motivated and committed to excellence? Have you demonstrated that you consistently provide a high-quality service or work product to classmates, colleagues, and managers?

The resume: Getting started

If you've attended a resume-writing workshop or picked up a reference book on the topic, you probably already know that people who receive resumes don't spend a whole lot of time reviewing each one—at least not in the initial screening process. The exact amount of time and energy that's devoted to reviewing your credentials obviously varies depending on the person who's reading your resume, but a seasoned recruiter probably spends less than 30 seconds deciding your fate.

It might strike you as miserably unfair that you must spend so much time writing, revising, and perfecting your resume while the person who receives it spends less than 30 seconds looking at it—and may not even read it at all. The good news is that a thoughtfully written resume can convey an image of who you are, what you're capable of, and how you have used your capabilities to accomplish results—all in 30 seconds or less.

If this seems like a lot to accomplish, remember there are ample resources available to get you started. If you're a student, take advantage of the services your on-campus career placement office provides. Many of them compile binders of resumes from current and former students, which you can consult to get ideas. Once you've been inspired to write your own, you can schedule a resume consultation or attend the resume- and cover letter-writing workshops offered by many campus career centers. Discussing your experiences and qualifications with an expert—particularly if you've never drafted a resume before—can help you figure out what information to include and how to package it in an effective way. Even if you already have a working copy of your resume, it never hurts to have a second (and more objective) pair of eyes on your work.

Whether you're a student or not, it's worth asking family and friends—especially those who are already working in the industry you hope to break into—for guidance. They may even be willing to send you the resumes they used to land their current positions. At the very least, they'll be able to give you an honest assessment of whether your resume is well-written, error-free, and easy to understand. As a rule, successful job-seekers take all of the help they can get when it comes to "packaging" themselves for prospective employers, so don't be afraid to ask for help!

Resume content

An effective resume has—at most—three sections: "Education," "experience," and (sometimes) a third section for relevant information that doesn't fit into either of the other two categories. The optional third section goes a few by different names: "activities," "additional information," "interests," "other," or "personal," depending on what you've included in the section. The order in which the sections appear usually depends on how much work experience you've got; if you are still in school or if you are a recent graduate, the education section should come first unless your professional experience is uniquely relevant and warrants emphasis (for example, you were a summer intern at the firm to which you're applying). If you're more than a few years out of school, the "experience" section should come first. The longer you've been out of school, the less resume space your education section should occupy. After a few years, you'll need to include only the basic information (institution, degrees conferred, honors awarded, and year graduated). Information on your grades, extracurricular activities, and research projects will eventually get bumped off the page in favor of a beefier experience section. If you include an "other" section, it should always appear last.

Some resume books—and career planning offices at some colleges and universities—suggest that candidates include an objective, overview, or summary at the top of the resume, immediately after the candidate's name and contact information. However well-intentioned the advice, we suggest you leave it out; your resume should already be a concise snapshot of your professional and academic experience to date, so it's redundant to summarize it even further. A career objective doesn't need to take up valuable real estate on your resume, either. If you're not applying for a particular job but are sending your resume to indicate your interest in an organization, it's virtually impossible to write an objective with the appropriate level of specificity. Resume objectives that are too broad not only end up sounding silly ("To be gainfully employed by a respectable firm so that I can afford to live in the city of my choice while avoiding incarceration and simultaneously utilizing my interpersonal, analytical, and leadership skills as well as my corporate wardrobe"), but they don't really tell the reader anything useful. At the other end of the spectrum, including an objective that is too specific introduces the risk you'll be knocked out of consideration if there are no available openings that meet your criteria. If you are responding to an advertised job posting, it should be fairly obvious your objective is getting that job—otherwise, why would you be applying for it? Your interest in a particular firm or your intention to apply for a specific job can instead be outlined in your cover letter.

The optional third section

The question of whether to include a third section ("activities," "interests," "other," or "personal") is one over which reasonable people can disagree. If you're still in school or have graduated within the past year, you're probably fairly safe including a section on the extracurricular activities you've pursued in college. Otherwise, stick to information that's relevant to the position for which you're applying or that distinguishes you in some way from other candidates (professional associations or memberships, for example, or proficiency in one or more foreign languages). The issue of whether to include personal interests or hobbies is another gray area; as a general rule, those that are fairly common (cooking, travel, jogging, and reading, for example) probably won't win you any points because they appear in resumes so frequently. Lines like "traveled extensively through Europe" almost never achieve their desired effect for the same reason. They won't disqualify you from consideration by any means, but they're unlikely to advance your candidacy either. If you're trying to choose which items to include in this section, include the ones most likely to pique the genuine interest of the recruiter.

Resume format

Now that you've figured out the type of information you'll include in your resume, you'll need to package it in a clean, easy-to-read, and error-free way. Keep in mind that conformity is a good thing when it comes to resume formatting: Anyone who picks up your resume should immediately be able to identify the two main sections (education and experience), and, within each of those sections, it should be easy for the reader to understand your achievements and qualifications. Adding too many stylistic bells and whistles—or packing your resume too tightly—just makes it more difficult for the recruiter to identify your credentials. To make your resume easy on the eyes, keep these resume format basics in mind.

- Keep it to one page. Writing a resume requires careful consideration of which achievements warrant mention, which can be described more concisely, and which should be scrapped altogether.

- Stick to a single, easy-to-read font (Times New Roman and Helvetica are safe choices) in a legible font size (10 to 12 points).

- Use one-inch margins on all sides; don't try to "buy" more space by shrinking the margins.

- Label major sections (education, experience, and other) clearly and leave line spaces between them.

- Write in bullets, not paragraphs. Recruiters won't take the time to weed through densely packed prose. Use the active voice rather than the passive voice, leave out first-person pronouns, use qualifying adjectives and adverbs sparingly, and keep dependent clauses to a minimum—it will help keep your writing focused, action-oriented, and concise.

- Use boldface type, italics, or small caps sparingly. Overusing these features defeats the purpose of calling attention to critical information.

- Within each of the major sections, use a reverse chronological listing. Either the name of the organization or the dates worked should appear on the left (your approach should be consistent throughout the resume).

- For hard copies of your resume (these are a dying breed, but you still need to take a few copies with you when you interview), use high-quality bond paper in white or off-white.

The Magic Bullet

Make no mistake about it: Writing a resume is not the same as writing one of those family newsletters you stuff into holiday cards at the end of the year (and if you don't send these, chances are you know someone who does). You know the letters we're talking about: the ones that typically feature self-indulgent use of the third-person perspective and lots of unnecessary exclamation points. Your resume is a far more objective, achievement-driven, results-oriented summary of your qualifications in which the bullet point—not the sentence or the paragraph—is the primary component. To help you make sure your bullets hit their targets, we've consulted career management expert and author Douglas B. Richardson, who offers the following tips for making your resume stand out from the crowd:

- **Don't overdo qualifying adjectives.** Descriptions of "major contributions," "dynamic programs" and "significant improvements" aren't objective reality. They're the writer's opinion and are discounted as such. Use high-action adverbs sparingly, too—words like "aggressively," "proactively," "progressively."

- **Avoid the use of "wimpy" verbs.** Use verbs to communicate action and achievement: Manage. Execute. Analyze. Create. Organize. Let the other drip be the one who "aided," "participated in" or "helped bring about."

- **Emphasize your past achievements by using titles, numbers, and names.** Titles show that someone else had enough faith in you to invest you with responsibility. That proves something, and yet many people leave it out.

- **Quantify your achievements wherever you can.** Numbers serve two functions. First, they show magnitude of achievement. The person who "increased plant output 156 percent in seven months" is more impressive than the one who merely "increased productivity." And "managed technical-design staff of 350" is better proof of your skills than "headed engineering group." Second, numbers offer concrete evidence that's rarely questioned.

- **Names carry clout the same way numbers do.** IBM isn't a "major data processing firm." It's IBM. Working there isn't the same as working at Marty's Software Heaven. Imagine if George Washington's resume simply stated: "Played significant role in planning and implementation of major country."

- **But if you can't rely on name alone, provide a description.** Descriptions such as "*Fortune* 100 Company" or "world's largest shoelace maker" can make an enormous difference in how you—and the quality of your achievements—are perceived.[1]

One size does *not* fit all

If you are job hunting in more than one field, or considering different types of positions within the same field, you will need to have more than one version of your resume. For example, let's assume you are applying for two jobs: one as an account representative at an advertising agency and one as an editorial assistant at a publishing house. For each position, you need to emphasize different skills. For the account rep job, you'll need to emphasize your interpersonal, communication, sales,

1 Douglas B. Richardson. "Skeptical Resume Reader Tells How He Really Thinks." *CareerJournal* . July 30, 2001. www.careerjournal.com.

and marketing skills. For the editorial assistant slot, you'll need to stress your attention to detail, ability to work under deadline pressure, and skills as a proofreader. Naturally, there will be some overlap between the two resumes, but the thrust of each should be very different. You should also have a more generic version of your resume available, which you can use for networking purposes. This will come in handy when you meet a contact who wants to know more about your background, but isn't necessarily offering you any kind of employment opportunity.

Electronic resumes

Once you've crafted the perfect resume, you'll need to save three electronic versions of it. That way, you'll be ready to send off your resume regardless of whether it needs to be e-mailed as an attachment, in plain text in the body of an e-mail, or uploaded onto an online database.

- **Microsoft Word (or other word-processing software) document.** This is the version of your resume that you'll e-mail to hiring personnel when you're instructed to send it as an attachment. It's also the one you'll print out and take with you on interviews. And though the days of sending a hard copy of your resume by FedEx are all but over, this is the version you'll use if need to send a paper copy for any reason.

- **ASCII format with line breaks:** ASCII (American Standard Code of Interchange) allows databases and data recognition software to read your resume without the confusion caused by formatting. The "with line breaks" option is critical for e-mailed resumes because there is no standard e-mail program that everyone uses; if the recipient's e-mail program doesn't automatically wrap line breaks, your resume could appear as a single line of horizontal text on the receiving end. By clicking the "insert line breaks" option, you'll avoid this potential problem. Your word-processing software will force line breaks so that no single line will exceed 65 characters of text. In Microsoft Word, use the "save as" tab, save your resume (name it differently from the first version), and save the file as plain text. When the dialogue box appears, choose "other encoding" and select US-ASCII. Also click the "insert line breaks" checkbox.

- **ASCII format without line breaks:** Use this format when you're instructed to upload your resume to an online database and to cut and paste into preset fields. Unlike the version you'll paste into the body of an e-mail, the version for web-based forms should not have forced line breaks (the text should wrap instead). Why is this? Because if you copy and paste a plain-text resume to an online application form and it has line breaks manually inserted, the end result will be a jagged effect. Each webmaster has a different default setting for how many characters constitute a single line of text, so if your resume exceeds this limit, your resume will look terrible. If you create an ASCII resume without line breaks, the text will instead "wrap," which means you won't have to manually reformat your resume once you've pasted it in the appropriate box. In order to save a version of your resume suitable for online application forms, follow the directions for "ASCII format with line breaks" above, but skip the last step.

Joanna C. Bloggs

Present address
903 Laurel Dr., Apt. #5C
Princeton, NJ 08648
(609) 555-7124
E-mail address: joanna@bloggs.net

Permanent address
1234 Hollyhock Lane
West Chester, PA 19382
610-555-7089

EDUCATION

Princeton University   Princeton, NJ • GPA: 3.9
- BA expected June 2005. Double major in history and English. Extensive course work (approximately 15 credits each) in business/management and public policy departments.
- Secretary of Class of 2005. Elected by peers to plan activities that promote class spirit and unity among 1200 undergraduates. Head publicity committee to promote major class events.

Henderson High School   West Chester, PA • GPA:4.0
Graduated May 2001. Class valedictorian. National Merit Scholar. Completed advanced-placement courses in English, calculus, physics, and Spanish.

WORK EXPERIENCE

Crane Communications   New York, NY
Public-relations Intern
Summer 2004
- Worked with senior account executives to manage relationships with clients in emerging high technology and health care industries.
- Assisted with the writing, editing, production, and distribution of press materials, including press releases and fact sheets.
- Conducted account-related research and compiled findings into complete coverage reports.
- Developed and maintained media lists and editorial calendars.
- Collaborated with office staff to devise publicity strategy and coordinate publicity logistics for major client events.

Chester County Community Center   **West Chester, PA**
Director of Youth Programs
Summer 2003
- Led the start-up and development of a youth volunteer program that connects 50 high schools with community organizations in need of volunteers.
- Conducted extensive research to identify participating community organizations, interview organizations' leadership, and determine their most immediate volunteer needs.
- Created a comprehensive database of area schools that enabled program to effectively match student volunteers and community groups.

Princeton University Library   **Princeton, NJ**
Library Staff
September 2001–May 2002
- Managed front desk and circulation records.
- Worked part-time while completing first year of college. Worked an average of 10–15 hours per week while maintaining a full course load.

PERSONAL
- High degree of competency in written and spoken Spanish (founded high school Spanish club; received first-place honors at State Declamation Foreign Language Championships, 2000).
- Demonstrated interest in community-service initiatives (president of high school volunteer organization; honored at 15th Annual Volunteer Awards of Chester County).

After you've spent hours tinkering with your resume to make it a visual masterpiece, you might cringe at the thought of saving it—and sending it, for that matter—in an ASCII format. Don't despair: You can minimize the damage by taking the following steps:

- Replace bullets with asterisks (*).

- Offset category headings with a row of tildes (~), a row of equal signs (=), or capital letters.

- Change your margin settings to 2 inches; 60 characters (including spaces) is the maximum line length. Setting a wider margin allows you to control where the line breaks occur.

- Select a fixed-width typeface like Courier and use a 12-point font size.

- Add white space for readability.

- Do a test run. Send a copy to a friend—or yourself—over e-mail to see how it looks.

JOANNA C. BLOGGS

Present address:
903 Laurel Drive, Apt. #5C
Princeton, NJ 08648
609-555-7124
E-mail address: joanna@bloggs.net

Permanent address:
1234 Hollyhock Lane
West Chester, PA 19382
610-555-7089

EDUCATION

Princeton University
Princeton, NJ
- BA expected June 2005.
- Double major in history and English.
- Extensive course work (approximately 15 credits each) in business/management and public policy departments.
- Secretary of Class of 2005. Elected by peers to plan activities that promote class spirit and unity among 1200 undergraduates. Head publicity committee to promote major class events.
- GPA: 3.9.

Henderson High School
West Chester, PA
- Graduated May 2001.
- Class valedictorian. National Merit Scholar. Completed advanced-placement courses in English, calculus, physics, and Spanish.
- GPA: 4.0.

WORK EXPERIENCE

Crane Communications
New York, NY
Public-relations Intern
Summer 2004
- Worked with senior account executives to manage relationships with clients in emerging high technology and health care industries.
- Assisted with the writing, editing, production, and distribution of press materials, including press releases and fact sheets.
- Conducted account-related research and compiled findings into complete coverage reports.
- Developed and maintained media lists and editorial calendars.
- Collaborated with office staff to devise publicity strategy and coordinate publicity logistics for major client events.

Chester County Community Center
West Chester, PA
Director of Youth Programs
Summer of 2002
- Led the start-up and development of a youth volunteer program that connects 50 high schools with community organizations in need of volunteers.
- Conducted extensive research to identify participating community organizations, interview organizations' leadership, and determine their most immediate volunteer needs.
- Created a comprehensive database of area schools that enabled program to effectively match student volunteers and community groups.

Princeton University Library
Princeton, NJ
Library Staff
September 2001–May 2002
- Managed front desk and circulation records.
- Worked part-time while completing first year of college. Worked an average of 10–15 hours per week while maintaining a full course load.

PERSONAL
- High degree of competency in written and spoken Spanish (founded high school Spanish club; received first place honors at State Declamation Foreign Language Championships, 2000).
- Demonstrated interest in community service initiatives (president of high school volunteer organization; honored at 15th Annual Volunteer Awards of Chester County).

Cover letters

If you were to conduct a survey of recruiters and hiring managers, you'd probably be hard-pressed to find one who could remember a truly exceptional cover letter (or an exceptionally good cover letter, anyway). The truth of the matter is cover letters are rarely read closely. As we mentioned earlier, they're more frequently skimmed. In fact, a cover letter is a little bit like a passport photo: Having a really good one is nice, but it isn't going to get you anywhere unless your other paperwork is in order. You can't get very far if you don't have one at all, though, and having a bad one is just plain embarrassing. In short, it's worth taking the time to make sure yours is great.

Your cover letter doesn't need to be a literary masterpiece, but it does need to be concise, well written, polite, at least somewhat personalized, and error-free. "We get so many applications from people claiming to be great writers and editors," says Diane, an HR professional at a magazine publishing company. "I'm always shocked at how many of them include poorly written cover letters with multiple typos." Not only should your resume be flawless, but it should include all the required information: the position to which you're applying, the primary reason for your interest, and a brief overview of the one or two qualifications that make you a compelling candidate. At the end of the letter, you should (politely, never presumptuously) suggest a possible next step—usually a brief telephone conversation or an in-person meeting.

By the time you've covered each of these points, you'll probably have reached the desired cover-letter length: no more than one page in hard copy, and no more than one screen shot if you're sending your resume via e-mail. The following guidelines will help you ensure that your cover letter gets the job done:

- **Address it to a particular person by name.** Be sure to indicate how you obtained that person's contact information. If you were referred by someone who already works at the company, mention that person's name early on; when a recruiter scans a cover letter or e-mail, he's more likely to take the time to review your credentials if he recognizes a colleague's name in the text.

- **Keep it brief.** Remember that the purpose of the cover letter is to set the stage for your resume, not to explain anything on it— or worse, repeat it. The longer your cover letter, the more likely the recruiter is to skim it (which effectively defeats the purpose of including more detail). This is not the forum to explain the genesis of every academic or professional decision you've made to date, nor is it the place to regurgitate your resume in clunky, densely-packed prose.

- **While we're on the topic of regurgitating,** we should point out that the cover letter isn't the place to spit content from the company's website—or, even worse, the posted job description— back at the recruiter. While we absolutely recommend that you conduct background research on the company before making contact about a job, paraphrasing information that's readily available on the company's website isn't enough to establish that your interest is sincere. On the other hand, if you've taken the time to speak with current employees or attend an on-campus information session at your college, you can—and absolutely should—describe what in particular sparked your interest.

- **Show you're a giver, not just a taker.** No matter how brief, the cover letter shouldn't be lopsided. While you should mention one or two specific things that have attracted you to the company, you should balance your approach by describing why the company should be attracted to you. Your cover letter should imply that hiring you would be a mutually beneficial decision. Don't just talk about what the company can do for you: Explain what skills and qualifications would enable you to make a positive contribution to the company.

- **Watch your tone, missy.** We know we just told you that your cover letter should describe your potential contributions to the company, but it should do so politely. Scott, who works in the publications office of a major university, recalls an interview in which the hiring manager commended him on the polite cover letter he had sent her by e-mail. "I was surprised that it had made such an impression," he explains. "But she told me I'd be shocked at how many e-mailed cover letters she received that weren't polite or respectful." While you shouldn't be shy about mentioning your achievements and qualifications, you should never assume a presumptuous or self-aggrandizing tone. There's definitely a fine line separating confident and obnoxious—if you're having trouble deciding whether you've navigated it successfully, ask a friend for an objective, third-party assessment.

- **Take the thyme two proofread.** Because hiring managers often don't read cover letters with the same scrutiny they read resumes, you may be tempted to relax a little bit when it comes to editing yours. Believe us: It's worth the few extra minutes it will take to make sure that your cover letter is error-free. Use the spell-check function, but don't rely on software alone. Spell-check is famous for letting things like misused contractions (you're versus your, it's versus its, etc.) fall through the cracks, and it certainly won't let you know if you've misspelled the name of the company or recruiter (and believe us, a missing comma or hyphen in the company or recruiter's name might just tip the scales against you). Spell-check also won't protect you against the famous "mis-merge" that has sealed many a candidate's fate (you've described how your fastidious attention to detail will make you a valuable asset to Random House—in your cover letter to Scholastic).

Sending your resume and cover letter via e-mail

In a relatively short period of time, the prevalence of e-mail has completely transformed the way job candidates communicate with prospective employers. It's easier and faster than ever to send resumes and cover letters, but ensuring that your correspondence is flawless—and that it ends up in the right hands—is no less important. The ease and informality of e-mail can (and often does) trip up job-seekers who forget that the way they communicate—even electronically—creates a first impression that will affect how hiring managers view their candidacy. Don't let this happen to you: Put the same care into e-mailed cover letters and follow-up e-mails that you would into any other type of formal correspondence. Because e-mails are transmitted almost instantaneously—and because there's no way to control how quickly or widely they're forwarded—it's virtually impossible to contain the damage the smallest error or impropriety can cause. To play it safe, complete the "To:" field last if you're communicating with a potential employer over e-mail. This way, you're covered if you accidentally click "Send" before your message is ready. Remember, there are no "do-overs" when it comes to e-mails: "Ignore last message!" and "Oops!" e-mails are ineffective and can damage your credibility.

Avoiding the recycle bin

Thanks to the havoc wreaked by both spam and computer viruses, there's no guarantee your message will reach its intended recipient. Many companies use sophisticated spam filters to guard inboxes from suspicious e-mails. Typically, these filters delete suspected spam or divert it into folders that automatically trash e-mails that go unchecked for a certain period of time. In an effort to minimize the serious threat of computer viruses, some companies restrict employees from opening e-mail attachments (including resumes) from external sources. In some cases, their servers may even delete attachments automatically as a precaution.

Overzealous spam filters and stringent external e-mail policies can definitely work against you, so it's critical that you follow the directions when responding to a job posting. If you've been instructed to e-mail your resume as an attachment, use Microsoft Word (or a comparable basic software package). Unless specifically instructed to do so, don't send it as a compressed file or as a PDF. Trust us: If the recipient can't open your file successfully the first time around, she's not going to chase you down to request another one. Make sure to include your name (at least your last name) in the name of the file (e.g., Jane_Doe_resume.doc). Many recruiters and hiring managers save all the resumes they receive for a given position in a specific folder; many also forward resumes to other colleagues or hiring personnel at their organization. A descriptive file name that includes your name ensures that your resume can be easily located and identified regardless of where it lands.

If a company has explicitly instructed applicants not to send e-mail attachments, don't do it. Not only do you run the risk that your message will end up in the recycle bin unopened, but blatantly disregarding the instructions immediately gives the recruiter a reason to eliminate you from consideration. (Trust us: He's already looking for ways to whittle down that inbox, so there's no need to tempt him with another one.) If you can't send it as an attachment, you'll need to send it in the body of your e-mail in plain-text format. It's true that plain-text resumes sent via e-mail aren't the most attractive ones out there, but what they lack in beauty they make up for in reliability. When you don't have specific instructions, sending your resume this way is the safest course of action.

If you're e-mailing your resume, the cover message that introduces it should be in plain text, too. (When you send it in HTML format, there's a slight risk the person on the receiving end won't have an e-mail program that can properly read the HTML formatting—which means they won't be able to read what you've sent. The more significant risk, though, is the spam filter: HTML messages are more likely to trip up spam filters than plain-text messages.) Here's how to double-check if you're in plain text format: if you're writing an e-mail in which you can alter the appearance of text—i.e., you can italicize, underline, or change the font—you're not in plain text format. Some e-mail providers only allow users to write in plain text; if you're still unsure and you're using Microsoft Outlook, click on "format" in your new message window and be sure that "plain text" is the selected format.

Don't forget about the "Subject" field when sending your application materials. If you're sending your resume in response to an online job posting, you'll often be told exactly what to include in this field. If left to your own devices, remember this: The less your e-mail looks like a spam message, the less likely it will be diverted. With this in mind, never leave this field blank. Instead, include a subject line that is short and descriptive and immediately identifies you as an applicant. If you can, include the job title or requisition number in the subject line (remember that the recruiter receiving your message may be responsible for filling multiple positions). Otherwise, include only your name and the position applied for (e.g., "Zach Glass, Case Manager"). Leave punctuation marks—especially exclamation marks—out of the subject line, and don't use all capital letters in an attempt to grab the recipient's attention.

Finally, you should avoid using words in the subject line—or even in your cover message—that will convince the company's spam-filter technology that your resume belongs in the trash bin, along with e-mails promising enlarged body parts or cheap prescription drugs. You probably have a pretty good idea of what key words we have in mind (if you need a refresher course, take a break from reading this and log in to one of your web-based e-mail accounts). You're unlikely to use most of them in your cover letter or resume (if you need to, you've probably picked up the wrong guide). Still, remember that words like "free," "hard," "offer," "increase," etc. are often used by spammers, so keep them out of your correspondence if you can. If your e-mail address has several numbers to the left of the @ symbol, consider changing it: The numbers could represent something as innocuous as your birthday, anniversary, or the year you graduated from college, but, to a spam filter, they look like the type of tracking code that many spammers use.

As an added safety measure, you may want to ask any personal contact you have within the organization to forward your resume to the appropriate contact. Not only does this increase the odds you'll defeat the spam filter, but internal referrals typically boost your overall credibility as a candidate. If you don't have an internal point person who can forward your resume on your behalf, be sure to run every version of it through a few different spam filters before sending it off; send it to a few friends and family members—and include your own e-mail address or addresses in the CC field—to figure out whether it's going through. This might sound like a lot of trouble, and it is. There is an upside, though, to the omnivorous spam filter: You have a perfectly legitimate reason to follow up with the company and make sure your application materials were received.

"Power Jargon": Learning to talk the talk

Whenever you enter a new industry or company, you'll quickly find that each one has its own unique vernacular you must understand—and eventually adopt. Paying attention to the language insiders use to describe their industry and their specific roles should be part of your job-search preparation. If used subtly and judiciously, incorporating "power jargon" into your resume, cover letter, and interview can help influence the decision-maker in your favor; if you speak someone's language, they'll probably—perhaps subconsciously—consider you one of their own.

Interestingly, the purpose of power jargon is slightly different depending on the stage of the job-search process you're in when you use it. In the context of a resume, the purpose of industry jargon is getting your resume noticed—either by the human being who has the unenviable task of screening through thousands of resumes and deciding which ones make the first cut, or by the non-human resume scanner whose job it is to do basically the same thing by identifying and counting specific key words in resumes. In the context of a cover letter or an interview, the purpose is less to get noticed than, ironically enough, to blend in. And once you arrive for your first day of work, the purpose of power jargon is knowing what the heck you're supposed to be doing.

To illustrate the importance of understanding jargon before your first day on the job, consider the experience endured by Monica—now a 30-year old associate editor—on her first day of freelance proofreading at a food and wine magazine. "I had no idea that in the magazine biz, the term 'hot' means that something is extremely urgent," she says. "So someone came up to my desk and asked me if I'd finished proofreading a particular story. When I said that I hadn't, she politely reminded me that it was 'pretty hot.' Not knowing what she meant—that I needed to get it done ASAP—I thought to myself, 'What's she making such a big deal about? The story's about *coleslaw* for God's sake—what's so trendy about that?'" This is why it's important to do your homework early on in the process—preferably before you make contact with a company about a job.

Understanding the importance of key words, however, doesn't give you license to use them recklessly. Power jargon can be, and often is, overused in resumes, obscuring the very credentials the candidate was hoping to highlight in the first place. And if you use jargon without understanding what it means, you may use it in the wrong context and sound uninformed when you intended to sound savvy. Our advice for avoiding potential power-jargon pitfalls? Have someone who's in the know take a look at your resume and cover letter to alert you to any egregious misuses of industry or company terminology. In the interview, play it safe—your goal is to use power jargon to blend in, not stand out. Overusing jargon (or using it in a forced, contrived way) won't win you any points, especially with hiring managers who've logged countless hours interviewing candidates. Not only will experienced interviewers see right through your attempt to sound like an expert, but they'll often go to great lengths to put you back in your place. "That happened to me once," says Thomas, an assistant editor for an academic journal. "I was interviewing for my first editorial job, and I mentioned that I was familiar with the *Chicago Manual of Style*. My interviewer said, 'Oh really? Which edition do you normally use?' I was completely stumped. I had no idea which edition it was—I had to look at my copy when I got home (it was 11, incidentally). Even though I had to admit that I didn't know, I got the job anyway. After a few months in the office, I eventually found out that none of the copyeditors knew exactly which version they were using, either. The interviewer had just been doing that to rattle my cage, I guess, and figure out whether I was bluffing."

Even though this story has a happy ending, it still offers a valuable lesson: Don't use terminology you don't understand, and if you are asked a question you don't know the answer to, just say that you don't know. If your interviewer calls your bluff, you've not only lost face, but you've potentially lost a job. It's not worth the risk.

What's the magic word?

In the 1991 remake of the film *Father of the Bride*, Steve Martin's character, George, snoops through the home of his future son-in-law's parents, only to be confronted by a pair of growling, snarling Rottweilers who seem poised to eat him alive. He knows there's a one-word command that will make them go away, but he can't quite remember what it is—only that it begins with "re." He tries a few: "Relent. Re-Recoil . . . Reverse," but they only make the dogs angrier. (The word he was looking for was release). As George found out with the attack dogs, using correct keywords is important. For him, it meant he wouldn't get devoured; for you, it means your resume won't get discarded because you appear not to have experience relevant to a particular job.

Keywords are almost always nouns or short phrases. They name the characteristics, skills, tools, training, and experience of a successful candidate for a particular job. As you may already know, many organizations use resume scanning software to identify qualified candidates among a sea of online applications; by scanning resumes for certain words and phrases, scanning software is intended to streamline the resume review process for time-starved recruiters, who may receive literally thousands of applications for a single job posting. If your target company uses this type of software as a preliminary screening tool, you'll want to be sure your resume includes the relevant key words. The number of "hits" (times the key words appear in any given resume) will often determine which resumes are actually read by a human being.

How do you know which keywords to include? Well, writing a resume in a scanner-friendly way is definitely more an art than a science—and it requires common sense, good judgment, and a little bit of research. Before you submit a resume online, visit the company's website and pay attention to the language used to describe what the company does, what it's looking for in potential employees, and the job requirements it lists for specific positions; the job description and the list of qualifications associated with the position are also great resources when tailoring and tweaking the version of the resume you use.

As is the case with any job-search advice we provide in this guide, it's best to temper your enthusiasm for power jargon with a healthy dose of good judgment. Particularly if you're applying for a position through an on-campus recruiting process or through an internal referral that forwards your correspondence directly to the hiring manager, your resume may be initially reviewed by a human being—not a scanner.

A rose by any other name . . . might be something else entirely

To make matters even more complicated, there are a couple of different levels of jargon you'll need to weed through to use it effectively. There's both industry jargon and company-specific jargon. At the industry level, seemingly identical processes or functions will be described differently depending on the industry in question. For example, book publishing uses different terminology than magazine publishing, and academic and financial publishing each use a different lexicon entirely. If you looked at a "blueline" (the last version of a publication editors have a chance to review before it goes to print) at a magazine publisher, you'd be looking at the "blues," but if you looked at one at an investment bank, you'd probably be looking at a "red." And if you say "blackline" instead of "blueline" because you worked at a law firm one summer and you're still in the habit of saying it, you're going to look pretty silly in your magazine-publishing interview.

At the organizational level, power jargon might include something as seemingly insignificant as the use of acronyms and abbreviations (and it seems the larger the organization, the more acronyms there are to remember). The names of groups, functions, even job titles may be abbreviated so widely within an organization that you'll stand out if you don't use them when you communicate with your potential employer.

Is your head spinning yet? Don't worry. When it comes to power jargon, there are plenty of ways to pick it up so you're at least conversant by the time you apply for a job. When you speak with industry insiders in the context of networking or conducting informational interviews, pay attention to the terminology they use to describe what they do and where they work. (In fact, the ability to pick up on power jargon is one of the many good reasons you should be focused on listening rather than talking when it comes to informational interviews). If your industry insider uses a term you're not familiar with, don't just nod as though you are—ask what it means! Remember, you're not being evaluated during your informational interviews or networking conversations; you're there to learn and ask questions. If stopping to ask what something means during one of these conversations means you actually know what it means when it comes up later in a job interview, then asking was a worthwhile investment. In addition to one-on-one conversations with insiders, you can pick up power jargon by paying attention to the lingo used in trade publications, on industry-specific websites, and in job listings for similar positions at other companies in the industry.

When it comes time to interview with a specific company, your understanding of that organization's terminology is just as important as your fluency in industry lingo. Before you walk out the door to meet with your prospective employer, you should understand the jargon the company uses in the following contexts:

- **Its name**—Know when a company goes by its initials and when it's abbreviated some other way when its own employees refer to it. We'll illustrate our point using an example from the financial services world: If you were working on Wall Street, you would never call Goldman Sachs or Merrill Lynch "GS" or "ML." If you were an employee—or an industry insider—you'd refer to them as "Goldman" and "Merrill," respectively. However, you would refer to Credit Suisse First Boston as "CSFB."

- **Its job titles**—If everyone at a particular firm always says "RA" instead of "Research Associate," it will ever so subtly work in your favor if you refer to the job that way, too (even though it still might mean "Resident Advisor" to you). The same goes for support roles—sometimes, assistants are just that: assistants. At other organizations, they're called "admins" or "PAs" If you're applying for one of those jobs, know what you'll be called (how else will you know when someone's talking to you?)

- **Its organizational structure and hierarchy**—It sounds almost silly, but pay attention to how employees and insiders refer to the specific department with which you're interviewing. Is the custom publishing department referred to as "custom pub?" Is the book publishing division referred to as "BPD" or simply "books"? Even more importantly, how are roles and job titles described? At some companies, "analyst" is a more senior role than "associate," for example, while at others, the exact opposite is true. Know which level and job title would apply to you; if you don't, your ignorance might be misinterpreted as an inflated ego.

INTERVIEWING

If the primary purpose of a great resume is to get an interview (which it is), then it seems as though the point of the interview would be to land the job. But, in reality, that's only half right. One of your goals during the interview process is to tell a compelling story—to present your life (educational, extracurricular, and otherwise) as an entirely logical series of decisions in which this particular job is the obvious next step. The other (equally, if not more important) objective is to learn as much as possible about the position you're applying for, the culture of the organization you're interviewing with, and the extent to which the job fits with your personal and professional goals.

Because you're working hard to present yourself in the best possible light, it's easy to forget that interviews aren't entirely unilateral. When you're being grilled about your resume, your motivations, and your choices, it will undoubtedly seem as though your prospective employer is the one calling the shots. But the interview is also a chance for you to learn about the organization and the position for which you're applying. It's the best opportunity you have, prior to your first day on the job, to fill in any gaps between the pieces of info you gleaned through networking and informational interviews. It's your chance to ask questions, to get a sense of whether or not the organization's culture is one in which you'll fit, and to figure out whether the specific position is one in which you'll be challenged and rewarded for your efforts.

In this section, we'll give you suggestions for making the most out of your interviews. We'll tell you what interviewers will be looking for during your conversations, and we'll describe the types of interview questions they're most likely to ask as they evaluate you. We'll also tell to you how to prepare for interviews—how to anticipate the topics (and questions) you're most likely to confront and how to craft compelling responses. Along the way, we'll give you practical advice—guidance on everything from arriving on time to wearing the right shoes—so you can truly put your best foot forward.

What are interviewers looking for?

Earlier in this section, we listed the personal characteristics organizations value most in potential employees. As we said earlier, the list is intended to be a starting point for your interview preparation; it stands to reason that the relative importance assigned to each of these attributes will vary significantly depending on the industry, the company, and the specific job for which you're interviewing. You may even find, when you interview with multiple people for a single position, that each interviewer emphasizes slightly different things. Across the board, however, the people who interview you are basically trying to answer the following three questions as they evaluate your candidacy:

- Are you capable of doing the work?
- Do you really want to do the work?
- Would they enjoy working with you?

As a general rule, the less directly applicable your past experience is to the job you're hoping to get, the more emphasis your interviewer is likely to place on the first question. If you've more or less proven your ability to do the work through similar professional, academic, or extracurricular activities, your interviewer is more likely to probe the second two.

Recruiters will be on the lookout for certain intangible qualities throughout the entire interview, too: qualities like confidence, conviction, enthusiasm, poise, presence, and sincerity. For example, do your eyes light up when you talk about your educational background, your professional experience, or (most importantly) the role for which you are interviewing? Do your answers sound heartfelt and impassioned, or is it obvious you've rehearsed them so many times you could recite them in your sleep? Are you comfortable and self-assured talking about your background and accomplishments, or does self-confidence quickly disintegrate into self-consciousness as soon as you step into the interview room? Interviewers don't necessarily measure these intangibles through specific questions, but rather through their well-honed intuition.

Preparing for your interview

Whether you realize it or not, you can predict the vast majority of the questions you will hear during an interview—provided, of course, you've done your homework on the industry, the organization, and the position you've got your eye on. Some questions (e.g., "Why are you interested in this job?") arise so frequently in one form or another you'd be foolish not to take the time to outline your responses well in advance. Though no amount of preparation will enable you to predict the questions verbatim, you can predict the themes the interview is likely to cover. Nine times out of ten, you're going to be asked to discuss the following:

- Why you are interested in this type of work, and why you want to work with this organization specifically
- How your academic, extracurricular, and/or professional background relates to the job for which you're applying
- The extent to which you've developed realistic expectations about the job you're considering, and whether or not you know enough about the company to make an informed decision about joining it
- Whether certain gaps or inconsistencies on your resume are likely to turn into vulnerabilities on the job

Know Your Achilles Heel

So how do you know which part of your application is likely to be perceived as a gap or inconsistency? It really depends on the nature and level of the job for which you're applying; hopefully, your informational interviews will have shed some light on the gaps that might exist between the ideal set of credentials and your own (if not, the job posting and/or description will certainly provide some clues). But across industries and jobs, there are a few common red flags that might raise questions about your ability and desire to do the work. If any of these apply to you, give some thought to how you might address them in your interview.

- **Disparity between professional/academic background and desired job**

  This is the most obvious—and perhaps the most prevalent—of all the instant red flags. If the position for which you're applying bears little or no resemblance to the work you've done in the past—or to the work you're currently doing—then your prospective employer will probably ask a few questions. They'll go something like this: If you really want to do this type of work and are so well suited to do it, then why haven't you done it already? Or, at the very least, why haven't you studied it? To be completely honest, these are perfectly legitimate questions.

- **Time gaps**

  Keep in mind that the person reviewing your resume might check to see if you've taken off between school years or jobs. Time off is not necessarily a bad thing. Recruiters know that while you're building a career, life can pull you in other directions: people start families, spouses get relocated, family members get sick, and professionals take time off to consider a career change or simply recharge their batteries. Still, you need to be prepared to explain any lapses. You needn't feel compelled to offer a lot of personal detail, but you should be honest, direct, and prepared if questions about time gaps arise. In your response, focus on what you accomplished during that time—not the ground you lost by taking a break.

- **Inconsistent or poor academic performance**

  This includes lower-than-average GPA, test scores, or grades in specific classes. If your accomplishments appear strong in one area but weak in another, you should expect questions about the disparity. The interviewer will want to know the reason behind any low grades (did you work part-time during school?) or a discrepancy between your GPA and standardized-test scores. Be prepared to explain any circumstances that affected your performance, but avoid undue personal detail.

- **Job- (or major-) "hopping"**

  If your resume includes seemingly disparate work experiences, or if you've been at several companies in just a few years, you risk being perceived as a job-hopper. This is unlikely to be much of an issue if you're still in school, but keep in mind that switching majors multiple times might be viewed with comparable skepticism. Frequent course changes (of either the professional or academic variety) sometimes give the impression that a person has difficulty sticking with a situation, working through problems, or committing to a job. If you're applying for a job when you've only been at your current one for a short period of time, prospective employers might wonder if you're likely to jump ship if they hire you, too. If your jobs to date have been short-term by nature (because they've been summer jobs or internships), make sure you've stated that clearly somewhere on your application.

- **Geographic concerns**

  If you've spent most of your academic and professional life in one place, you may be questioned about your interest in a job that's somewhere else. Not only will a company probably question whether you're serious about relocating if you're offered the job, but they have practical and logistical issues to consider when it comes to interviewing you in person. A firm that must fly you out for an interview will probably quiz you over the phone to gauge your level of commitment before extending an invitation. Firms also know there's a good chance you may decide not to relocate even if you get the offer—and if you do, it'll probably take some time before you can physically move yourself to your new city and get settled in. All in all, an out-of-town candidate is generally considered a riskier—and potentially costlier—prospect than an applicant close to home.

You'll probably find that thinking of your interview as a conversation intended to address these themes is more effective than thinking of it as a series of questions for which scripted and rehearsed answers are expected. You'll be able to adapt quickly to different interviewing styles and formats, and you won't be thrown off when asked a question you didn't expect.

In the following pages, we'll give you a number of sample questions that tend to arise across industries and companies. Don't let the number of questions overwhelm you—you're not expected to prepare a scripted answer to every possible question or to memorize the list of interview do's and don'ts. In fact, if you take away only one thing from the following pages, it should be this: *Knowing the job for which you are applying—and knowing exactly how your experiences and achievements relate to that position—is the single most important thing you can do to prepare for job interviews.*

Types of interview questions

Even though most interviewers will be trying to gather the same kind of information, the format of the questions will vary significantly depending on the job, the interviewing philosophy of the organization, and the person sitting across the desk from you. We've outlined the three most common types of interview questions below.

- **Resume-based questions**

  No surprises here: Resume-based questions focus on the one-page life summary that landed you the interview. It goes without saying, but we'll say it anyway: You must know your resume inside and out, and you should be ready to talk intelligently and confidently about anything and everything on it. Arrive at your interview with two or three talking points about each line item on your resume. If there's something particularly unusual on it (e.g., you wrote a novel while you were an undergraduate student, you speak seven languages), you can be sure it will come up again and again. Consider the points you'd most like to convey, and make sure you know them cold. If you're asked to summarize your resume, stick to just that: a summary. Use your response as an opportunity to connect the dots (especially if the story wouldn't be obvious to someone reviewing your resume for the first time), not as an invitation to cram in all of the information you couldn't fit onto one page.

- **Behavioral questions**

  Other questions require you to cite experiences—professional, academic, and personal—in which you've actively demonstrated specific attributes. This approach is called behavioral interviewing, and it's based on the premise that patterns of past behavior most accurately predict future performance. Advocates of behavioral interviewing report that the technique enables interviewers to most accurately assess whether a candidate possesses the requisite skills and personality for on-the-job success. The logic is appealing: Anyone can rattle off a list of attributes commonly sought by employers in their field, but successful candidates can readily substantiate these claims with examples of competency in a given area. A behavioral prompt would be: "Tell me about a time that you took on a responsibility that perhaps wasn't part of your official job description." In response, you could choose to point out that at your previous job you designed a comprehensive training program for new employees, organized guest speakers, and gathered feedback when the program was over to gauge how effective its participants thought it was. Or you might choose to highlight your involvement in a freshman-year economics study group, in which you took up the flag for an ailing team member and wrote a presentation that technically fell outside the scope of your assigned duties. Either example works, as long as it shows that you've taken initiative in the past.

With this in mind, don't simply compartmentalize your achievements into "work experiences," "educational background," "extracurricular activities," and "personal interests" as you prepare for interviews. Instead, think about each of your endeavors in terms of the skills, abilities, and attributes it enables you to demonstrate. For example, which ones helped you develop a strong team-player mentality? How about exceptional leadership skills? Which ones demonstrate your quantitative aptitude and your facility with numbers? Which ones show that you can learn from your mistakes? We've said it before, but we'll say it again: You should know your resume inside and out, and have an arsenal of experiences ready that can prove you're a rock star in any number of areas.

- **Case interview questions**

  For years, management consulting firms have used case interview questions as part of their recruiting processes. Designed to gauge candidates' problem-solving skills and general business acumen, these questions are a more highly evolved version of the word problems you were introduced to in third-grade math class. But even if you're not interviewing for jobs in management consulting, you're not necessarily off the hook where these types of questions are concerned. For better or worse, companies in many industries serve up their own version of the case interview question, hoping to approximate the demands of the job to whatever extent possible in an interview setting. If it's a research job you're interviewing for, you may be asked to walk your interviewer through a hypothetical research project, explaining the steps you would take to complete the assigned task. If the position requires a great deal of public speaking, you shouldn't be caught off guard if you're asked to make an impromptu presentation on a given topic. Not surprisingly, writing, editing, and proofreading tests are often administered as part of the interview process for publishing jobs. Part of your research process should involve figuring out what those tests are likely to be.

Tips for winning interviews

In the following pages, we provide hypothetical interview questions covering a range of topics and themes. There are a few interview best practices, however, that transcend boundaries of interview question category, context, and scope. Keep the following guidelines in mind regardless of the particular questions interviewers lob your way.

- **Honesty is the best policy.**

  This little nugget is definitely one to remember during interviews. As your mother probably told you shortly after you learned to speak: When you tell one lie, you have to tell five more lies to cover up the first one. For each of those lies, you have to tell five more, and so on. Mom was right about this one; interviews are stressful enough when you're telling the truth, so don't make it harder on yourself by coloring the edges of your resume with fictional experiences, skills, or interests. The truth almost always prevails in the end, so don't tempt fate by bending it—even a little.

- **Be honest, but emphasize the positive.**

  Being honest about your screw-ups and weaknesses doesn't mean that you can't spin them in a positive direction. If you're asked about a perceived weakness or mistake, you can be candid while emphasizing what you've learned from each experience. You can use the infamous "what's your biggest weakness?" question, for example, to prove that you're constantly working to overcome your Achilles heel (or, better yet, you could provide a specific example of an instance in which you overcame it).

- **Remember the three C's.**

  No matter how much you've prepared for your interviews, make sure your responses are conversational, casual, and concise. While we can't overemphasize the importance of researching the industry, organization, and position before you arrive—and anticipating the interview questions you're most likely to confront—you shouldn't give the impression you're reading your interview responses off of cue cards. In fact, if you sound too rehearsed your interviewer may suspect you've got something to hide. Remember: "Canned" is not one of the three C's.

- **Answer the question you've been asked.**

  We know it sounds obvious, but it's easier said than done (particularly if you're a rambler). If you're immersed in a full-time job search, chances are you'll have more interviews than you'd care to remember. Some candidates get so accustomed to fielding certain questions that they become robotic: They hear a few key words, and they're off on their unintentionally well-rehearsed pitch. Interviews will indeed begin to sound the same, but don't forget to listen to the question!

- **Keep it short and sweet.**

  On a related note, keep it brief. If you ramble, you're considerably more likely to lose your way—and more likely to exhaust your interviewer in the process! Remember, it's easier for an interviewer to ask a follow-up question than it is for her to rein you back in after you've gone off on a tangent.

- **Pay attention to your interviewer's style.**

  A one-size-fits-all approach doesn't work especially well during the interview process; even within the same company, interviewers adopt substantially different styles to figure out whether you're a good candidate for the job. Some are more intense, while others treat the interview as a more relaxed, get-to-know-you session. The more promptly you can pick up on your interviewer's particular style, the better off you'll be, so pay attention.

- **Don't be critical of previous employers or colleagues.**

  In fact, you should be wary of sounding even the slightest bit sour on your previous work experiences. Not only would doing so suggest that you're generally negative and cynical, but if you use the interview as an opportunity to vent about a previous employer, your interviewer will wonder how you'll talk about his company when given the opportunity.

- **Keep track of the questions you're asked.**

  If a question comes up in one interview, it's quite likely it will come up in another. Particularly if you feel you haven't answered a question effectively, take a minute or two after the interview to jot down the question and outline what you would say if given a second chance. You'll be glad you did when you hear the same question again in subsequent rounds.

- **Keep your audience in mind.**

  This is an interview, not a confessional. Don't delve into anything you wouldn't (or at least shouldn't) discuss on a first date: your political views, religious beliefs, or anything else known to spark controversy. Along these lines, remember to temper your honesty with a healthy dose of good judgment when addressing your strengths and weaknesses—try to steer clear of anything so incompatible with the job description it'll make your interviewer head for the hills.

- **Give off a positive vibe.**

    We know interviews are inherently stressful, but interviewers simply won't rally behind a candidate who seems uncontrollably nervous or just plain miserable. Keep reminding yourself that interviews are fun—when else do you have the opportunity do talk about yourself for 30 minutes straight?

Popular interview questions

As we said earlier in the chapter, it helps to remember that your interview is nothing more than a conversation with a specific purpose: Your interviewer is trying to figure out whether you can do the work, whether you want to do the work, and whether your prospective colleagues would enjoy working with you. In addition, they may ask questions designed to gauge your honesty, integrity, and ability to learn from your mistakes. And they may throw in a few miscellaneous questions to lighten the mood.

Interviewers can ask any number of specific questions in order to decide whether you're a compelling candidate: The sample questions we provide are not meant to be an exhaustive list, but they'll give you a head start in your pre-interview research process. We've grouped the questions according to the qualities they're usually used to gauge. (Talking to insiders in advance of your interviews will help you figure out which specific areas your interview is likely to emphasize.) You'll have a huge leg up on other candidates if you've taken the time to research and prepare answers to the most frequently asked questions.

Aptitude questions (Can you do the work?)

Aside from allowing interviewers to gain insight into your initiative, motivation to succeed, and your work ethic in general, questions in this category seek to answer the question, "Can you do the work?" As we mentioned earlier in the chapter, the relevance of your past work experience and academic studies typically is inversely related to the emphasis your interviewer will place on answering these questions. In other words, the less directly applicable your past experience is to the job in question, the harder you'll have to work to prove you can excel at it.

Unless you're applying for a job that's directly related to your undergraduate studies (and many first-time job candidates with liberal arts degrees are not), you should be prepared to convince every prospective employer that your achievements outside of the industry in question will translate to success within it. As we've said before, the interview is your golden opportunity to explain perceived gaps or inconsistencies in your resume so they're viewed in a different (and hopefully more favorable) light.

If your GPA is on the low side, for example, you should be prepared to talk about it (and even if your GPA is stellar, you should be ready to talk about any rogue C's or the absence of course work related to the job you'll be doing). If you don't have extensive work experience, be prepared to explain how other pursuits—extracurricular activities, sports, or independent research projects, for example—might give you an edge on the job. Whatever the chink in your professional armor, it's important to consider it in advance of your interview, rather than weeding your way through it once you've gotten there.

Questions designed to gauge your ability to do the job include the following:

- Tell me about a time when you worked on a highly quantitative or analytical project. Describe the context, the project, and the outcome.

- What is the greatest challenge you've faced to date? How did you overcome it?

- What motivates you?

- Describe a time when you achieved a goal that required significant personal sacrifice. How did you stay motivated to achieve the goal, despite the hardships that it involved?

- What classes did you find the most difficult in college? Why do you think that's the case?

- Describe any classes you've taken in college that were highly quantitative or analytical in nature? How did you do in those classes? Are you comfortable working with numbers?

- Give me an example of a project (either academic or work-related) that required significant attention to detail. Do you consider yourself a detail-oriented person?

Because your interviewers are assessing your fundamental ability to do the work, questions in this category tend to be the most confrontational. Don't be caught off guard by interviewers who ask you to explain why you chose to study Renaissance language and literature or why you spent a summer lounging in the Caribbean. There's nothing inherently wrong with either of those choices, but be sure you're prepared to convince your interviewer that they're not inconsistent with your interest in the job. Remember, no one expects all of your experiences to be directly related to the position; that said, recruiters want to be sure you're really interested in the work and not just dabbling.

Along similar lines, you should be prepared to discuss your choice of major, particularly if you're applying for a job unrelated to your degree. If you sense your interviewer is skeptical about the relevance of your academic background, your response should be respectful, but not apologetic. Stand by your academic and professional decisions, and share your decision-making process with your interviewer. Don't get carried away, though: Many liberal arts undergraduates fall into the trap of saying things like, "The skills required of [whatever the job in question is] aren't that hard to learn. It's not rocket science, and I'll obviously just learn it on the job." Keep in mind that your interviewer may not have been a liberal arts major, and therefore might not agree with your assessment. So rather than dismissing the intellectual rigor required of other disciplines, emphasize that you're eager to learn things you didn't necessarily study during your undergraduate years.

Suitability/commitment questions (Do you *want* to do the work?)

Whereas the aptitude questions described in the previous section are designed to establish that you can do the work, commitment questions are intended to figure out whether you genuinely want to do the work. First and foremost, your interviewer is trying to figure out how serious you are about the job itself, and whether the company's particular culture is one in which you'll fit—and eventually thrive. By far, the most commonly asked commitment question is, "Why do you want to do this job?" followed closely by, "Why do you want to do this job at this specific organization?" Here are a few other favorites in this category.

- Walk me through your resume and tell me how you decided to pursue this job/career track.

- What are you looking for in your next job? If you could create any position for yourself, what would it look like? What do you look for in a potential employer?

- Explain your role in such-and-such job listed on your resume. What did you learn from that experience that would be relevant to you here?

- What other industries/companies/positions are you considering? Are you actively interviewing elsewhere? Are you presently considering offers at any other organizations? If you are considering multiple offers, how will you make your decision?

- Why are you leaving your current job?

- Why should we hire you? Why do you think you'd be good at this?

- What do you think you would like most/least about this job?

- Where do you see yourself in five years?

- Walk me through what you think a typical day at the office would be like if you were hired for this position.

Your ability to provide solid, thoughtful answers to these questions—responses firmly grounded in realistic job expectations—will definitely advance your candidacy. While no one expects you to have known your professional destiny since age six, or to have made every significant decision over the last two decades with this job—or any job—in your sights, you will be expected to describe your professional and personal endeavors as a rational sequence in which this position at this company is the next logical step. You should be able to articulate exactly what you hope to gain—both personally and professionally—from the experience and to demonstrate your preparedness for its challenges and demands. Keep in mind that the delivery of your message is important here: you have to believe your own story, or no one else will.

There are multiple "right" answers to the question of why you're interested in a specific job, there are universally bad answers, too. Don't even think about suggesting that you consider it a stepping-stone to something else, that you stumbled across it, that you're ready to take just about anything because you've been out of work for so long, or that you generally think the industry is pretty cool. If you're interviewing for positions that represent a broad spectrum of functions and industries, you aren't obligated to tell your interviewer.

If, on the other hand, the job is one you're really excited about, questions like these give you an opportunity to make that clear. Perceived commitment to (and enthusiasm for) a specific company—not just the industry in general—always influences the choice between two (or more) otherwise comparable candidates. Companies love to be loved, and with good reason: They know that if you've done your homework and genuinely want the job, you're more likely to thrive at the organization and less likely to turn around and leave once you get there. You not only present yourself as a low-risk hire, you also reaffirm your interviewer's choice of company and career (and stoking your interviewer's ego is never a bad thing).

To gauge whether you're not only enthusiastic but committed, interviewers will often ask you to describe how you see your career evolving in the long term. Give some serious thought to how you'll attack questions about what you see yourself doing one, five, or ten years from now. While no one expects you to know for certain what you'll be doing several years into the future (the earlier you are in your career, the less sure people expect you to be), you should at least be able to present a credible scenario that includes the job in question. Taking the time to consider where you'd like to be down the road isn't just interview preparation—it's an opportunity for self exploration, too. If you find you're trying a little too hard to convince your interviewer that this is a job you want—or you find it necessary to convince yourself of it—then it's probably time to reassess whether your heart is in it.

Team-working/Attitude questions (Do we want to work with you?)

Questions in this category are designed to assess your interpersonal skills, and—as the name suggests—your ability to work as part of a team. Through questions like these, your interviewer is trying to figure out whether she would enjoy working with you, and whether your prospective colleagues, managers, and team members are likely to enjoy working with you. The questions themselves focus on your ability to build and maintain relationships, inspire confidence among clients and colleagues, and resolve interpersonal conflict (not to mention your ability to avoid conflict in the first place). Not surprisingly, these questions reveal an emphasis on teamwork—you might be expected to describe your firsthand experience on teams, and you'll often be asked to discuss the characteristics of effective and ineffective work groups. In addition, interviewers may ask you about your interests and achievements to figure out what makes you tick and what makes you an interesting person to get to know. Here are a few common questions in this category.

- What role do you typically assume when you work in a team setting? Describe the last time you worked on a team and the role you assumed.

- Tell me about a situation in which you've had to work with someone that you didn't particularly like or get along with. How did you overcome personal differences to achieve your goal?

- Have you ever worked on a team that wasn't successful meeting its goals? What do you think went wrong?

- Describe an occasion when you persuaded someone to do something they didn't want to do.

- How would you characterize your leadership/management style?

- What achievement are you most proud of?

- What are you passionate about?

Regardless of the specific questions you encounter in your interview, the way in which you respond to the questions is often just as important as the answers themselves. When interviewers assess a candidate's interpersonal effectiveness, the intangibles we mentioned earlier in the chapter (e.g., confidence, enthusiasm, poise, polish) are especially critical. Of course, you should be ready to provide solid examples that establish your comfort and efficacy in a team-based work environment, but your ability to build a rapport with your interviewer will solidify your case. Recruiters will look for signs you're self-assured, professional, and generally pleasant to work with.

A word about teamwork

There are definitely jobs out there that don't require a lot of human interaction, but they are far outnumbered by positions that do. If the job you're considering requires a substantial amount of teamwork, you'll want to draw your interviewer's attention to the team-oriented pursuits on your resume. Keep in mind, though, that it may not be immediately obvious to your interviewer which activities depended on your ability to interact effectively with people. For example, you may feel your experience as a staff writer for the student newspaper is highly relevant because you managed multiple deadlines for a high-maintenance editor and leveraged relationships with key contacts to obtain hard-to-find information, but "staff writer" may not scream "team player" to your interviewer. Be on the lookout for opportunities to highlight relevant experiences, and don't expect your interviewer to read between the lines. At the same time, don't overstate your team contributions or pretend you've never met anyone you didn't get along with famously—your interviewer will conclude that you're not credible.

Questions on honesty and integrity

Interviewers look for more than just team-working ability and charisma when trying to decide whether you'll fit in. They place a great deal of emphasis on your honesty and integrity, too (as the list of attributes most commonly sought by employers at the beginning of this chapter attests). They'll sometimes ask questions regarding your mistakes and failures to determine whether you're honest and accountable when you screw up (and we all screw up from time to time, so knowing when to admit it—and knowing how to mitigate the damage—is key). Questions like these also examine your ability to learn from past experiences and continuously improve your performance—a skill that's crucial for professional success whether you're part of a team or not. Popular honesty and integrity questions include the following:

- Tell me about a time you made a mistake. How did you handle it?
- Tell me about your biggest failure.
- What is your biggest weakness?
- Describe an ethical dilemma you faced in the past. How did you resolve it?

The way in which you answer these prompts will say a lot, as questions regarding mistakes and failures require diplomacy and tact—two qualities employers value highly. Of course, you should be honest when you answer questions such as these. We all want to present the best possible image of ourselves during job interviews, so it stands to reason that none of us particularly enjoys talking about our faults. Still, if you're asked about your past mistakes or biggest weakness, you have a unique opportunity to distinguish yourself. If you can demonstrate your maturity, humility, and sense of humor about your foibles, your likeability (and credibility) will skyrocket.

Miscellaneous questions

In an ideal world, all organizations would approach their recruiting processes with the same level of thoughtfulness and sophistication we're advising you to bring to your interviews. Sadly, this isn't the case. In fact, we'd be remiss if we didn't point out that some interview questions will have little or no relevance to the job. At best, these questions are intended to put you at ease, to give you a breather in the midst of an otherwise stressful interview, and simply to allow an interviewer to get to know you a little better. At worst, they can reveal your interviewer's inexperience in a recruiting role. Only you will be able to guess which one applies to your interview. Elisabeth, now an alumni-relations officer at a West Coast business school, was asked the following question when she interviewed for an administrative position on campus: "If you were stranded on a desert island and could bring three CDs, subscribe to three periodicals, and order three television channels, which would you choose and why?"

Make no mistake about it: There's very little an interviewer stands to learn about your ability to do the job by asking you a question like that. "I got the impression that she had never interviewed anyone for a job before, and she got a kick out of being on the other side of the desk or something," Elisabeth told us. You may encounter novice interviewers who enjoy throwing curve balls your way. If you do, be a good sport and humor them—at the very least, the questions might spark some interesting conversation at a future cocktail party.

When it's your turn to ask questions

Toward the end of the conversation, your interviewer will probably ask if you have any questions for her. There are a few different schools of thought on how candidates should approach this part of the interview: Some insiders insist that you should always ask a question when offered the opportunity, and that your question should prove to your interviewer how much research you've done on the industry and the specific firm.

Although this advice is well intentioned, it can easily backfire (especially if you come across as a know-it-all trying to challenge your interviewer). If you approach the interview as a learning experience, then it follows that you should stick to those questions you'd genuinely like answered. Make the most of the opportunity to ask the questions that require insider insight. If you really want to know why your interviewers chose to work at the company you're interviewing with, ask away. You're not likely to lose points for asking questions that aren't insightful or penetrating enough, provided your questions don't display blatant ignorance regarding the industry, the company, or the specific position. The list of informational interview questions in the previous chapter includes topics that would be appropriate to explore if you have the opportunity. The following list may also prove helpful:

- I wondered if you could describe your own career path to me. How did you arrive at this organization, and how did you end up in your current role/department?
- What do you think it takes for someone to be good at this job, and what do you think it takes for someone to really enjoy it?
- What are your three most important strategic objectives for this year?
- I want to be sure I have a clear understanding of how this role fits into the organization as a whole. How would the specific responsibilities of this position fit into the bigger picture of what your department does? How does your department fit into the larger organization?
- Can you tell me how job performance is evaluated with regards to this position? How do you assess whether someone is on track and meeting expectations? Do you have a formal review process? Could you describe it to me?
- Is this a new position or would I be replacing someone?
- What is a typical career progression for someone in this particular role?
- Can you outline the organizational structure in this department? Division?
- What are your company's key competitive concerns?
- How would you describe your firm's culture? What do you think is different/better about working here than anywhere else? What things do you think the company's leadership team takes particular pride in?
- Are there a lot of opportunities for training and development here? Are rotations into different functional or geographic areas fairly common?

Danger ahead: Proceed with caution

Even though it's generally safe to ask questions you'd sincerely like answered, there are some you should probably avoid, no matter how badly you'd like them answered. (At the very least, you shouldn't ask them in an evaluative setting such as an interview). Stay away from questions in the following categories:

- **Presumptuous questions,** such as "How quickly will I be eligible for a pay increase?" or "When can I expect to have my own clients?" Questions like these will give your interviewer the impression that you consider the job offer a done deal, which could make her predisposed to prove you wrong.

- **Questions that suggest you have underlying concerns about the job,** such as "I heard that this job involves a lot of late nights and weekend work. Is that true?" You may have legitimate concerns about the position, but it's probably best to ask someone other than the person evaluating your candidacy for the inside scoop.

- **Questions that imply you've already got one foot out the door,** such as "what do people typically do once they leave your firm?" Unless you're interviewing for a contract job or a position that has a specific start and end date, you should probably avoid giving your interviewer the impression you've already got your sights set on bigger and better things.

While crafting questions of your own, keep one last thing in mind: Most of your interviewers will be on a fairly tight schedule, either because they've got other candidates to speak with or because they have their own jobs and schedules to get back to. Learn to read your interviewer: If it's clear she is trying desperately to wrap things up, don't feel pressured to ask your questions simply because you've prepared them. If you sense she's trying to move things along, a diplomatic response might be, "Thanks. I'm sure you're on a tight schedule, so if it would be better to contact you later with any questions, I'd be happy to do that." This way, you've left it up to her— if she's indeed at the end of her interview tether, she'll take you up on your offer. If she's got plenty of time, she'll invite you to ask away (and she'll be impressed that you respect her schedule, which will win you extra points).

Learning from your interview

As we said at the beginning of the chapter, the interview process will usually leave you feeling as though your prospective employer has the upper hand. And, quite honestly, they probably do. But that doesn't mean you shouldn't be evaluating the company just as rigorously as they're evaluating you—you just can't do it as overtly. As the conversation evolves, ask yourself if your interviewer is someone you would like to work with—does it seem like he would make a good mentor, teammate, or manager? As you learn more about what you'd be doing on a daily basis, do you feel yourself getting more or less jazzed about the job? In general, does the company's approach towards the recruiting process seem organized and professional? We spoke with one jobseeker who recalled an interview experience that quickly changed her impression of a particular firm. "I was supposed to meet with three different people during a single office visit," she explains. "But one of my interviewers just never showed up! I was left sitting in a lobby for an hour and 25 minutes until the third person came to meet me. They ended up scheduling a phone interview a week later, but no one ever explained or apologized for the no-show. It didn't leave me with the best impression of the company."

Though such egregious breaches of interview etiquette are pretty rare, you can still learn a lot about an organization by the way it approaches its recruiting efforts. And we know it sounds a little bit *Oprah,* but listen to your inner voice when it comes to your interviews. If your enthusiasm for a job starts to wane as you learn more about it, pay attention to those feelings. As a general rule, people are never quite as enthusiastic about a particular job as they were before they were offered it; if you become less excited about a position as you learn more about it, chances are it won't grow to be more appealing once it actually starts. One of the few downsides of cultivating exceptional interview skills is the risk of talking your way into jobs that don't necessarily match your skills or interests. So while it absolutely pays to do your research, know your resume, and invest time preparing for each individual interview, it's equally important to trust yourself when all is said and done.

Thanks for the memories

It's true in tennis and golf, and it's true in job interviews, too: Once you've taken a swing at the ball, it's essential to follow through. Whether you interviewed in person or over the phone, and whether it was a first-round screening interview with HR or a final-round cross-examination by the senior vice president of Global Widget Marketing, you need to send a thank-you note at the completion of the interview process. Sending a thank-you note isn't just a polite way to recognize the time and courtesy someone's extended to you, but it's a way to reiterate your interest in the position, jog your interviewer's memory of your conversation, and highlight one or two specific things that make you a compelling candidate for the job. Apply the same sensibilities to your thank-you note you would toward your cover letter: think polite, concise, personalized, and absolutely error-free. Make sure your proofreading efforts extend beyond spelling and grammar; after all, you worked hard to establish your credibility and interest during the interview—you don't want to undo it all by making an embarrassing slip-up in a thank-you note. If you were introduced to multiple people during your office visit, make sure you get their names and titles correct. This is important whether you're sending them individual thank-you notes or mentioning them by name in the note you send your primary contact. "I once sent a thank-you note to a hiring manager after a series of interviews with multiple people," says Sarah, a 26-year old research associate at a consulting firm. "One of the people I met with was named Edwin Famous. But I hadn't taken his business card or written down his name immediately after the interview, so, when I sat down to write a thank-you note to my primary contact, the name that stuck out in my head was—for some reason—'Amos,' rather than 'Edwin.' I thanked the hiring manager profusely for not only taking the time to speak with me, but for introducing me to Miriam and Amos as well.

Unbeknownst to me, the entire office—including the person whose name I botched—found out about my error and found it extremely entertaining. It didn't cost me the job or anything—not only did I get an offer, but I accepted it. But from the day I started until the day I left two years later, I was the one who got the name wrong in the thank-you note. I'll never do that again." When you were little, you may have been told that if you couldn't think of something nice to say, then you shouldn't say anything at all. Well, when it comes to writing thank-you notes to interviews, the rule is this: If you can't get all of the names right, then it's better to not to include them at all. Of course, the best approach of all is to collect business cards from every person with whom you meet—and to proofread your thank-you correspondence diligently before sending it.

While your thank-you notes should always be flawless, they don't have to be written by hand and sent via snail mail to be effective. It was once considered gauche to send anything other than a hand-written note on quality stationery, but most hiring professionals these days agree that a prompt, well-written e-mail (sent no more than two business days after the interview) generally gets the job done. We've said it before, but it bears repeating: Don't let the ease and informality of e-mail give you a false sense of security. Like your cover letter or resume, your thank-you note is an opportunity to convey a confident, competent, and professional image to potential employers; don't waste that opportunity by regurgitating the same spiel you used in your cover letter. If anything, your thank-you note can be a more powerful tool for advancing your candidacy because you can use what you've learned in your interview to write a personalized, targeted note. In it you should mention one or two specific topics discussed during the interview that reinforced your interest in the position. If your interviewer described the specific attributes or qualities the position requires, mention one or two achievements that prove you possess them. And, finally, offer to send any additional information the hiring manager might require in order to make a decision. (Chances are they would have asked if they needed anything, but it's nice to offer nonetheless.)

Cultivating a Professional Appearance

You've put a lot of time and energy into preparing for your interview, so wouldn't it be great if you could rely solely on your impressive achievements and your sparkling personality to get you the job of your dreams? Sadly, you can't. Putting your best foot forward means not only proving you have the academic and professional chops for the role, but looking and acting the part, too. According to a recent report by the National Association of Colleges and Employers (NACE), a candidate's professional appearance does influence hiring decisions. "Job candidates need to remember that their overall grooming and choice of interview attire project an image," says Marilyn Mackes, the organization's executive director. "They are marketing themselves to the employer as a potential employee, and part of marketing is the packaging." The two most important appearance-related factors, according to the NACE study, were personal grooming and interview attire.

- **Grooming**—Nearly three-quarters of NACE's survey respondents said that a candidate's personal grooming would strongly influence their hiring decision. The term "grooming" might sound a little Kennel Club, but it means that your hair should be clean, neat, and brushed. The same goes for your teeth—no one should be able to tell that you had a Caesar salad for lunch. If you're concerned about your breath, you can pop a breath mint or chew a piece of gum—but nothing should be in your mouth by the time you meet your interviewer. If you share your house with a furry friend, be sure the evidence isn't all over your suit; invest in a lint-roller and give yourself a once-over before heading out the door. Your nails should be clean, trimmed, and not brightly painted. Be sure your clothes are clean and neat, without any missing buttons, wrinkles, tears, or stains (check under the arms).

  Speaking of underarms, remember that decades-old deodorant commercial that advised, "Never let them see you sweat"? That's good advice for your interview too: Gentlemen, wear a short-sleeved white cotton t-shirt under your dress shirt to mitigate any possible sweat effects. For women, a nice sweater shell underneath your suit jacket instead of a button-down dress shirt will achieve the same thing (you won't have to worry about ironing that way, either). Remember that natural fabrics like wool and cotton are generally more breathable than synthetics, so keep that in mind as you select your interview duds.

  If you choose to wear perfume or cologne, don't overdo it; your personal fragrance shouldn't arrive at the interview room before you do. And while we're on the topic of odor, don't ever smoke outside before you walk into the office building. One of the many drawbacks of this habit (don't worry, we aren't here to lecture you) is the lingering smell.

  The "less is more" guideline applies to makeup, ladies. Candidates of either gender should steer clear of flashy or excessive jewelry.

- **Interview attire**—Approximately half of all employers who responded to the NACE survey indicated that nontraditional interview attire would strongly influence their opinion of a candidate; another 38 percent said it would have a slight influence. For women, traditional interview attire means a well-tailored suit in a neutral color (black, gray, navy, and dark brown are all safe choices) and conservative shoes (no stilettos, open toes, or even peep-toes). For men, it means a suit in a dark, neutral color (black, navy, or dark gray), a white or light blue dress shirt (no flashy stripes or patterns), a silk tie with a conservative pattern, socks that match the trousers (no white!), and conservative, polished dark shoes.

While a suit is definitely a safe choice, keep in mind that relatively few companies observe a business-attire dress policy these days. You shouldn't assume that the rules that will apply once you've gotten the job will pertain to you as you're interviewing for it, but it's entirely possible that the person scheduling your interview may let you know that a suit is not de rigeur for your office visit. If this happens, consider yourself freed of the suit requirement. You should still err on the side of conservatism, though. The personal grooming guidelines still apply, and even a more casual ensemble should be clean, pressed, and well tailored.

Source: National Association of Colleges and Employers. "Employers Say Appearance Counts for Job Candidates." www.naceweb.org/press/display.asp?year=2006&prid=236.

Arriving on Time

Whether the setting is an urban jungle or a corporate park in the 'burbs, and whether you're driving or taking public transportation, you'll need to do some planning to make sure you arrive on time for your interview. Try to arrive at least an hour in advance—that way, you've left ample cushion time in case you run into traffic, encounter public transport delays, can't find a parking place, or get lost en route. In the event your journey goes smoothly and you arrive an hour in advance, you can visit the closest coffee shop and use the extra time for focused interview preparation. You can review the company information you've collected and take one last look at the questions you hope to ask during the course of the interview. And—especially if the trip has left you looking a little less pristine than you did when you left home—you can use the time to tidy up your appearance before you walk in the door.

NEGOTIATING THE OFFER: A CHECKLIST

Congratulations! Your thorough preparation and solid credentials have landed you a job offer. Now what? Well, the same truth that applies to marriages applies to job offers: Just because the ring's on the finger doesn't mean things can't still unravel. You still have more preparation and work to do to ensure that you live happily ever after. You may have heard the age-old wisdom that when it comes to negotiating salary, the first one to cite a number loses. There's some truth to this nugget, but negotiating a pay package that's both attractive and fair is a little more complicated. Here are our top tips for making sure your employment offer is a win-win proposition.

- **Wait your turn.** Until you've actually been offered a job, it's not appropriate to initiate a discussion of salary or benefits. If you're asked in preliminary conversations or early-round interviews what salary you're hoping to earn (or what salary you've made in the past), try to keep it vague; mentioning a specific figure too early in the process is a no-win situation. If you name too high a figure, they'll question whether you're likely to accept the job if it's offered to you; if you name too low a figure, you'll leave money on the table. To continue with the poker metaphor, play your cards close to the vest and don't show your hand too early.

- **Know your worth.** When you apply for a job, you're essentially selling services to a prospective employer. You can't possibly negotiate an offer if you don't know the going rate for those services. Take the time to figure out what people in positions comparable to yours are earning. Web-based tools such as Salary.com and SalaryExpert.com make it easier than ever to obtain a baseline figure for a given job title in a specific geographic area. This should only be a starting point, however (as we said before, the ranges these sites provide are necessarily broad). If you can, check with your contacts in the industry—friends, acquaintances, networking groups, professional associations—to hone in on a salary range you can reasonably expect.

- **Know your bottom line.** Base salary is only one component of the total-compensation picture, but (particularly early in your career) it can be the most important piece. If that's the case for you, have a bottom line—in other words, the lowest base salary at which you'd be willing to accept the position—in mind. Other compensation-related factors (performance-based bonuses, paid time off, company-sponsored retirement plans, paid relocation expenses, and employer-paid health insurance, to name a few) can help you evaluate the offer, but give some thought to the relative importance you assign to those factors in advance of your discussions.

- **Manage your expectations.** The strength of your negotiating position is determined by supply and demand. The more specialized your skills—and the higher the demand for those skills—the more leverage you'll have. In general, the more entry-level the position, the larger the pool of qualified candidates the employer can choose from. The sector you're considering plays a role, too. If you're considering jobs in academia or the public sector, there's usually room to negotiate; if the hiring manager must work within established pay-grade levels, he will have less discretion when it comes to deciding how much to pay.

- **Manage *their* expectations.** If you ask for more money and get it, remember that you'll be expected to make a proportionately greater contribution to the organization you're joining. This isn't necessarily a problem—provided you keep up your end of the bargain. If your performance is less than stellar, however, you'll have damaged your credibility—and your subsequent pay increases and advancement opportunities will probably suffer as a result.

- **Take a long-term view.** Whether it's getting the job offer in the first place or negotiating your salary and perks, it's easy for "winning the game" to become your top priority. But know that the best job opportunity isn't always the one with the fattest paycheck—it's the one that offers the best experience. Consider whether the position will enable you to develop skills that will make you more marketable down the line. Consider the position's promotion potential, learning opportunities, and the extent to which it makes good use of your skills and abilities. Your career is an investment; don't give up long-term career opportunities for short-term financial gain.

- **Keep the big picture in mind.** Know, too, that while paying rent is important, compensation is only one piece of the pie when it comes to your job satisfaction (and your overall mental health, for that matter). Other factors—such as work/life balance, job security, and geographic location—should influence your assessment of the job offer, too. Don't forget that the company's culture—and the quality of your managers, mentors, and colleagues—will have a significant impact on your experience. If you can't stand the thought of going to work every day, no amount of money—either now or five years down the line—will make it worthwhile.

- **Mind your manners.** One of the things that makes negotiating a job offer different from negotiating the price on a used car is the need to preserve the relationship with the party you're doing business with (in this case, your future employer). With that in mind, your negotiation approach should never be confrontational—nor should you give the impression you're unreasonable or greedy. Even if the initial offer falls short of your expectations, be polite and gracious about it. Begin any counter-offer discussions by saying you're appreciative of the offer and the opportunity—and mean it.

- **Play fair.** There's no doubt about it—negotiating your compensation is tricky business. Aim too high and you run the risk of damaging your credibility or pricing yourself out of the market entirely. Settle for too little and you'll always be playing catch-up (and you'll probably feel under-valued and unappreciated down the line). So, when it's time for negotiations, keep "fair and reasonable" in mind as you evaluate specific terms. It's in your best interest to earn fair compensation and it's in your employer's best interest for you to feel you're compensated fairly for your efforts.

Thanks, but no thanks: Learning from rejection

As a matter of personal and professional pride, we'd all like to get an offer for every job for which we apply. But, in reality, most of us don't. Sometimes, you know exactly where you went wrong: It's usually the point in the interview where the room starts to get really hot, the walls seem to close in around you, and everything starts to happen in slow motion. "I've had interviews where I knew things were going downhill right from the start," says Paul, who recalls an on-campus interview for a research job at a university. "For some reason, I thought my interview was at 10:30 A.M., and I left myself plenty of time to find the building on campus where my interview was taking place. But, when I walked in, my interviewer introduced herself and said, 'You know, we were expecting you at 10:00 A.M. Did you get lost?' It turns out I had gotten the interview time wrong. Five minutes into the interview, my cell phone started ringing because I'd forgotten to turn it off. So within 10 minutes I was completely distracted and flustered, and I felt I couldn't recover. It wasn't entirely surprising that I didn't get the job."

In situations such as these—where you know your interview didn't go exactly as you'd hoped or planned—the best thing you can do is value the experience as an opportunity to learn. It might not be much consolation at the time, but you'll be far less likely to make the same mistakes (in Paul's case, showing up late and leaving his cell phone on) again, and you'll only refine and improve your approach as you go along. The interview process shouldn't be a game you're determined to win; instead, it's a unique opportunity to learn about yourself, polish your presentation skills, and explore one of the literally thousands of career possibilities available to you.

What do you do when you've been passed over for a job and there's no "smoking gun"—you knocked every question out of the park, got along famously with every person you met, and still didn't get the offer? How do you figure out what went wrong so you can learn as much as possible from the experience?

First, understand that there are times when even the most meticulous research and thorough preparation aren't enough to land an offer with a particular company. It's entirely possible that you did do an outstanding job during the interview process—it might just be that another candidate did it a little bit better. Or maybe the successful applicant went to the same college as two or three of the people who interviewed him. Or maybe you felt there was chemistry between you and your interviewers, but one (or more) of them didn't feel the same way. There are dozens of possible reasons, and it's just not worth the emotional energy to figure out which one it's most likely to be.

However, if you decide to ask for feedback after you've gotten a "no, thank you," do keep a couple of things in mind:

- **Accept that you might not get what you're looking for.** Even if you ask nicely, you might not get constructive feedback. No one likes to be the bearer of bad news—not even HR folks or hiring managers, who have to deliver it on a daily basis. In the overly litigious society we live in, no one wants to get sued, either; so it's really no surprise that employers are typically reticent when it comes to justifying their hiring decisions. You need to be prepared for the stock answer, which is "We were overwhelmed by the number of qualified applicants for the position and have offered the position to the candidate whose experience and background most closely matched our hiring needs."

- **Remember that timing is everything.** The best time to ask for feedback is when the decision-maker (or, in many cases, the messenger) calls you to tell you you're not getting the job offer. Of course, rejection phone calls are more the exception than the rule these days; in many cases, companies will choose a more passive-aggressive route and send you an e-mail or letter, or not get back to you at all. If you get a rejection e-mail, the best time to ask for feedback is immediately after you receive it.

- **Cross-examinations are not appropriate.** You're far more likely to get meaningful feedback if you steer clear of questions such as "Why aren't you hiring me?" which immediately puts the other person on the defensive. Though it might seem as if you're beating around the bush, you're probably best served saying something along the lines of: "Thanks very much for getting back to me and letting me know. Since I'm still in the process of interviewing with other organizations, I was wondering if you could give me any advice or feedback that might help me with future interviews."

- **Don't ever argue—ever.** If your HR contact or recruiter does give you feedback that you disagree with, it's never appropriate to engage them in a debate about the merit of their decision. No matter how watertight your argument might be, it won't change the outcome; it will just protract an inherently awkward and uncomfortable conversation. You want to keep the conversation short, sweet (or at least bittersweet), and polite. Most employers have zero tolerance for confrontation in this scenario.

- **Take a hint.** If you leave a voicemail or send an e-mail message asking for feedback and you don't get a reply, leave it at that. Don't send follow-up messages or phone-stalk your contact trying to get them to speak with you. If they don't want to give you feedback, they don't have to—and you've got nothing to gain by trying to beat it out of them.

It's not you, it's me: Declining an offer

If, on the other hand, you receive an offer from an organization but choose to decline it for any reason, you should be just as gracious turning it down as you would be accepting it—or negotiating its terms. Let your prospective employer know as soon as you've decided it's not the right opportunity; as a candidate, you may already know how frustrating it is not to receive word after you've invested a lot in an application process. While it may be tempting to delay a potentially unpleasant conversation, letting your contact know promptly about your decision is the gracious, professional thing to do, especially since the organization still has a position that needs to be filled. Just as the first step in negotiating an offer is thanking your contact profusely for extending the opportunity, the first step in declining the offer is also expressing your appreciation. Then, offer a brief explanation—in however much detail you feel comfortable—of why you have decided to decline it. As far as personal information is concerned, leave it out if you're at all in doubt. Feel free to stick to the basics—i.e., "It's just not the right opportunity for me at this particular time."

In some instances, the employer may probe you for more specifics, so be prepared to politely say enough but not more than you feel is appropriate or judicious to reveal. Of course, never bad-mouth any organization—or any individual interviewer or employee with whom you met. Again, thank them for the time they spent speaking with you about the position and tell them you very much enjoyed meeting with them and learning about the role and the organization.

Though it's never quite as much fun to decline a job as it is to accept one, remember that it's okay to decline a position that's not right for you. It's also perfectly acceptable to decline an offer if you just want to wait to see what else is out there in your job search—it's better to be out of a job a few extra weeks or months than quit one six weeks after you started because it's just not working out. Trust your gut as well as your evaluation of the job's criteria. If something just doesn't seem right for you, follow your instincts. Even if your friends, parents, and significant other are telling you what a great opportunity it is, you're the one who's got to go to work every day.

CHAPTER 6

Q & As with Former History and Political Science Majors

A Final Word From Us...

By now you should be feeling pretty darn confident about the many opportunities that are available to you as a history or political science major. This book has sought to show you that the skills and knowledge you gained in your studies have market value in the "real world." We have also given you the tools you need to get in the door, whether the next step is advanced study, fellowships, or launching a successful job search.

But don't take our word for it. We spoke with several former history and political science majors from all walks of life to find out how their degrees have helped and/or hindered their professional career paths. Some of these folks work in academia, others in business, others in media, and still others in education and/or various creative fields. You'll get to hear straight from them about how being a history or political science major has affected their professional growth. We asked them why they chose to major in history or political science, what they learned, how those skills have been useful/not useful in the real world, about internships, their first job search, their current job, the best career advice they received, tips for current history or political science majors looking to transition into the professional world, and more. Remember—this is only the beginning. The next several years will be full of exciting ups and downs, as your future kicks into high gear. So buckle up. And remember to enjoy the journey.

Good luck!

Q & A with Former History Majors

The following professionals dedicated their time to answering our questions:

Angelo Araimo is the chief enrollment and planning officer at a small residential liberal arts college.

Elisabeth Nevins works in museum education.

Jessica Walter works in college development and fundraising.

Richard Nevins is a former lawyer, currently teaching history at a parochial high school in Connecticut.

Lauren Hull does campus recruitment across Europe for a major U.S. investment bank.

Why did you major in history?

Angelo: I switched from economics to history at the end of my second year when an advisor suggested I major in "what you enjoy the most."

Elisabeth: History was the subject I did the most consistently well in during high school, so I figured I must be pretty good at it. And the parameters opened up so widely in college—the number of courses and variety of topics, both focused and broad, were very inspiring. I realized that I really just enjoyed exploring history more than anything else that was available to me.

Jessica: Entering college with an undecided major, I was pleased to know that Princeton University encouraged undergraduate students to major in their preferred area of study, purely based on their interest in learning. Embracing this liberal arts vision and mission, I was confident that I could later pursue advanced study for a particular field or career. I took a fantastic history course in the spring semester of my freshman year. Recognizing that the majority of my upperclassman courses would be in my major's department, I decided that I would most like to take several history courses—purely based on my personal interest—as opposed to other courses.

Richard: I enjoy dynamic activity. The study of history is as simple or complex a process as you want to make it. If you are a curious person, and I am, there is always more to learn/analyze and think about when you study history.

Lauren: For no more grandiose reason than I had always done well in this area at school and knew it left my career /further study options pretty open.

What skills or information learned in college do you find yourself making the most use of?

Angelo: It is amazing how often I still use the basic research and writing skills learned in college. Preparing an analytical report is very similar to doing a research paper. Also, I learned how to prepare and make an oral presentation in college and now I do that all the time.

Elisabeth: My field is pretty closely tied to my major so I find most of what I learned as a college history major useful. My research skills have come in pretty handy over the years as I've had to educate myself about many specific periods and topics in American and local history so that I could ultimately educate others. And I find that I follow a similar model that a history professor would with a class, starting by exploring a topic through more general sources and then focusing in on the specific themes or information that best meet the criteria for the project that I am working on.

Jessica: My writing skills improved exponentially in college. I recall learning freshman year that I didn't have a grasp of how to create a true thesis statement in my papers. This shocked me, since I had previously thought that I was a strong writer. Being a history major, I was graded almost solely by papers; I even selected courses because there were final papers in lieu of exams/tests. I knew that I had to write well or I'd get poor marks in all my courses, and I'm a much better writer for it now. I take it a bit for granted, but colleagues at both my previous and current job have complimented me on my writing ability and style, and I realize that I am in the minority with this skill set.

Richard: Patience, avoidance of jumping to conclusions, and the seeking of quality sources were skills that I developed in college and which are still with me. Information about "Classical Knowledge" has proved to be very valuable. Selective use of time is also a necessary skill to learn and use.

Lauren: The analytical and skim-reading skills well honed during far too many hours in the library during finals term and the art of debate/negotiation or maybe just the plain ability to argue (I like to think rationally) without end until everyone else gives up or falls asleep . . . that, and the art of thinking on your feet—also known as making it all up on the spot—jointly useful during a seminar when you didn't even dent the reading list and also during a presentation when the slides you were sure were loaded on your laptop have disappeared.

What skills or information learned in college do you find yourself *not* using at all?

Angelo: I rarely "cram" anymore (okay, occasionally I still do).

Elisabeth: It's hard to think of any skills that are completely useless to me. I certainly no longer write formal papers defending a particular thesis (thank goodness), but I try to create educational activities that explore history in an organized, balanced and well-thought-out manner so I continue to rely on the key elements of a strong paper even in less formal presentations.

Jessica: Nothing comes to mind.

Richard: I've had few occasions to utilize higher mathematical or scientific skills/knowledge in an applied manner, although the ability to explain their roles in our society is a vital necessity.

Lauren: Anything relating to England during the twelfth century.

Which internships or extracurricular activities that you pursued in college have been most valuable to you personally and professionally? Why?

Angelo: Unfortunately, I worked full-time throughout college and so had no internships.

Elisabeth: I applied for an internship at a museum near my hometown after my junior year of college. As chance would have it, they were mounting an exhibit on Samuel Colt and felt my history background would be useful in the education department as they created materials to help teachers use the exhibit with their students. I never knew that museums had education departments . . . it was a eye-opening experience that led me to my career as a museum educator. And I also worked with some wonderful people whom I still turn to, ten years later, for support and guidance.

Jessica: I participated in a number of extracurricular activities in college and I think almost every one of them shaped my success personally and professionally today. Namely, I was a tour guide, which highlighted my verbal communication skills and ability to speak before a group—this now enables me to deliver presentations internally in my department/office. I was also an officer for my eating club [upperclassman social club unique to Princeton University] and sorority and was responsible for conducting meetings, drawing up agendas, etc. which now aids me in meeting facilitation as well. Finally, I participated in a variety of club and coed recreational sports;

teamwork and group dynamic understanding are skills that are universally necessary and appreciated.

Richard: Athletic activities allowed me to interact with a great number of different individuals in a great many places providing for healthy attitudes physically and socially. Developing an awareness of the spiritual life at college has permitted me to be a more inquisitive person and at the same time one who is more tolerant of the differences in people around me.

Lauren: I continued working and commuting to work throughout university and took on more responsibility; this helped me avoid spending quite so many hours in the bar and professionally it meant I had far more experience than the average graduate when I completed my degree.

How did you decide which field, either in academia or the real world, to go into?

Angelo: Upon graduation, I decided to explore areas that were "related" to my major. In the five years after college I worked in travel, high school teaching, and library research (and continued to tend bar to actually make a living). I also completed a master's in history during this time. Eventually, I decided I loved education but not necessarily adolescents, and entered the world of higher education.

Elisabeth: My interest in history has always been about trying to understand everyday people and their motivations. And though I loved exploring the past—doing research and such—I knew I would never make it as an academic: I'm just not that focused. And I'm much too social. I'd go nuts sitting around in my study all day writing or whatever. My summer internship in the education department of a museum opened my eyes to a field where I could study the past and share my passion with others through teaching. It was a perfect fit for my strengths and my interests.

Jessica: I worked as a student "dialing for dollars" to make money for textbooks in college. I was later asked to be the lead fundraising volunteer for my class after graduation, which continued my relationship with Princeton University's Development/Annual Giving Office, for which I now work.

Richard: In the real word, the legal profession beckoned because of its inherent intellectual and social context. Applying legal principles to actual life problems is very rewarding. In the academic world, I later changed to the teaching of history in high school because it requires daily interaction with youths who, if you gain their trust, will push you to do your very best.

Lauren: At present I have yet to decide where I am actually headed but I targeted a company/sector that I knew would be advantageous for me in terms of my personal goals (i.e. moving and working internationally in the short-term future). It also helped that I had a few years of experience in this sector so I didn't have to start right at the bottom of the ladder.

Did you have a mentor when you entered the workforce/graduate school?

Angelo: A number of faculty members provided guidance for me.

Elisabeth: Yes, my supervisor during my internship had attended Bank Street, the graduate school I went to. She introduced me to their museum education program. I didn't end up going to grad school immediately, but when I was ready I knew where to look. Also, I stayed in touch with the head of the internship program and she advised me on other programs I might be interested in and served as a reference.

Jessica: No.

Richard: My older brother, who was a practicing attorney, provided great insight and guidance as I adapted to the work force. Prior to that, in military service, a superior officer provided me with a great amount of guidance. In the educational field, I have been mistaken for the experienced teacher—while I am the true learner.

Lauren: No—not sure I believe in shaping your life around the advice of someone who has simply been there and done it all before. I'd rather make my own mistakes and attempt to learn from them.

What's the number-one bit of advice you wish you were given before you entered the job market?

Angelo: Find a career you truly enjoy because if you are not happy at work you will be unhappy most of the time.

Elisabeth: If you have to justify taking a job to yourself, it's probably not something you really want to be doing. Most of my friends and I had moved on to our second job by the end of our first year out of school. Of course, we were lucky that the job market was strong and we had the option of trying something else. In retrospect I wish I had stood my ground and kept looking even though I was feeling pressure to get a job, settle down, and start paying the rent.

Jessica: At Princeton, everyone thinks they should go into consulting and investment banking because they're pretty much the only options that are presented to the senior class (with only minor exceptions). Initially, I fell prey to the same assumption though those fields really [weren't] for me.
The advice I'd offer is for students to be brave enough to explore career options in addition to what their Career Services office provides them. There are infinitely more options out there — go for something in which you are truly interested. Don't sell your soul to the consulting/I-banking devil unless you're truly sure that you want to do that.

Richard: Knowing the "culture" of the work place before you jump into a specific job is highly important, but this knowledge is not easily obtainable, or it may be disguised by a veneer of superficial behaviors. If a work environment uses up a great deal of your time in survivalist behavior, you'd be better off someplace else.

Lauren: Do not assume someone knows what they are doing just because they claim to.

What were your job-related expectations when you were still in school, and how did they match up with your experience of the "real world?"

Angelo: I guess I was surprised to learn how similar almost every organizational structure is. One always assumes some great mystery about the "real world" outside of college. Also, teachers always think the corporate world is very exotic and exciting; business people assume education is slower paced and more collegial, etc . . . I had some of these notions as well. But, I have found that most fields are similar—there are good and bad places to work within them—in regard to structure.

Elisabeth: Honestly, I didn't have any expectations. I just knew I needed to get a job and I wanted to be in New York City. Beyond that I saw my first few years out of school as an opportunity to fumble my way around being a grown-up for the first time. Unlike how it seems to have worked in the past, I had no illusions that I would pick a career, get a job, and stick to it for the next 40 years until I got my gold watch at retirement. I had no idea what it was like to be out on my own; I didn't want to hold myself back with preconceived notions of what my life would be. I was just going to have to get out there and find out . . . and I did.

Jessica: I pretty much got what I expected. I expected to be surrounded by other intelligent, driven individuals (which I was); I expected to be paid enough to enjoy wherever I was living (which I was/did); I expected to make new friends and learn from experienced individuals within the organization (yes on the former, only minimally on the latter); I expected to sample the business world in order to determine if I wanted to pursue that career avenue later in life (I did sample it and I decided that the corporate world wasn't for me).

Richard: In a somewhat naïve way, I never connected with the fact that you could get paid well for doing something you liked doing. Consequently, the real world surprised me with its economic rewards. As a corollary, I was quite impressed with individuals in the work force who had only the economic reward in mind as motivation for their daily activities. I never found myself in between these two polarities.

Lauren: My expectations were and still are pretty high in terms of what I can learn from the situations my job puts me in as opposed to what I gain materially (although of course that is a part of the equation too). I worked before and during my degree so the 'real world', as it is mostly referred to by those who have been ground down by the nine-to-five and who look bitterly upon fresh-faced college graduates, was nothing new to me.

What was your first job out of college? How did you find that job?

Angelo: I was working at a bar in Manhattan and a group of folks about my age would come in every Friday afternoon for a drink. They worked at a company that produced exotic tours to Asia, Europe, and Latin America. They all had liberal arts degrees and interests in travel. One thing led to another and I went to work there as a customer service rep.

Elisabeth: My first job out of school was as an account executive at a very tiny ad agency in New York City, five people total. How I got the job . . . totally bizarre story. My friend Sara from college was at a summer mixer for recent grads of our school. She ran into Angela, a woman who had sung in the same singing group that we had, and learned that she and her partner were looking to hire someone. Sara gave them my name, they called me that night, and I was on a bus to New York the next morning. By the end of the day they had offered me the job. It all seemed so serendipitous, and they were so nice, I took the job.

Jessica: My first job was as a research associate for the Corporate Executive Board in Washington, DC. It was a less-hardcore-than-consulting-or-I-banking entry-level business position for liberal arts kids. I researched business-y topics through a number of databases and online, sometimes held interviews with business professionals about various business practices and then wrote it up in a cute little "brief" report format. I was recruited for the position through my school's Career Services program in the winter of my senior year.

Richard: My first job out of college was that of a soldier; it found me through the draft. I ended up in military intelligence work largely because of my academic record. After service and law school, I worked as a public defender; I found this job by obtaining recommendations from influential people. My first job as a teacher was as a long-term substitute. I got the sense that most public school hiring staff felt that I was overqualified for the jobs, or perhaps, too expensive due to the place I would be put on the unionized salary scale, thus, initially I had to prove my durability.

Lauren: Recruitment associate—working for a medium sized consultancy providing outsource recruitment/occupational psychology solutions to a range of UK public sector departments. This was a natural progression from the three years I worked at the same company, undertaking a variety of roles including management, before and during my degree studies.

If you went straight into the workforce after receiving your bachelor's degree, do you wish you had attended graduate school first? If you went on to grad school, do you wish you had worked first? In either case, why?

Angelo: I sort of did both simultaneously and am glad I did.

Elisabeth: No! No! No! I went straight to work and am very happy with that decision. First, there was school burnout. I needed to do something different. And I learned so much about myself during the three years I was out of school. Just knowing that, at 22, I could take care of myself was important to learn. My experiences also confirmed my strengths and interests so when I finally did go to grad school I was sure it was the direction I wanted to take things . . . a good thing to know as you sink yourself deep into student debt.

Jessica: No, I am glad that I went into the workforce after undergraduate college, because: 1) it was really nice to make some money and be able to afford to go out to restaurants and bars for a change, 2) it was nice to work nine-to-five and not have papers and things hanging over my head over weekends/holidays/vacations/etc., 3) it was nice to have weekends off, paid holidays, paid vacation days, etc., 4) I wanted a chance to enjoy reading for pleasure and without a highlighter in one hand, and 5) I knew that I wasn't ready to decide my career/grown-up "fate" and thus, I didn't want to go into tens of thousands of dollars of debt arbitrarily picking a course of advanced study. I wasn't mature enough then to decide "what I wanted to be when I grew up" so I thought it best to check out the real world first, to get a sense of what was out there, so I could later make a more educated decision. I also didn't agree with classmates who were going to law school in order to avoid the real world for another three years, when they already knew/suspected that they didn't want to be lawyers.

Richard: I went to law school right from college, although that activity was interrupted by the war in Vietnam. Prior to college, and right through college and law school, I worked in a great number of temporary jobs: garbage collector, postman, housepainter, gas station attendant, community college lecturer, substitute teacher, warehouse-truck-loading laborer, legal intern and highway construction laborer. I regret that most of these jobs were "local" because that limited my geographic experiences. Ultimately, I expect work experience can give one a sense of maturity that the academic world appreciates more today than in the 1960s.

Lauren: I have no regrets about skipping grad school at this stage—to me it would have been a pretty pointless exercise given that I was pretty fed up with studying by the time I sat finals at Oxford and was unsure where to direct my academic focus. That said, I intend to complete further study within the next five years but have yet to decide whether this will be in a field directly related to the undergraduate degree I have, or in something new or even possibly related to my work.

What's the best piece of advice you've received from a colleague?

Angelo: "Always remember the people are the most important part of any organization."

Elisabeth: "Go to law school." Someone I used to work with told me that. She was kind of joking but kind of not. After many years working in the nonprofit world, I think she was warning me away from a similar path; telling me to sell out, make lots of money. Why was it the best advice I've gotten? Because I realized that law school or "selling out" wasn't an option for me. I may never make a zillion dollars, but I'm happy with my choices.

Jessica: None comes to mind.

Richard: I have been told many times to slow down. Most people are already where they need to be; if you slow down, you can share yourself with those around you.

Lauren: Switch off your blackberry when you leave the office, or better yet, leave it in the office.

What's the smartest move you've made since receiving your bachelor's degree?

Angelo: Marrying my wife, Mary. And, a long way back to second, realizing that I was much more cut out to be a college administrator than a teacher.

Elisabeth: I've had many jobs—five since I graduated nine years ago, plus I took time off to get my graduate degree. Sometimes I worry that I look a little flaky on paper. But I've always tried to make choices that are going to make me happy in the long run and so far my strategy has paid off. Probably the best move I made was leaving the high-paying but totally unsatisfying job that I took immediately after grad school after only nine months, to work my dream job (for a big pay cut). Totally worth it. Not only was it my dream job, but it was with a very respected institution, so it's a great job to have on my resume.

Jessica: Leaving the corporate world and entering the land of academia. I don't do academic work, but I love the atmosphere and energy of being on a college campus, full of gifted, intelligent, young people and fantastic opportunities to experience cultural shows, concerts, lectures, etc.

Richard: I learned to trust and confide in and work with intelligent [people].

Lauren: Temping in an investment bank in a business area unrelated to what I wanted to do in order to gain insight into the corporation as a whole and then be ideally placed to target the role I wanted originally. Never underestimate the power of strategizing when it comes to job-hunting.

Describe your current job and its major responsibilities.

Angelo: I am the chief enrollment and planning officer at a small residential liberal arts college. As such, I oversee recruitment, admissions, financial aid, and institutional research. I also oversee our strategic planning process.

Elisabeth: I recently moved to Boston with my husband and am working part-time as a museum teacher while I look for a full-time position. My previous job was Coordinator of middle and high school programs for the Connecticut Historical Society Museum. I was responsible for two large projects, History Day and a Teaching American History (TAH) federal grant. History Day is a national competition, like science fair, and I was responsible for running the program on the state level. For the TAH grant I researched, wrote, and produced a series of seven history kits for the Hartford Public Schools using local history and primary sources.

Jessica: I am responsible for annual fundraising campaigns for approximately a dozen alumni classes at Princeton University. I work with lead volunteers to recruit teams of callers to reach out to every member of these alumni classes and solicit them for a gift to Annual Giving by phone. I script e-mail solicitations to be mass sent to nondonors in the class. I update and send spreadsheets to volunteers so that they have a sense of the proper prioritization of their work. I help set goals for the classes and for individuals within the class with large capacity for giving. I motivate and inspire volunteers through written communication throughout the year. I write agendas for lead volunteers to use when facilitating conference calls with volunteer teams.

Richard: At present, I teach history/social studies in a Connecticut parochial school. The courses are AP European History and World History. I have also taught humanities and law. I am the moderator of the Student Council and the advisor to the Model UN Club, as well as the union negotiator and building representative. I have approximately 100 students on the [freshman] and senior level.

Lauren: Junior recruiter for campus recruitment across Europe for a major U.S. investment bank. This entails planning and facilitating all campus recruitment and summer/off cycle internships each year, forming strong working relationships with bankers at all levels from analyst to managing directors and across all divisions, screening applications in the thousands, arranging interviews and assessment days, managing two assistants and their workload, supporting my manager in the budget creation process, arranging and attending presentations and events across Europe (between September–December this year we are running 168 of these events), assisting in planning diversity initiatives and attending these where possible.

What experience was required for it?

Angelo: The combination of teaching (which I did for seven years) and numerous administrative positions (from entry-level recruiting and advising, to being a manager of an office), over a fifteen-year period.

Elisabeth: The position required a foundation in the principles of museum education which focus on experiential learning, strong research and writing ability, knowledge of the realities of teaching in an urban setting, ability to work with and manage a variety of personalities, and—most of all—organization, organization, organization.

Jessica: No experience was necessarily required, but previous fundraising experience was preferred. Overall, my current employer was looking for smart, personable individuals to work with Princeton alumni in order to raise money. It wasn't necessary for me to have experience asking people for money (though I did). They were looking for highly capable, independent people to take ownership over the fundraising campaigns of several Princeton alumni classes. And superior written and verbal communication skills were a must.

Richard: Technically, I needed a bachelor's degree and a plan for becoming certified and obtaining a master's degree. While life experience is an intangible, I believe it played an important role in my obtaining this job.

Lauren: Previous recruitment experience was essential but it also helped that I had temped in another area of the company so knew the team, had read up on their activities, and built relationships during the previous four months.

To what extent has your degree helped you in your current role?

Angelo: Early on it gave me a knowledge base and the communication skills to feel confident and to move forward in a variety of positions. Coupled with my graduate degree, it has also given me the breadth and depth required to serve students, lead staff, and work collaboratively with faculty and administration at the college level.

Elisabeth: My education, both undergrad and graduate, is very important to my work. My BA in history helps me with all the historical research that I do and my MSEd in museum education grounds me in the educational theory that I need to turn this research into engaging and effective activities and programs for students.

Jessica: I communicate through written correspondence with my volunteers (clients) on a daily basis. The strength of my writing skills causes my volunteers to forget my age (since I'm younger than most of them by a generation or more) and be confident in my work.

Richard: It was necessary then, and (with the No Child Left Behind Act, in order to be highly qualified) it is more necessary now. I teach history, and although my law degree progresses me on the pay scale, to be qualified to teach history, one should have a history degree. (To make this more relevant, one should have a history degree and not just an "education" degree.)

Lauren: To a large degree the bare bones of historical knowledge I acquired have yet to be utilized (although it is at times fascinating to note just how similar office politics are to the Machiavellian world of the Tudor Royal court) but what I do draw on are the communication and negotiation skills built during one-to-one tutorials and the analytical skills developed by needing to read and absorb 50 different accounts of one historical period in a week or less. The sheer resilience I learnt from getting two 2,000 word papers a week written while balancing work and a social life also helps.

What do you like most about your current role?

Angelo: I love interacting with students, helping them make decisions about college, and solving some problems when I can. I really enjoy working at something that helps shape the future in such a tangible way. Also, the diversity of issues that one tackles regularly in this position keeps it very exciting. And never leaving college is a great thing.

Elisabeth: There are many things I like about my field—getting paid to study history and hang out with kids to name two. But what I like most is teaching history in creative ways. The academic world is all about "publish or perish." Classroom teachers are burdened with standardized tests and administrative busy work. My job as a museum educator is simply to think up fun ways to get kids excited about learning history. It's very liberating.

Jessica: I love working with people. I enjoy the quality of my colleagues in the office and I feed off of the Princeton alumni—with their love and enthusiasm for the school, for providing a great experience for future generations of Princetonians.

Richard: Everyone went to high school and could write a Hollywood script of (real-life) extraordinarily amusing/embarrassing adventures. I'm author and actor, producer and director, to some extent, in these dramas at this point in my life. At the same time, this position requires an intellectual, a social, and a moral presence. It's challenging.

Lauren: My colleagues and the opportunity to learn from them and their experience.

What aspect(s) of your current role do you not like?

Angelo: I am getting older and everyone around me is getting younger.

Elisabeth: Working at a nonprofit, the specter of limited funding always looms. There can be a good deal of busy work surrounding grant applications and reports that I could do without. But I also recognize it is an essential part of the equation. It's good to be held responsible for how we've spent the money we've been given; it can just be tedious at times.

Jessica: In all honesty, nothing really comes to mind.

Richard: I am in my tenth year of teaching, and I have yet to find things that I dislike that are different from the things that I did not like when I was a soldier, a lawyer, or a garbage man. Rudeness, arrogance, self-centeredness, an unwillingness to compromise etc. (you should, by now, get where I'm going), are features of people, regardless of age, gender, or position that show up in all avenues of life regardless of profession. I'm sure I have not been immune to behaving that way myself. Self-corrective behavior is sometime myopic, however, because there is always tomorrow, the day that you will change. Perhaps, if someone took some good advice from a wise person there would be less to dislike in the workplace.

Lauren: The hours and the sheer stress of it all.

What skills have you had to acquire that your bachelor's degree did not help you cultivate?

Angelo: All the "skills," perhaps better described as virtues, that come with life experience, such as patience and humility. Of course, since I graduated college in 1982, all of my computer skills have come postcollege as well.

Elisabeth: My graduate degree in museum education obviously provided me with the background I needed to apply my interest in history within the museum setting. In addition, I taught myself how to use design software, which has come in really handy in a variety of settings. I ended up designing all seven of the history kits I created, which saved time on a lot of back and forth with an outside designer. I've also gotten pretty comfortable using computers and technology generally. So often I become the go-to girl when someone's having a problem and doesn't want to hunt down the IT department. It's a blessing and a curse.

Jessica: Understanding of financial concepts, particularly with individuals' management of their personal wealth, the process by which companies go public, rules and restrictions involved with charitable giving, etc.

Richard: Public speaking is a powerful tool. While I did study rhetoric in college, it was more in the context of a historical perspective, rather than as a practical subject.

Lauren: None as yet that I didn't already have from my previous experience.

What suggestions would you have for those still in college? Are there any "optional" elements of the undergraduate experience that you would recommend they explore?

Angelo: First, be as broad as possible at the undergraduate level. It may sound like a cliché, but college is really your last chance to become broadly educated—and I believe fewer and fewer students are taking advantage of this opportunity, and such an education truly is valuable. Also, there is so much opportunity now for college students to complete internships, do off-campus service and study abroad. Each of these opportunities expands your knowledge and awareness of the world in which you will contribute.

Elisabeth: My advice would be to explore as much as possible. There are so many opportunities for learning right at your fingertips: classes, professors, extracurriculars, and other students. My biggest shock in graduating to the "real world" was realizing how much harder it was to find interesting people and experiences. In college there is such an amazing amount of intellectual energy concentrated into a relatively small geographic area. Walk out of your dorm room and you'll bump into a learning opportunity. Enjoy that energy. Immerse yourself in it for as long as you can.

Jessica: Current students should be sure, every semester if possible, to take at least one course purely out of interest in the topic. Not because it fulfills any prerequisite, not because they think it'll look good on a resume later, not because their parents want them to take it—they should take art history if they love museums, they should take a new language if they've always wanted to learn it, they should take religion if they're just curious, they should take international studies just to learn more about what the heck is going on in the world around us these days. Students should have *fun* with at least one course per semester.

Richard: Perhaps this is from a too-distant perspective, but there seems to be a party attitude nearly all the time in college these days. Parties are great; people need to not be serious. The pursuit of intellectual matters should prevail some of the time and not merely so one can emerge from the stupor into the proper job setting. Enlightenment can be a goal in and of itself.

Lauren: Make the most of your time studying and focus on the areas that interest you—they are the only ones you will remember. Only make time for the "extracurricular" activities that truly fascinate you; doing anything and everything simply to bulk up your resume just makes you look like you're trying too hard and will make you resentful that you are not elsewhere doing something, anything, more interesting.

Do you have any tips for those entering the workforce/graduate school now?

Angelo: Be practical, but be idealistic at the same time. It is just as easy—and much more rewarding—to do good while you are doing well. And it is more likely that you will do both if you follow your passions and not obsess about what the current "market" is.

Elisabeth: I'm not a big fan of the straight-to-graduate-school path, unless of course you've known you wanted to be Perry Mason since age three. Even then, I think it's important to get out there, get a job, pay the electric bill, buy groceries, and work for "the man" for a year or two. It's amazing what you learn about yourself and what you really want your life's work to be. And try to enjoy the experience. All you may learn is that you hate your job, but that's important to know and now you can try something else.

Jessica: Don't fall prey to your Career Services office's limited opportunities. Try to connect with history alumni at your school to ask them what they did postcollege and to recommend other career paths for you about which you might not have even thought.

Richard: As I am facing the prospect of financially retiring, although it is unlikely that I will ever retire from work (carpentry has became an avid pursuit at the moment), my advice is to save for the future, not necessarily with money, but perhaps with your attitude about what is necessary in your life. At the same time, get to know your "boss." Perhaps she or he can give you the mentorship that all of us need.

Lauren: Travel first if you can, get out there and see the world and learn something about yourself and how you cope outside of college/away from your family and friends before you get stuck into building a career.

What's the best way to get a job in your field?

Angelo: Certainly try to do an internship while still in college. It gives you knowledge of the field, it gives you a reference in the field, and it allows you to learn what the field is really like.

Elisabeth: An internship is probably the best way to start, to see if you really like the work. And internships are great ways to make connections within the field. It seems a graduate degree is becoming more and more desirable as well. There are many good museum studies/museum education programs in the country. Find the one that fits your needs best. Networking is also key, and this is where graduate school also helps. Many grad programs require an internship, offer lots of field trips to meet with museum professionals, and have alumni networks. These are the people who will hire you.

Jessica: Every college has a Development/Advancement/Fundraising office. If you're still in school, ask to intern there—they'll always bring you on board to help with various things. If you're already out of school, look for other fund-raising opportunities—with your alma mater, with your high school, with your church, with a nonprofit, with various charities. Fund-raising differs from place to place, but it's great to get a feel for the fundraising world, no matter where you work.

Richard: In the legal field, if you want to work in the major firms, you have to have the pedigree (educationally or connectively) and/or the recommendations of someone who is already in the arena. In the educational field, you unfortunately have to be young and willing to sacrifice a few years for paltry sums of money with the expectation that only the love of what you do will reward you in the end.

Lauren: Experience.

What mistake do history grads often make?

Angelo: History graduates are often led to believe that their choices are teaching or some form of "research." These graduates often do not explore the more creative benefits of their degree.

Elisabeth: Go to law school?

Jessica: They choose to go into education, because when they tell people "I'm majoring in history" everyone responds "Oh, are you going to be a history teacher?" Teaching is a noble and wonderful career, but it's not the only option for history majors. We know how to read, write, and communicate. Those are universal skills that can be used everywhere.

Richard: They have failed to see history as a dynamic (non-Marxist from my point of view) process that examines human conduct. History is a bridge; it's never an end in itself.

Lauren: Presuming they have to go into journalism, law, or teaching. That or procrastinating by doing more and more study until they forget how to function without an essay deadline hanging over them.

What's something that you think more history grads should do to advance their careers?

Angelo: Try to match your academic passion (degree), with other interests or skills you may have. For example, history graduates who love to travel and to meet and speak with new people often make great sales professionals. And many corporate leaders have begun in the sales area of their companies. But an added plus would be identifying another interest and looking for a sales position in that area. So, a recent graduate I know who was a great choral singer is now in sales and marketing for a music company. I just hired a recent history major who loved his college experience here as an admissions recruiter.

Elisabeth: Keep learning and keep looking. Extracurriculars aren't just for students. Make sure you live a varied and busy life beyond work. You never know what opportunities are out there . . . keep your eyes and ears open.

Jessica: No answer; it's totally dependent on the individual and the career they choose.

Richard: If they have read good historians, they should be able to write well; they should develop their writing skills and demonstrate them in all possible avenues.

Lauren: Take a more active interest in gaining work experience where possible during their degree. This doesn't have to be of the organized internship variety, volunteeer work or job shadowing can be just as useful.

Who is in the best position to offer a history graduate help with his or her resume and cover letter?

Angelo: I believe, for most liberal arts graduates, the Career Development office—especially at small colleges—is in the best position to help. But colleges also now have alumni mentors in most areas. And still, as in my case, faculty in history can be great mentors as well.

Elisabeth: The best person is definitely someone who looks at and evaluates resumes for a living. I'm lucky—my mother-in-law worked in Human Resources for years and has been extremely helpful in advising me over the years. I also participated in the resume review sessions sponsored by my college Career Services department. They tend to bring in good people and I got some useful feedback.

Jessica: Other history majors who have already graduated college—try searching through your school's alumni database for contacts.

Richard: Those individuals who have taken history and used it as a bridge to another profession, whether it be law, education, medicine, etc.

Lauren: A career advisor or in-house recruiter at the type of firm the graduate is applying to.

What pitfalls should history graduates avoid when applying to and interviewing for positions?

Angelo: Get help preparing your resume and write a formal, well-edited cover letter. I am amazed at how many sloppy letters I receive from recent graduates. Why would I hire someone who is either too lazy to compose a good letter of interest, or incapable of doing so? Also, avoid promising things on the interview that you cannot deliver (true working knowledge of a foreign language is one that springs to mind). You might actually get the job and then have two weeks to learn what you said you already know.

Elisabeth: Perhaps selling themselves short and not realizing how important studying the past is to understanding our world today. Having a good grasp on what has happened in the past—what motivated people to make the choices they have and understanding the consequences of those choices—is a real skill that can be relied upon in any number of work situations. Use your history degree as a selling point when looking for a job; don't apologize for it.

Jessica: Be prepared to explain your skill set and why those skills perfectly align you for whatever position you're interviewing.

Richard: Ironically, despite what I've said above, it would be avoiding the fact that a main topic of discussion should be your history interests. If you've clearly defined them in your studies, and have worked at them, then your history specialties should interest nearly everyone you speak with; perhaps not for hours, (don't bring videos) but at least for a portion of any interview you participate in. Demonstrate the relevance of history; otherwise why study it in the first place?

Lauren: If a job ad asks for an application form and not a curriculum vitae, do not send a curriculum vitae. This will be thrown away. Avoid turning up having done no research—you look lazy and unprofessional if you cannot answer simple questions as to why you're interested in this role/sector/firm/career. Be polite to everyone, and I mean everyone, you meet. Interviewers have been known to quiz receptionists over candidate's general behavior.

When an interviewer asks you a question make sure you answer it, do not recite the answer you had rehearsed for the question you were hoping they would ask. Have something interesting to ask at the end of the interview to leave the positive impression that you are inquisitive and intelligent.

Avoid putting anything on your curriculum vitae for which you cannot provide further detail when asked. Avoid putting anything on your curriculum vitae that is totally irrelevant in the hope that it will "pad" it out and provide a picture of the well-rounded candidate you are (by irrelevant I generally mean anything you achieved under the age of 16 unless you were a child prodigy or climbed Everest unaided).

If an interviewer gives you their business card feel free to follow up with a simple "thank you for your time" e-mail—however do note that they are not your friend and will most likely not appreciate 300 words on why they are so great and why you simply must work for them really, really soon.

Q & A WITH FORMER POLITICAL SCIENCE MAJORS

The following professionals dedicated their time to answering our questions:

Dan Rosenfield is the Dean of Enrollment Management at the University of Louisiana at Lafayette.

Graham Mackenzie is a program manger for the United States Treasury.

Hardy Spire is a senior producer for the CBS News *Early Show*.

Lawrence Kaufman owns a New York-based real estate advisory firm.

Michael Marcus works in marketing/advertising for ESPN Digital Media.

Why did you major in political science?

Dan: I majored in political science as an undergrad and later got a master's in educational counseling.

Graham: I majored in political science because the discipline included advanced work in classes I did well in and liked in high school, and I thought it would prepare me for a career in law.

Hardy: I majored in political science because I realized it fit my lifelong love of politics and current events. At the time I had no idea what I wanted to do postcollege but knew when I declared that for me to have any chance of success in school my major needed to be in an area of intense personal interest to me.

Lawrence: I was a political science and economics double major. I started off interested in economics and pursued that major and took a number of poly sci courses because I found the topics very interesting. Before I knew it, it was senior year and realized I only needed a few more credits to get a degree in that major as well.

Michael: There was no science behind my decision to major in political science. At the time, I felt it would be the best opportunity to stay abreast of current events, government, law, and policy. It seemed to be the most practical knowledge that could be applied to real life.

What skills or information learned in college do you find yourself making the most use of?

Dan: Communication skills and analytical skills primarily. I think most folks would tell college-bound students that the value of higher education is much more about personal growth and skill development than facts/information (except perhaps in the very vocationally-oriented fields).

Graham: Waiting until the last minute and staying up late to finish a project.

Hardy: As far as my political science education I find my background in political theory to have given me some context for much of what I encounter now . . . but the classes in the American presidency and campaign politics were the most fascinating and now apply directly to my daily work.

Lawrence: I think the "soft science" majors teach a person how to think. I gained an ability to think critically, analyze a lot of information and boil it down to its essence (talking points). I think I also learned that there are often numerous ways of looking at an issue and the answer is not always "black and white."

Michael: For me, it was more about personal growth, interpersonal skills, development of my own personal belief system and convictions. College was probably the most significant phase for personal growth and maturity.

What skills or information learned in college do you find yourself not using at all?

Dan: The limited math and science course work I did has little to do with my everyday work (but I will always be thankful for taking "chemistry for poets," which brought me together with my wife).

Graham: There isn't anything I learned in college that hasn't proved useful somewhere . . . even if just playing Trivial Pursuit with friends.

Hardy: I don't use my music history or astronomy knowledge very often . . . or information learned in my "biological basis of human sexuality" class . . . but I don't regret taking them. They were part of my overall effort to get as diverse an education as possible.

Lawrence: I do not use calculus. I do not need the skills to produce a 15-page research paper—in fact quite the opposite—there is not enough emphasis placed on quick gathering of information and brief analysis and presentation.

Michael: Quite frankly, it's a lot of the core classroom/academic material. Everyone carries with them varying degrees of knowledge and expertise, no doubt some of which is learned in the classroom. The most valuable information for me was learned outside the classroom, simply by living life, developing relationships, and meeting people with diverse backgrounds.

Which internships or extracurricular activities that you pursued in college have been most valuable to you personally and professionally? Why?

Dan: My experience working on college newspapers and in college radio was most valuable because both helped me learn to manage time and develop communications and organizational skills.

Graham: My involvement in athletics and fraternity life was the most rewarding because they provided close friends for life. Many of us talk weekly and routinely get together two or three times year. Even though we're in different fields and try to avoid it, discussions of work inevitability come up which sometimes provide a solution to a business problem, or even a new business opportunity.

Hardy: My internship at NBC News in New York City was incredibly significant. I became addicted to the excitement of television, particularly live television, and I still can't shake it. I also spent much of my extracurricular time at our campus radio station. The idea that my voice and music were being broadcast via ten massive watts of broadcast power was thrilling even though the signal had a range of about a thousand feet. Today my work is seen by three million people nationwide each morning, which is pretty exciting too.

Lawrence: The summer jobs I had during college were closely related to my interests (real estate) and were good preparation for entering the job force after college.

Michael: I interned at a sports radio station and sports cable network—both were valuable simply from the standpoint of getting experience on the resume. You don't always have the most meaningful work, but it's more about establishing contacts and getting exposure in the workplace. Fraternity life was fairly significant as well. I gained experience establishing camaraderie through sports, building a sense of unity, and serving as treasurer for one year.

How did you decide which field, either in academia or the real world, to go into?

Dan: I pretty much fell into education after deciding to "try it" until I figured out what I wanted to do. After that, I pretty much fell into my current field after being asked to fill in for someone on medical leave. As they say, "Man plans, God laughs."

Graham: Going to law school was Plan A, but I didn't get accepted. I prepared myself for Plan B by student teaching and obtaining a teaching certificate in college but decided against going that route. I ended pursuing Plan C, entering the business world, by getting an MBA.

Hardy: At a moment of complete confusion following my graduation I realized the only consistent theme throughout my life was an interest in working in television. From my childhood idea of life as a TV weatherman to my college internship, it was the common denominator of everything that interested me the most. I didn't realize it, though, until I graduated.

Lawrence: I always had a pretty good idea that real estate would be my field. Several family members were in the industry and I was exposed to it at an early age. I did not think/worry about how my college major(s) would help or hinder me in my pursuit of a position in real estate.

Michael: The job market was pretty tough and particularly competitive in the world of sports. I landed in media/advertising out of necessity. It was a close enough parallel to the world of sports/broadcasting and a nice introduction to the media industry.

Did you have a mentor when you entered the workforce/graduate school?

Dan: My father was very helpful when I wanted advice (and also when I didn't) and several of my grad school professors were very helpful.

Graham: Yes, in a way. A couple of fraternity brothers who graduated before me had gone to graduate school and gotten good jobs after getting their MBAs.

Hardy: I was surprised at how willing people were to give me advice and encouragement. I had several mentors when I began at CBS in 1993 and continue to get new ones as I progress in my career. There are always people who are willing to share their wisdom, and you're never too old to learn from it.

Lawrence: No mentors per se.

Michael: No official mentor, but the closest would be my fraternity advisor. He was influential not only in the fraternity (helped me establish a financial plan as treasurer), but also for personal growth (letters of recommendation, career advice, life issues, etc).

What's the number-one bit of advice you wish you were given before you entered the job market?

Dan: That people do not have to have a long-range career plan and should not necessarily take a narrow focus. Start off doing something about which you are passionate (if you can) and continue to look for growth and options.

Graham: Pick a specific function and become expert in it. Grow, and if possible, expand your career from a strong functional base of expertise.

Hardy: Be willing to take any job in the area that interests you, no matter how low on the totem poll. First jobs never last for very long, and you can't get the job you want until you figure out a way to get in the door. Also, don't count on any of those contacts you made as an intern to pay off unless you use them immediately after your internship is over.

Lawrence: Create a three-to-five-year plan, and think about how what you are doing today will help you get to the next step in fulfilling that plan. The focus of the plan can shift, but having one helps to keep you focused on always moving forward—wherever that leads you.

Michael: Take some time to travel/explore the world for a few months—don't stress about finding a job.

What were your job-related expectations when you were still in school, and how did they match up with your experience of the "real world?"

Dan: I thought I'd work in education for a few years and then perhaps go to law school or explore other professions.

Graham: In college, I wanted to go to law school, but that didn't happen. In grad school my job-related expectations were to get an interesting position in a large corporation where I could apply the skills I had learned in school, learn the business, and move up the ladder into positions of increased responsibility.

Hardy: I expected to be able to find a well-paying job right away. My friends all talked about the jobs they already had lined up prior to graduation, so I thought I'd be able to do that too, but it didn't work out that way. I spent a few months goofing off before settling into a job search. Nothing turned up until the end of December of that year.

Lawrence: I had the feeling that I would enjoy working more than school life—and I was right. I felt much more productive, energized about what I was doing and how my future looked when I graduated and started working.

Michael: Pretty much on par with reality. I stated repeatedly throughout college that I was looking forward to working in the real world. I always felt I'd be happier working, rather than sitting in a classroom.

What was your first job out of college? How did you find that job?

Dan: I sent out about a hundred resumes and registered with several teacher placement agencies and wound up working at a small boarding school for under-achievers in the Berkshire Mountains of Massachusetts. For $4,000 a year plus room and board, my duties included teaching, coaching basketball, and periodically supervising in the dining hall, in evening study hall, in the residence halls, etc. My hourly wage was probably far less than I would have earned flipping burgers, but I loved the job and soon decided to stay in education.

Graham: I answered an ad and accepted a job as a marketing assistant for a company that was the leading supplier of buttons to the fashion industry and fabric stores in the country. I knew it wouldn't lead to a career, but it was fun and a great motivator!

Hardy: My first job was as a CBS page working as a "temp" throughout CBS television in New York City for $7.50 an hour. Responsibilities ranged from working on the news desk at CBS News to seating the audiences for *Geraldo* and the *Late Show with David Letterman*. I got a call on Friday, December 17 from Drew classmate Alex Haynes who was working as a page in New York. She told me they needed someone to start immediately, so I packed a bag and drove from Maryland to New York to start the following Monday morning.

Lawrence: I was a leasing associate for a large commercial real estate firm. I got the job through a friend of a friend of my father. The person who ultimately hired me made me work hard to get the interview—a test I have not forgotten (in 15 years).

Michael: Through a recruiter, I ended up taking a three-month temp job with the ad sales office of Court TV in Chicago. It wasn't sports, but it was in the media world and a great foundation for my career. That was my foray into advertising, and I've been in the field ever since.

If you went straight into the workforce after receiving your BA, do you wish you had attended graduate school first? If you went on to grad school, do you wish you had worked first? In either case, why?

Dan: I went straight to work, a good decision for me because I was not yet committed to grad school or a particular field. In fact, my best guess would have probably been that I'd go to law school after working in education for a few years. However, it is harder to go to grad school when married and older, as I was, so I'd recommend that folks with more "focus" consider going straight to grad school.

Graham: I worked for two years before going to grad school and am glad I did. Work experience made the MBA classroom and text material relevant. Without the experience I would not have gotten as much out of the program as I did.

Hardy: I'm satisfied with my decision not to go to grad school right away. I have no idea what I would have studied, and I needed to get away from the school atmosphere. Now the idea of grad school is very appealing. I think I'd be more successful now if I were to go back to school. I'm still not sure what I would study, though. Perhaps journalism . . . but maybe history.

Lawrence: I was happy to go into the workforce straight after school. What I learned from working could not be replicated in a classroom.

Michael: I did not go to grad school and have no regrets. The real world (outside of academia) always had greater appeal to me. I don't think I had enough focus and discipline to take on more years in a classroom setting.

What's the best piece of advice you've received from a colleague?

Dan: Better to take chances than to be afraid of making decisions and/or changes. Or, it is sometimes better to ask for forgiveness than to ask for permission.

Graham: Actually there are four: Do the right thing, do things right, don't take it personally, and keep it light.

Hardy: Never ever burn a bridge with anyone above you . . . below you . . . or at your level. No matter how big an industry you are in, you never know when that intern you ignored might one day come back to be your boss.

Lawrence: Don't be afraid to work hard.

Michael: Move to New York City.

What's the smartest move you've made since receiving your BA?

Dan: Maybe deciding that rooting for the Knicks and Giants is masochistic and very self-destructive. Or, maybe, buying a poodle. You can't be unhappy for long with a poodle in your household.

Graham: Getting my MBA.

Hardy: The smartest move was probably being willing to take that first job despite the low pay, inconvenience, and overwhelming fear of moving to New York City. It meant spending the first few months living with my girlfriend's parents and later in her dorm room, but it was worth it.

Lawrence: Marrying my lovely wife, Melody. (Good one, right honey?) More to the point of the question, developing and maintaining a good network of contacts.

Michael: I took the advice and moved to New York from Chicago nearly seven years ago. Landed the dream job, and have been here ever since.

Describe your current job and its major responsibilities.

Dan: As Dean of Enrollment Management at the University of Louisiana at Lafayette, I work with the office of the registrar, office of admissions, office of enrollment services, office of financial aid, and scholarship office. As a result, I am involved in recruiting students and serving them after they have enrolled.

Graham: I'm a program manger for the United States Treasury Department and manage a portfolio of financial smart card applications that support U.S. military cash management needs around the world.

Hardy: I'm the senior producer in Washington, DC for the *CBS News Early Show.* I supervise a staff of seven producers and associate producers responsible for coverage of breaking news and feature stories for the network's daily national morning news broadcast.

Lawrence: I run a small real estate advisory firm. The primary business is to find real estate investment opportunities for investors and manage the assets after we buy them.

Michael: I am responsible for creating sponsorship packages for ESPN Digital Media. [This] includes ESPN.com, wireless, podcasting, fantasy games, video programs. I serve as a liaison between National Ad Sales and Editorial/Design/Production. I am also responsible for articulating sponsorship opportunities to sales. Presently, I manage a team of three people.

What experience was required for your current role?

Dan: For the most part, folks who do what I do have had on-the-job training/experience in one or more aspect of college administration.

Graham: I had over 22 years of experience at ExxonMobil Corporation in a variety of positions and locations where I acquired problem-solving and communication skills, knowledge of card-based payment systems, retail operations, information systems, pricing, marketing, accounting, banking, enterprise solutions, and emerging technology.

Hardy: I needed many accumulated years of experience producing news and feature stories for a network newscast, covering breaking news, production of video tape, news writing, and logistics. I also spent several years learning to manage people as a fill-in for previous senior producers.

Lawrence: My various positions in real estate over the past 15 years all contributed to the knowledge base needed to successfully execute my duties and responsibilities.

Michael: College degree, work experience and fluency in media marketing/advertising, specifically online advertising. Passion for sports, organizational and communication skills.

To what extent has your degree helped you in your current role?

Dan: My education and training has certainly helped me in many ways, but a degree in any number of other areas could have done the same. In fact, others doing the same job hold degrees in all sorts of areas.

Graham: My undergraduate and graduate degrees were instrumental in positioning me to succeed in a wide variety of rewarding positions in both corporate and government sectors including, financial analysis, pricing, planning, operations, accounting, marketing, payment systems, administration, program management, and senior management.

Hardy: To the extent that I cover politics, it has helped me a great deal.

Lawrence: I think my analytical skills (not just financial) were honed because of my degree. I often must take a variety of disparate information, arrive at a conclusion, and present it to a client in a concise and meaningful manner.

Michael: I don't know that my political science degree specifically has helped, but I think the broad-based liberal arts education has been beneficial. It was more about the total college experience, a good education, broad background of knowledge, and developing maturity to function in the real world.

What do you like most about your current role?

Dan: Lots of contact with a variety of on-campus and off-campus folks, the opportunity to work for an institution with an essential mission, and the ability to help students improve their lives, and the lives of others, via education.

Graham: The fast pace, volume, and diversity of projects I deal with.

Hardy: I'm proud of my alma mater and pleased I was able to turn my liberal arts degree into a career.

Lawrence: Every day is different and every property is different.

Michael: The fact that it's always changing. I began with a focus on creating marketing platforms for the internet (ESPN.com), and we've picked up responsibility for all emerging/digital media along the way. With the prevalence of wireless advertising, video, and podcasting, the job continues to evolve.

What aspect(s) of your current role do you not like?

Dan: I am sometimes disappointed by the limited resources available to education and public apathy about education.

Graham: I spend too much time in the office. Also, although it's extremely interesting and rewarding, my work takes me to some challenging locations (i.e., Afghanistan, Egypt, Iraq, Kuwait, Kazakhstan, Kyrgyzstan, Qatar, Saudi Arabia, etc.)

Hardy: I didn't get enough background in history. If I could do it all over again, despite how pleased I was with my political science education, I would give serious thought to majoring in history. I didn't realize at the time that the only way to truly understand the kind of stories I work on today, you have to put them in the context of what happened before today. I am now actually seeking out college and high school level textbooks in an effort to refresh my memory on a lot of world and U.S. history I missed along the way.

Lawrence: I prefer not to work on my own. I enjoy a team environment, where others can motivate you to think about an issue in different ways which, in turn, promotes creativity.

Michael: We've always been understaffed in the marketing group. We've never really had the number of people commensurate with the work that we're responsible for outputting.

What skills have you had to acquire that your degree did not help you cultivate?

Dan: So-called people skills are generally learned and improved outside of the classroom, as are management skills.

Graham: Attention to detail. I always thought the higher up the ladder you went, the less you had to know the details . . . in reality it's exactly the opposite.

Hardy: Not enough background in history.

Lawrence: Most importantly for my work, my financial analysis skills were all acquired after college—either on the job, through continuing education classes, or my subsequent MBA.

Michael: Simply learning the media math, vernacular, standards, and practices. Short of taking a specialized undergraduate course, or entering grad school, it's impossible to acquire this knowledge in college. In addition, the internet was just starting to take off when I was in college, let alone the growth of internet advertising. The prevalence of online advertising didn't begin to materialize until after I had graduated.

What suggestions would you have for those still in college? Are there any "optional" elements of the undergraduate experience that you would recommend they explore?

Dan: I'd encourage students to take a wide variety of courses that appeal to them and be open to new experiences and directions.

Graham: Learn to write concisely. Executives are bombarded with communications. You have to get your message and call to action out quickly and accurately. Use attachments to support your case.

Hardy: Look for courses or campus clubs that spark your curiosity: Music, languages, astronomy, film. . . . You rarely get another chance to focus so intensely on those things that you find interesting. If an internship is considered "optional," I think it should be recast as "required." There are few other ways to gain work experience—or a foot in the door—or something to write on your resume.

Lawrence: I think undergrads should try to get some real, hand-on experience in the field they think they are interested in pursuing. In every college town, there are businesses that will take on interns during the school year to help their business in some way. I worked for a furrier during one school year, and I got to see how a business was run. Not that it was my field but I had interactions with people (owners, coworkers, customers) that gave me good interpersonal skills to carry forward with me.

Michael: Internships for certain. They seem to be mandatory. Many of the people who end up filling entry-level jobs at ESPN served as interns here previously.

Do you have any tips for those entering the workforce/graduate school now?

Dan: Time management is critical. Pay attention to it and continue to try to use your time more efficiently. Make time your friend, not your enemy.

Graham: Be prepared to work hard and establish your credibility.

Hardy: For those entering the workforce now, once you get a job, be self-confident but humble. Listen to what's told to you by those whom you look up to. Absorb everything you can. And make as many friends as you can.

Lawrence: The best first/early jobs fall into two categories: (1) "peon" in a very large and established firm in a particular industry (preferably one in which you have an interest) or (2) a small but integral role with a small firm. The first option gives one the name/brand recognition when moving up the ladder in a particular industry, while the second option may give someone real hand-on experiences to take with them.

Michael: Patience. Your dream job may not come along right away, so be willing to take on something that might not be exactly aligned with your career goals. You have to gain experience somewhere before you become marketable, so just get in the ballgame. Over time, through networking, establishing contacts, and aligning yourself with the right people who can advance your career, you will hopefully end up in a happy place. Much easier said than done.

What's the best way to get a job in your field?

Dan: There are many entry-level positions open in higher education, particularly in admissions, financial aid, and residence life. Ultimately, a graduate degree will be required for significant advancement. Fortunately, identifying existing openings is easy, since most are published in a very limited number of publications and on a very few websites (which anyone in higher ed can point you toward). Also, most universities post their openings on their websites.

Graham: Personal referrals and internships are probably the best way, but don't ignore a well-written resume targeted to decision makers.

Hardy: Some people do what I did and start out as a page. Some people are able to turn internships into a permanent job after college. But the absolute best way to get into this business is to get a job at a small local station and learn the business from the ground up. Even though I've done alright so far, my one big regret is not getting local news experience. You can always tell who has it and who does not. That experience is highly valued by those who are in a position to hire.

Lawrence: Ideal way to get a good job in any field, at any level, is through connections that can make introductions to people other than human resources.

Michael: It's all about networking. Meet people, socialize, talk to friends and family. Through six degrees of separation, everyone knows someone in the business. It's really a function of who you know and being in the right place at the right time.

What mistake do political science grads often make?

Dan: Thinking they need a graduation to retirement career plan and not being open to different options/opportunities. Many of the happiest folks I know are in fields in which they never envisioned themselves.

Graham: Accepting a job, or staying in one, that's not right for them.

Hardy: I suppose the biggest mistake is thinking there is nothing they can do with their degree. In areas like media and politics there are hundreds of positions in which you can apply what you've learned.

Lawrence: I think it is tough to make a mistake immediately after college. Any job is a learning experience and will help you make a decision on how to proceed with your next career move. At some point, you need to become focused on a particular field and specialization.

Michael: Expecting too much too soon. Promotions, hefty salaries, and job titles don't happen overnight. Be a workhorse and be willing to do everything asked of you (no matter how trivial). Service with a smile. You might seem like a low man on the totem poll, but keep in mind that everyone has been there before. You'll look back fondly on your first job one day and know that you wouldn't have gotten to be where you are without that experience.

What's something that you think more political science grads should do to advance their careers?

Dan: Continue their education, attend meetings and seminars, and read.

Graham: Be honest with your potential and progress as time goes on. Assess potential reasons for lack of movement and adjust accordingly.

Hardy: Again, internships are key. Do them at network news, local news, newspapers, radio stations, a politician's office, a political campaign, a lobbying firm. It's the best way to meet people and to learn about what life is really like after college.

Lawrence: Do not stop learning—read industry periodicals, attend seminars, talk to colleagues, go to industry-related social functions, and the like.

Michael: You need to approach work with some passion, take pride, take ownership, and don't begrudge the smaller tasks. Be willing to do all the little things, demonstrating your ability to do whatever it takes to get to the next level.

Who is in the best position to offer a political science graduate help with his or her resume and cover letter?

Dan: Folks who hire people in the field of interest. Most professionals are happy to mentor others. Folks trying to break into a field should not be afraid to approach them and ask for advice.

Graham: A senior person in a related field.

Hardy: I would seek help from a supervisor wherever you are interning.

Lawrence: Approach a friend who has been working for eight to ten years and has been with at least four firms. These individuals will have the most insightful input for creating a good resume in the marketplace.

Michael: It could be a number of people really. Anyone from a college advisor/mentor to close friends/family. Anyone with a strong command of the structure and vocabulary required for a quality resume. If the resume is crafted towards a very specific career goal or job industry, it would be helpful to have someone who works in the industry offer assistance.

What pitfalls should political science graduates avoid when applying to and interviewing for positions?

Dan: Resumes and cover letters need to be well developed, flawless, and written specifically for individual positions. I could go on all day about resume/cover letter errors, but the most interesting example I can offer is of a bright, successful, professional who would have almost certainly had an interview here if he had not, in his cover letter, used the name of a similarly named university to refer to this one. In interviews, the biggest sins I see are poor overall communication skills, the use of trite answers, and poor listening skills.

Graham: First, make sure the resume is error free. Second, avoid giving yes/no answers in an interview. The interviewer wants to hear you speak and is listening to how you frame your responses. Use firsthand examples to support your position.

Hardy: People applying for entry level jobs—or any job right out of college—should avoid overselling themselves. Resumes should *never* be more than a page long at that level and should not embellish experience. Employers look for someone who can say a lot via their resume by not saying a lot.

Lawrence: Listen to the questions being asked at an interview. Often, the answers are "baked" into the questions which can lead to a more insightful and "appropriate" response. At the same time, one must be genuine about how they present themselves. Most important, is "getting into the room," and this requires diligence. If someone does not respond to an e-mail, call them and leave a message (and vice versa). Be persistent until you can speak to someone live on the phone or get some form of direct response via e-mail.

Michael: If it's a first-time job, show a willingness to start at the bottom and work your way up. Inquiring about career growth is okay, but don't overemphasize to the point where it appears you're already looking for the next promotion. Embrace the job at hand, get a foot in the door, and have faith that your hard work will be acknowledged and ultimately lead to advancement. Don't be too nervous, but don't be too cocky. Confidence is good, but has to be channeled in the appropriate ways so as not to turn people off. It's a delicate balance, but many people simply like someone who is grounded, humble, and articulate. The job skills can be learned in time. It's the personal qualities that are hard to teach.

GOOD LUCK.

Graduate Schools and Fellowships

GENERAL SEARCH ENGINES

GradSchools.com
www.gradschools.com

Peterson's Graduate and Professional Schools
www.petersons.com/graduate_home.asp?path=gr.home

The Princeton Review's Grad Program Search
www.princetonreview.com/grad/research/programProfiles/search.asp

FIELD-SPECIFIC GRADUATE SCHOOL INFORMATION

ALA-Accredited Master's Programs in Library and Information Studies
www.ala.org/ala/accreditation/lisdirb/lisdirectory.htm

Archival Studies Programs, Society of American Archivists
www.archivists.org/prof-education/ed_guidelines.asp

Association of Professional Schools in International Affairs
www.apsia.org/apsia/index.php

Association for Public Policy Analysis and Management: Advice on Policy Education
www.appam.org/education/students.asp

Council on Education in Journalism and Mass Communication: Journalism and Communications Graduate Programs
www2.ku.edu/~acejmc/STUDENT/PROGLIST.SHTML

Graduate Programs in Political Science
www.politicalindex.com/sect18.htm

History Departments Around the World
http://chnm.gmu.edu/resources/departments

National Association of Schools of Public Affairs and Administration
www.naspaa.org/students/students.asp

National Communication Association: Graduate Program Directory
www.natcom.org/ComProg/GPDHTM/Scripts/GradDir2.htm

The Official MBA Guide
http://mba.us.com/guide

"Preparing for Law School" prepared by the Pre-Law Committee of the ABA Section of Legal Education and Admissions to the Bar
  www.abanet.org/legaled/prelaw/prep.html

Teacher Accredited Training Programs
  www.ncate.org

FELLOWSHIPS

Asian Pacific American Institute for Congressional Studies Fellowships
  www.apaics.org/apaics_fellow.html

Boston College: Links to professional work fellowships
  www.bc.edu/offices/careers/jobs/strategies/fellowships

Congressional Hispanic Caucus Institute (CHCI): CHCI Public Policy Fellowship Information:
  www.chci.org/chciyouth/fellowship/fellowship.htm

Congressional Black Caucus Foundation Fellowships
  www.cbcfinc.org/Leadership%20Education/Fellowships/index.html

Echoing Green Fellowships for Emerging Social Innovators
  http://www.echoinggreen.org

Green Corps Leadership Training Program
  www.greencorps.org/training.asp?id2=19458

The Hispanic Journalism Foundation Fellowship
  www.hispaniclink.org/foundation/fellowshipinternship.htm

Idealist.org: Descriptions and contact information for a variety of nonprofit and public policy fellowships
  www.idealist.org/career/fellowship.html

Policy and International Affairs Program Fellowship Program for college juniors
  www.ppiaprogram.org/programs/jsi.php

Presidential Management Fellows Program for graduate students
  www.pmf.opm.gov

Wellstone Fellowship for Social Justice
  www.familiesusa.org/about/wellstone-fellowship-about.html

The Woodrow Wilson National Fellowship Foundation
  www.woodrow.org/fellowships.php

U.S. Department of State Fellowships
  http://careers.state.gov/student/progright/index.html

Jobs and Internship Resources

Alternative Teaching Credentialing Programs:

NYC Teaching Fellows: If you have not been certified to teach and hold a bachelor's degree, you have the opportunity to become a teaching fellow for a variety of schools located in New York City.
www.nyctf.org/prospective/mayteach.html

Project Pipeline: A two-year program designed to prepare college grads to teach in the classroom. Different programs for elementary and secondary teachers available.
www.projectpipeline.org

Public Allies: Opportunity to become a Public Allies Fellow or apply for the alternative licensure program, which will give you a three-year provisional license.
www.publicallies.org

Teach For America: Teachers will be provided with a paid salary plus education reward. A two-year teaching commitment is required.
www.teachforamerica.org

Education Job Listing Sites

Agent K–12: Jobs for teachers and administrators.
www.agentk-12.org

EdWeek Job Postings
edweek.org/ew/index.html

Jobs in Higher Education
www.academic360.com

Government, Politics, and Policy Job Listing Sites

Federal Jobs
www.usajobs.opm.gov

Finding an Internship in Public Service
www.naspaa.org/students/careers/service.asp#Finding%20an%20Internship%20in%20Public%20Service

Foreign Policy Association
www.fpa.org/jobs_contact2423/jobs_contact.htm

The Hill: Classifieds section includes policy jobs both on the Hill and within the greater Washington, DC area.
http://thehill.com/thehill/export/TheHill/Classifieds/Employment/index.html

National Association of Schools of Public Affairs and Administration: "Finding an Internship in Public Service"
www.naspaa.org/students/careers/service.asp#Finding%20an%20Internship%20in%20Public%20Service

Opportunities in Public Affairs
www.opajobs.com

The Politix Group: Political and government career resources.
www.politixgroup.com/dcjobs.htm

Public Affairs Council: Job listings in public affairs, mostly in Washington, DC.
www.pac.org/public/news/news_job_openings.shtml

Roll Call: A publication for Congressional news and information on Capitol Hill.
www.rcjobs.com

StudentJobs.gov: Links to student-employment pages for federal agencies.
www.studentjobs.gov

LAW JOB LISTING SITES

Findlaw: A website providing resources on the Internet for legal professionals and students, including job listings.
http://careers.findlaw.com

Law Employment Center
www.lawjobs.com

Lawyers Weekly Jobs.com: Paralegal positions searchable by state and by legal specialties.
www.lawyersweeklyjobs.com

MEDIA AND COMMUNICATIONS JOB LISTING SITES

American Copy Editors Society's Job Bank
www.copydesk.org/jobbank.htm

Bookjobs.com: Jobs within the book publishing industry.
www.bookjobs.com

Creative Hotlist
www.creativehotlist.com

Detroit Free Press: Links to journalism job banks and job-hunting advice for those interested in newspaper careers.
www.freep.com

Job Link: Print and broadcast listings including reporting/writing/editing, research, photography, and design.
newslink.org/joblink.html

Journalism Jobs: TV, radio, and newspaper jobs and internships.
www.journalismjobs.com

The Write Jobs: Writing jobs including journalism, editing, staff writing positions, technical writing, freelance.
www.writejobs.com

MUSEUM JOB LISTING SITES

American Association of Museums
http://museumcareers.aam-us.org/search/browse

American Historical Association
www.historians.org/governance/tfph/PublicHistoryEmployment.htm

Historic Preservation Internship Training Program
www.cr.nps.gov/hps/tps/hpit_p.htm

Museum Employment Resource Center
www.museum-employment.com

The Smithsonian Institution
www.si.edu/ofg/internopp.htm

NONPROFIT JOB LISTING SITES

Foundation for Sustainable Development
www.fsdinternational.org

Idealist.org: A project of Action without Borders, Idealist offers a global clearinghouse of nonprofit resources, including jobs, internships, mailing lists, and nonprofit resources by state and country.
www.idealist.org

InterAction: Coalition of U.S.-based international development and humanitarian nongovernmental organizations.
www.interaction.org

Opportunity Knocks
www.opportunitynocs.org

Union Jobs Clearinghouse: Staffing and trades positions in organized labor searchable by state and by union name.
www.unionjobs.com/staff.html

Appendix C

Career Advice and Resources

General Career Information

American Historical Association
www.historians.org/pubs/careers

American Political Science Association
www.apsanet.org/section_516.cfm

Occupational Outlook Handbook
www.stats.bls.gov/search/ooh.asp?ct=OOH

The Riley Guide
www.rileyguide.com/jobs.html

Communications

American Society of Newspaper Editors: "Is Journalism for You? Journalists Tell Their Stories"
www.asne.org/index.cfm?id=4847

Association of Newspaper Editors: "A Career in Newspapers"
www.asne.org/index.cfm?id=5260

The Association of Writers and Writing Programs: "Working in Publishing"
www.awpwriter.org/careers/hsmith01.htm

Reporter.org: Links to Journalism Organizations
www.reporter.org

Magazine Publishers of America: Career Resources
www.magazine.org

National Association of Broadcasters
www.nab.org/AM/Template.cfm?Section=Home&WebsiteKey=31cadfd9-b130-44b4-af2e-6603cbcc422b

Public Relations Society of America: "Careers in Public Relations: An Overview"
www.prsa.org

Education

American Federation of Teachers
www.aft.org

The Chronicle of Higher Education: News, articles of interest, and job listings in higher education.
http://chronicle.com

The Teacher's Guide: Links to teacher organizations.
www.theteachersguide.com/Educationassociations.html

GOVERNMENT AND POLITICS

10 Tips for Letting the Federal Government Know Your Worth
www.usajobs.opm.gov/EI64.asp

The Call to Serve Initiative: Dedicated to helping you learn more about careers in the federal government.
www.ourpublicservice.org

Federal Jobs Career Chat: Monthly e-Newsletter
www.fedjobs.com/index.html

Federal Jobs by College Major
www.usajobs.opm.gov/ei23.asp

National Association of Schools of Public Affairs and Administration: Profiles of Alumni
www.naspaa.org/students/careers/alumni.asp

The National Conference of State Legislators
www.ncsl.org/index.htm?tabsel=issues

National League of Cities:
www.nlc.org/Inside%5FNLC/Job%5FOpportunities%5Fat%5FNLC

The Politix Group: Political and Government Career Resources
www.politixgroup.com/dcjobs.htm

USA Jobs: Interest-specific career guides, designed to provide information about where specific types of jobs are found in the federal government.
www.dol.gov/oasam/doljobs/college-guide-apply.htm

LAW

American Association for Paralegal Education
www.aafpe.org

Careers in Mediation
www.mediate.com/careers

National Association of Legal Assistants
www.nala.org

National Federation of Paralegal Associations
www.paralegals.org

MUSEUMS AND LIBRARIES

American Association of Museums: "Museums Working in the Public Interest"
http://aam-us.org/aboutmuseums/publicinterest.cfm

American Library Association: Library Careers
www.ala.org/ala/hrdr/librarycareerssite/home.htm

Library HQ.com: Links to library organizations and associations.
www.libraryhq.com/orgs.html

Smithsonian Institution: Museum Careers
www.si.edu/ohr/museum.htm

Society of American Archivists: "So you want to be an archivist?"
www.archivists.org/prof-education/arprof.asp

NONPROFITS

Careers in Affordable Housing
www.nonprofithousing.org/actioncenter/careers/default.aspx

Human Rights Organizations: Human Rights Education Associates
http://hrea.org/erc/Links/index.php

InterAction: An alliance of U.S.-based international development and humanitarian nongovernmental organizations.
www.interaction.org/about/index.html

National Directory, Coalition for Asian American Families and Children
www.cacf.org/directories/national/index.html

The Young Nonprofit Professionals Network: Networking, information sharing, and job listings.
http://ynpn.org/careercenter

The OneWorld Partnership: 1,500 organizations promoting sustainable development, social justice, and human rights.
www.oneworld.net/section/partners

PUBLIC POLICY

American Association of Political Consultants
www.theaapc.com

The Association for Public Policy Analysis and Management:
www.appam.org/home.asp

Centers for Research Policy and Development, Maintained by the Kennedy School of Government, Harvard University
www.ksg.harvard.edu/library/orgs_tanks.htm

Directory of Conservative Think Tanks
http://policyexperts.org

Institute of International Education
www.iie.org/wcoast/links.htm

NIRA's World Directory of Think Tanks 2005 (NWDTT 2005)
www.nira.go.jp/ice/nwdtt

FINDING THE FUNDS

What you should know about paying for your graduate school educat

Furthering your education is an investment in your future. Laying down $120,000 — probably more — in exchange for a top-notch graduate school education requires just as much research and planning as deciding which school you'll hand that money over to.

The good news is that you still have a little time before you have to really worry about signing on the dotted line for any type of financial assistance. That gives you some time to research options, to properly calculate the actual costs of going to graduate school beyond just the sticker price, and to create a plan so that your potential future earnings cover your costs of living when you're out of school and using that degree you will have worked so hard for.

You're going to be responsible for the choices you make. Cutting your ancillary expenses for the next few years and building up an out-of-pocket school fund before you ever register for that first class might save you thousands of dollars in interest payments down the road. But how will you know if you don't come up with a plan?

No doubt you've accumulated some sort of credit history, most likely through undergrad student loans and/or some high-interest credit card debt, so you might think you have it all figured out when it comes to paying for graduate school. While you might understand the basics about how federal loans work and how scholarships, grants, and fellowships can help to cut down the final bill, there are lesser-known and fairly new options out there that can make your postgraduate life a little easier to enjoy.

OTHER PEOPLE'S MONEY

Scholarships and Grants

These are the best form of financial aid because they don't have to be paid back. Remember, though, that most scholarships require a minimum GPA and that some grants are good for only one year. When evaluating your payment options, make

> The government only lends money directly to you under the Federal Direct Loan Program. Lenders provide loans guaranteed by the federal government in the Federal Family Education Loan Program.

sure there is a reasonable expectation t the financial aid package being offered be available for the full term of the deg requirement or that you have a way of managing funds if they are not enough

Fellowships and Stipends

Fellowships come in many differe forms. Sometimes partial tuition scholarships are called fellowships. These university-sponsored fellowshi consist of a cash award that is prompt subtracted from your tuition bill. You earn the amount of the award by teac for a department or by completing research for a faculty member. The percentage of students who receive th type of fellowship and the amount pa each will vary depending on the inter degree and field, enrollment status (fu or part-time), and years of enrollmen

It is important to note that surviv on a fellowship alone is unlikely. Fellowships are taxable income—fede state, county, and city—and you may expected to pay for school fees, suppl and books out of your fellowship, as v as tuition. If the fellowship doesn't co the full cost of your attendance, you'l have to explore other financing optio

Employer-financed Opportunities

Some employers will offer a tuiti reimbursement or a limited financial for employees to attend graduate sch part time. Employers expect the adva degree to enhance your performance on the job or to make you eligible for a different job within the company. Be sure you understand all aspects of your employer's tuition reimburseme program before you sign on and be prepared to meet any commitments expected of you.

LOANS

When scholarships, grants, and fellowships don't cover the full cost o attendance, many students take out l to help out with the rest.

Avoid loans if you can. A loan can best be described as renting money. There's a cost and it may not be an easy cost to bear.

Here's an interesting anecdote. Many students graduate without knowing what types of loans they received, who the lender was and how much they owe. The first time many students become aware of the scope of their obligation is when they receive their first bill—six months after graduation.

This is often because students are passive participants in the financial aid process and do not educate themselves or ask questions. Most students receive a list of "preferred lenders" from their financial aid office and simply go with the lender recommended to them. Over the course of the previous year, relationships between financial aid offices and lenders have been called into question by State Attorneys General, the Department of Education, and regulators. Financial aid offices in certain cases received revenue from lenders in exchange for being placed on the "preferred lender list." Some schools have even rented out their name and logo for use on loan applications. These practices occur without disclosure to parents and students.

It is important to know that the "preferred lenders" may not offer the best deals on your loan options. While your financial aid office may be very helpful with scholarships and grants, and is legally required to perform certain duties with regard to federal loans, many do not have staff researching the lowest cost options at the time you are borrowing.

Remember that your tuition payment equals revenue for the school. When borrowing to pay tuition, you can choose to borrow from any lender. That means you can shop for the lowest rate. Keep reading. This will tell you how.

TYPES OF LOANS

The federal government and private commercial lenders offer educational loans to students. Federal loans are usually the "first resort" for borrowers because many are subsidized by the federal government and offer lower interest rates. Private loans have the advantage of fewer restrictions on borrowing limits, but may have higher interest rates and more stringent qualification criteria.

Federal Loans

There are three federal loan programs. The Federal Perkins Loan Program where your school lends you money made available by government funds, the Federal Direct Loan Program (FDLP) where the government lends its money directly to students, and the Federal Family Education Loan Program (FFELP) where financial institutions such as MyRichUncle lend their own money but the government guarantees them. While most schools participate in the Federal Perkins Program, institutions choose whether they will participate in either the FFELP or FDLP. You will borrow from FFELP or FDLP depending on which program your school has elected to participate in.

The Federal Perkins Loan is a low-interest (5%) loan for students with exceptional need. Many students who do not qualify or who may need more funds can borrow FFELP or FDLP student loans. Under both programs, the Stafford loan is the typical place to start. The Stafford loan program features a fixed interest rate and yearly caps on the maximum amount a student can borrow. Stafford loans can either be subsidized (the government pays the interest while the student is in school) or unsubsidized (the student is responsible for the interest that accrues while in school). Starting July 1, 2007, the maximum amount a student can borrow for graduate school is $20,500.

It is often assumed that the government sets the rate on student loans. The government does not set the rate of interest. It merely indicates the maximum rate lenders can charge. These lenders are free to charge less than the specified maximum rate of 6.8% for Stafford loans. There is also a maximum origination fee of up to 2% dropping to 1.5% on July 1, 2007. In some cases you may also be charged up to a 1% guarantee fee. Any fees will be taken out of your disbursement.

Historically lenders have hovered at the maximum rate because most loans were distributed via the financial aid office whereby a few lenders received most of the loans. The end result was limited competition. At 1,239 institutions, one lender received more than 90% of the number of Stafford loans in 2006.

The GradPLUS loan is a federal loan that is another option for graduate and professional students. GradPLUS loans can be used to cover the full cost of attendance and have a fixed interest rate. The maximum rate a lender can charge for a GradPLUS loan is 8.5%. GradPLUS loans also have an origination fee of up to 3%, and a guarantee fee of up to 1%. Any fees will be taken out of your disbursement. Getting approved for one might be easier than getting approved for a private loan, so long as you don't have an adverse credit history.

For either program, the borrower submits a federal application known as the Free Application for Federal Student Aid (FAFSA). The application is available online at www.fafsa.ed.gov.

Certain lenders offer rate reductions, also known as borrower benefits, conditioned on the borrower making a certain number of on-time payments. Unfortunately, it is estimated that 90% of borrowers never qualify for these reductions.

Last year, MyRichUncle challenged this process by launching a price war. The company cut interest rates on Stafford loans and Graduate PLUS loans and introduced widespread price competition. These interest rate cuts are effective when students enter repayment and do not have any further qualification requirements. In addition, students only lose the rate reduction if they default.

Your financial aid office is legally required to certify for lenders that you are enrolled and based on your financial aid package, the amount in Federal loans you are eligible to borrow. You are free to choose any lender even if the lender is not on your financial aid office's preferred lender list.

To shop for low cost Federal loans, call a number of lenders before applying to determine their rates and fees. This is an effective approach because your application will not impact the price. Once you are comfortable that you have the lowest cost option, apply and submit the Master Promissory Note to your lender of choice.

Private Loans

Private student loans can make it possible to cover the costs of higher education when other sources of fund have been exhausted. Additionally, when you apply for federal loans, you can borrow up to what your institutio has pre-defined as the annual cost of attendance. If your anticipated expens are above and beyond this predefined cost because of your unique needs, it will take a series of appeals before you institution will allow you to borrow m federal loans. Private loans help you m your true expectation of what you will need financially. Private loans can pay expenses that federal loans can't, such application and testing fees and the c of transportation.

When you apply for a private loa the lending institution will check you credit history including your credit sc and determine your capacity to pay ba the money you borrow. For individual whose credit history is less than posit lenders may require a co-borrower: a credit-worthy individual who also agr to be accountable to the terms of the While private loans do not have annu borrowing limits, they often have hig interest rates, and interest rate caps ar higher than those set by Federal loans Generally, the loans are variable rate l so the interest rate may go up or dow changing the cost.

To shop for a private loan, after you've researched several options, app as many of them as you feel comforta Once you are approved, compare rate Pick the lowest cost option.

EXTRA LESSONS

Borrow the minimum

Just because someone is offering to lend you thousands upon thousand of dollars doesn't mean you should necessarily take them up on that offe At some point, you'll have to repay th debt and you'll have to do it responsi Wouldn't it be better to use your mor for something more worthwhile to yo

Know your rights

Currently, student lending is an industry that is under heavy scrutiny. It is important, now more than ever, for parents and students to have an active voice and to make educational and financial choices that are right for them.

Some schools work with "preferred lenders" when offering federal and private loans. You are not required to choose a loan from one of these lenders if you can find a better offer. With respect to federal loans, the financial aid office has a legislated role which is to certify for the lending institution that you the borrower are indeed enrolled and the amount you are eligible for. They are not legally empowered to dictate your choice of lender and must certify your loan from the lender of your choice. You have the right to shop for and to secure the best rates possible for your loans. Don't get bullied into choosing a different lender simply because it is preferred by an institution. Instead, do your homework and make sure you understand all of your options.

Know what you want

When it's all said and done, you will have to take a variety of factors into account in order to choose the best school for you and for your future. You shouldn't have to mortgage your future to follow a dream, but you also shouldn't downgrade this opportunity just to save a few bucks.

Call us:
1-800-926-5320
or learn more online:
MYRICHUNCLE.COM/HISTORY

MYRICHUNCLE

Who we are:

MyRichUncle is a national student loan company offering federal (Stafford, PLUS and GradPLUS) and private loans to undergraduate, graduate, and professional students. MyRichUncle knows that getting a student loan can be a complicated and intimidating process, so we changed it. We believe students are credit-worthy borrowers, and that student loan debt should be taken seriously by borrowers and lenders alike. We propose changes in the student loan industry that will better serve parents, schools, and most importantly, students.

Why it matters:

Your student loan will be your responsibility. When you enter into a loan agreement, you're entering into a long-term relationship with your lender—15 years, on average. The right student loan with the right lender can help you avoid years of unnecessary fees and payments.

What we do:

MyRichUncle pays close attention to the obstacles students face. Removing these obstacles drives everything we do. MyRichUncle discounts federal loan rates at repayment rather than requiring years of continuous payments to earn the discount, which saves you money right from the start. We help you plan ahead, so you can choose the best loans and save.

Our credentials:

MyRichUncle is a NASDAQ listed company. Our symbol is UNCL. In 2006, MyRichUncle was featured in FastCompany Magazine's Fast 50 and in Businessweek's Top Tech Entrepreneurs. MyRichUncle and its parent company, MRU Holdings, are financed by a number of leading investment banks and venture capitalists, including subsidiaries of Merrill Lynch, Lehman Brothers, Battery Ventures and Nomura Holdings.

NOTES

NOTES

More expert advice from The Princeton Review

Also available:

Available everywhere books are sold or at PrincetonReview.com